WHO'S WHO
IN THE BIBLE
ILLUSTRATED

'And when the queen of Sheba heard of the fame of Solomon,
she came to prove Solomon with hard questions at Jerusalem, with a very great
company, and camels that bare spices, and gold in abundance, and precious stones:
and when she was come to Solomon, she communed with him of all that was
in her heart.' *(II Chronicles 9:1)*

WHO'S WHO
IN THE BIBLE
ILLUSTRATED

SAMUEL T. JORDAN

CHARTWELL
BOOKS, INC.

PUBLISHER'S NOTE

Every effort has been made to ensure the faithfulness of the information presented
in this book. The publisher will not assume liability for damages caused by the data
and makes no warranty whatsoever expressed or implied. The publisher welcomes
comments and corrections from readers, which will be considered for
incorporation in future editions.

HALFTITLE ILLUSTRATIONS
Page 9: Moses and Aaron before Pharaoh.
Page 163: The apostles Peter and John healing and teaching at the Temple.

ENDPAPER ILLUSTRATIONS
Front endpapers: left, Abraham leads his family from Ur of the Chaldees
on a journey that will take them to Canaan; right, Joseph prepares Egypt
for the famine to come.
Back endpapers: left, Christ with his disciples; right, Paul is taken
under guard from Jerusalem to Caesarea.

Contents

God and Satan, 6

Who's Who in
The Old Testament, 9

Who's Who in
The New Testament, 163

Characters in the Holy Bible with
No Recorded Names, 237

God and Satan

GOD The absolute, creator of the world and all that is, who made order out of chaos. The Bible begins majestically with this fundamental statement: 'In the beginning God created the heaven and the earth' (*Genesis 1:1*), and *The Gospel of John* begins: 'In the beginning was the Word, and the Word was with God, and the Word was God … All things were made by him … In him was life; and the life was the light of men.' (*John 1:1*) 'I am Alpha and Omega, the beginning and the ending, saith the Lord, which is, and which was, and which is to come, the Almighty.' (*Revelation 1:8*) All-seeing, all-knowing, omnipresent and the judge of all things, he holds in his hands the fate of humankind. He is the source of good in the world, constantly fighting the forces of darkness and evil.

God has many names in the Bible, and many have been added in later times. To Noah, he was simply 'the Lord', 'And when Abram [Abraham] was ninety years old and nine, the Lord appeared to Abram, and said unto him, I am the Almighty God.' (*Genesis 17:1*) When He spoke to Moses from the burning bush, 'God said unto Moses, I am that I am … Thus shalt thou say unto the children of Israel, The Lord God of your fathers ...' (*Exodus 3:13–15*) Later, 'God spake unto Moses, and said unto him, I am the Lord: And I appeared unto Abraham, unto Isaac, and unto Jacob, by the name of God Almighty, but by my name Jehovah was I not known to them.' (*Exodus 6:2–3*) It was the Jewish tradition not to enunciate the name of God, and His name was represented by the Tetragrammaton, the Hebrew name for God transliterated in four letters, Y H W H , and articulated as Yahweh or Jehovah.

Other appellations include that in *Isaiah 6:3*: 'Holy, holy, holy, is the Lord of hosts', while in the New Testament, Jesus calls him 'Abba, Father' (*Mark 14:36*), and this is echoed in *Romans 8*: 'we cry, 'Abba, Father', and also in *Galatians 4:6*.

He made man in his own image, but man was never permitted to see his face: to Moses at Sinai, 'he said, Thou canst not see my face: for there shall no man see me, and live.' (*Exodus 33:20*) As the Hebrews set out upon their epic journey from the Red Sea to the Promised Land, God preceded them: 'And the Lord went before them by day in a pillar of a cloud, to lead them the way; and by night in a pillar of fire, to give them light; to go by day and night.' (*Exodus 13:21*)

After Moses, God spoke to his servants often in visions or dreams: Isaiah, for example, reports that 'In the year that king Uzziah died I saw also the Lord sitting upon a throne, high and lifted up, and his train filled the temple. (*Isaiah 6:1*)

God's special relationship with his people was set out in the Covenant that he made with Noah (*Genesis 6:18*), Abraham (*Genesis 15:18*), Isaac (*Genesis 17:21*) and Jacob (*Genesis 28:12–15*). The laws of the Covenant were passed to Moses on Mount Sinai (*Exodus 19–40*). At the heart of these laws stand the Ten Commandments, which begin: 'Thou shalt have no other gods before me.' (*Exodus 20:3–5*)

Much of the Old Testament describes His peoples' failure to adhere to His laws, while prophets exhort the people to keep faith with Him and warn them of the punishment that will result if they do not heed these warnings. Those punishments inevitably follow: when God perceives the wickedness of Man he destroys all but Noah and his family in the Deluge; the lack of faith of the Hebrews in the wilderness is punished by a forty-year extension of their wandering; and the indulgence of false gods is repaid by the destruction of Jerusalem.

God will preside over the Last Judgement: 'When the Son of man shall come in his glory, and all the holy angels with him, then shall he sit upon the throne of his glory: And before him shall be gathered all nations: and he shall separate them one from another, as a shepherd divideth his sheep from the goats: And he shall set the sheep on his right hand, but the goats on the left.' (*Matthew 25:31–3*)

This is also described in John's great vision in *Revelation 20:11–15*.

While in the Old Testament God is a very active participant, in the New Testament His presence is manifest in the person of Jesus Christ.

SATAN The personification of evil, the Devil symbolizes and personifies humanity's own sinfulness and weaknesses. He is the enemy of God and humankind and sometimes a divine embodiment of God's wrath. He deceives and tempts, inducing man to sin and turn away from the love of God – luring them into hell. In the New Testament he is the opponent of God and rules over other demons with the ability to cause harm to mankind. In the dualist concept of the conflict between good and evil, God is light, and Satan represents the forces of darkness.

The word 'Satan' comes from the Hebrew for 'adversary', while 'devil' finds its origin in the Greek word 'diabolos', or slanderer. In an exchange between the pharisees and Jesus in *Matthew 12:24–8* he is referred to as Beelzebub, prince of the devils. This name (Greek Beezeboul, equating to the Hebrew Baal-zebel (Lord of Filth), emerged into English from 'Baal-zebub the god of Ekron' [Lord of the Flies] in *II Kings 1:2* when King Ahaziah was ill and wanted to know whether he would live.

In *II Corinthians 6:15* Paul refers to Satan as Belial: 'And what concord hath Christ with Belial? or what part hath he that believeth with an infidel?' In *Revelation*, he is referred to as 'the angel of the bottomless pit, whose name

'Then the devil taketh him up into the holy city, and setteth him on a pinnacle of the temple, And saith unto him, If thou be the Son of God, cast thyself down.'

in the Hebrew tongue is Abaddon, but in the Greek tongue hath his name Apollyon'. (*9:11*) Only in *Revelation* is the connection made with the serpent in the garden of Eden who seduces Eve into eating the fruit of the tree of the knowledge of good and evil. *Revelation* identifies him as a fallen angel, driven from heaven after a battle with the archangel Michael. (*12:7–9*) In *Revelation 20:1–8* John sees Satan fettered for a thousand years.

In *Isaiah 14:12–17* there is an identification of the King of Babylon with the Devil, here named Lucifer: 'How art thou fallen from heaven, O Lucifer, son of the morning! how art thou cut down to the ground, which didst weaken the nations!'

In the *Book of Job*, where the eponymous hero is tested to breaking-point, it is to Satan that God gives power to wreak havoc with Job's life: 'And the Lord said unto Satan, Behold, all that he hath is in thy power; only upon himself put not forth thine hand. So Satan went forth from the presence of the Lord.' (*Job 1:6–12*) Satan then inflicted a series of disasters.

In the essentially narrative books of *Genesis, Exodus, Joshua, Judges, Kings, Chronicles* and *Samuel*, neither 'Satan' nor the Devil is mentioned save when Satan instigates David's numbering of the men of Israel, to God's displeasure: 'And Satan stood up against Israel, and provoked David to number Israel.' (*I Chronicles 21:1*) Many more references to the devil/Satan are to be found in the New Testament, where the word word 'Satan' is used more than thirty times.

The Devil is also the tempter who offers

Jesus an alternative to carrying the great burden of being the Messiah. Later, upon the return of the seventy disciples: 'the seventy returned again with joy, saying, Lord, even the devils are subject unto us through thy name.' (*Luke 10:17–18*)

When Jesus tells Peter of Judas' coming betrayal he refers to the traitor as a Devil: 'Jesus answered them, Have not I chosen you twelve, and one of you is a devil?' (*John 6:70–1*) This is repeated at the account of the Last Supper in *John 13:2* 'And supper being ended, the devil having now put into the heart of Judas Iscariot, Simon's son, to betray him', while in *Luke 22:3*, this becomes Satan: 'Then entered Satan into Judas surnamed Iscariot, being of the number of the twelve.'

It is Satan whom Jesus warns (Simon) Peter about when he tells him that at his arrest the disciple will deny him thrice before cock crow: 'And the Lord said, Simon, Simon, behold, Satan hath desired to have you, that he may sift you as wheat: But I have prayed for thee, that thy faith fail not: and when thou art converted, strengthen thy brethren.' (*Luke 22:31–2*)

'And as he was yet a coming, the devil threw him down, and tare him. And Jesus rebuked the unclean spirit, and healed the child, and delivered him again to his father.' (Luke 9:42)

The use of the word 'devil' is also generally used to indicate a possessing spirit – 'When the even was come, they brought unto him many that were possessed with devils: and he cast out the spirits with his word.' (*Matthew 8:16*) One such was Mary Magdalene, whom Christ healed: 'And certain women, which had been healed of evil spirits and infirmities, Mary called Magdalene, out of whom went seven devils.' (*Luke 8:2*) Jesus gave this healing power also to his disciples: 'Then he called his twelve disciples together, and gave them power and authority over all devils, and to cure diseases.' (*Luke 9:1*) However, this led the pharisees to conclude that Jesus was in league with the devil himself: 'But the pharisees said, He casteth out devils through the prince of the devils.' (*Matthew 9:34*)

Elmyas the sorcerer is described by Paul as 'thou child of the devil, thou enemy of all righteousness.' (*Acts 13:10*) In the case of Annias and Sapphira, who kept back part of their donation to the church, 'Peter said, Ananias, why hath Satan filled thine heart to lie to the Holy Ghost, and to keep back part of the price of the land?' (*Acts 5:3*)

In *II Corinthians 4:4*, Paul sees Satan as the prince of worldliness, the god of this world. In John's gospel: 'Now is the judgment of this world: now shall the prince of this world be cast out.' *Ephesians 2:2* refers to Satan as 'the prince of the power of the air, the spirit that now worketh in the children of disobedience'.

In the *Epistle to the Hebrews*, Christ's death is said to be the victory over the devil and the forces of evil: 'that through death he might destroy him that had the power of death, that is, the devil'. (*Hebrews 2:14–15*) Christians are exhorted to constant war against the Devil and all his works: the first *Epistle of Peter* (*5:8*) warns: 'Be sober, be vigilant; because your adversary the devil, as a roaring lion, walketh about, seeking whom he may devour.' But Paul in *Romans 16:20* confidently asserts that 'the God of peace shall bruise Satan under your feet shortly.'

The Old Testament

A

AARON The brother of Moses, born three years earlier, just before Pharaoh's edict to murder all the newly born male children of the Hebrews.

When Moses was called by God to lead the Hebrews out of Egypt, he protested that he was not a sufficiently eloquent speaker, and so Aaron became his spokesman in all dealings with Pharaoh. Aaron was at Moses's side subsequently, and his wooden staff played a significant role in the history of the Hebrews. To demonstrate the power of the Lord before Pharaoh, it was turned into a serpent, and, when the Egyptian magicians did the same, Aaron's staff/serpent ate them all. He was the first High Priest of the Hebrews, a position confirmed by the planting of staves in the ground representing each of the twelve tribes; Aaron's alone was found next day to be miraculously sprouting and bearing almonds.

He was with Moses and the Hebrews in the epic journey from Egypt through the wilderness on the way to the Promised Land and accompanied his brother at his first meeting with God on Mount Sinai to seal the Covenant.

His wife Elisheba bore him four sons, Nadab, Abihu, Eleazar and Ithamar. The first two became priests like their father, but perished at the hands of the Lord, punished for burning incense in the Tabernacle.

Aaron failed God twice: first when Moses was on the mountain receiving the Ten Commandments, and the impatient Hebrews agitated for an immediate god to worship. He collected jewelry from the people and made a golden calf, which they then proceeded to worship. Only his penitence and Moses' intercession prevented God's wrath falling

Top: Aaron's staff turns into a serpent to show Pharaoh the power of God.

Above: Aaron burns sacrifice before the golden calf.

Left: In confirmation of Aaron as High Priest, his staff sprouts.

upon Aaron. His second transgression, in league with his sister Miriam, was to question Moses' leadership. Again, he was forgiven. But, like his brother, Aaron did not live to enter the Promised Land – he died on Mount Hor, near the southern end of the Dead Sea, in the Desert of Sin. (*Exodus 4–7, 29, 32, Leviticus 8, 9, 10, 21, Numbers 16, 17, 20*)

ABDON Tenth judge of Israel, son of Hillel the Pirathonite. (*Judges 12:13-55*) Possibly identical with Bedan. (*I Samuel 12:11*)

ABED-NEGO (Jewish name Azariah) A Jewish noble and one of Daniel's companions, educated by the Babylonians for high office in the administration. When Nebuchadnezzar erected a golden idol, they refused to worship it and as punishment were placed into a fiery furnace; but they were not harmed. Nebuchadnezzar, awe-struck, promoted them. (*Daniel 1:6–7,11–21, 3*)

ABEL Adam and Eve's second son, a shepherd, murdered by his brother Cain. He was the first human to die. (*Genesis 4:1–16*)

ABIATHAR High Priest with Zadok at the time of King David. He was the son of Ahimelech, who perished at the hand of Doeg during the massacre at Nob, ordered by King Saul as punishment for giving refuge to David, who had fled the court. Abiathar escaped to join David, and when David became king he appointed Abiathar and Zadok, as High Priests. When Adonijah attempted to usurp the throne, he and Zadok took the Ark of the Covenant from Jerusalem, but David sent them back to act as his spies during Adonijah's brief time in power. However, Abiathar was one of those who, unlike Zadok and Nathan, supported Absalom's plans to take the throne during the last years of David's reign; he was spared by Solomon but deposed as High Priest. (*I Kings 2*)

ABIGAIL David's second sister. (*II Samuel: 17:25*)

Abed-nego emerges from the fiery furnace untouched by the flames as Nebuchadnezzar watches in amazement.

Cain and Abel make sacrifices to the Lord, Cain the fruits of the field, Abel a lamb. But the Lord was displeased with Cain's sacrifice, which drove him to murder his brother.

Abigail: Her husband Nabal failed to give David the respect he was due, but she intercepted his men and appeased David. Nabal died soon after.

ABIGAIL Second wife of David, and widow of Nabal of Carmel. When Nabal refused to recompense David's protection, Abigail pacified the King and later married him. *(I Samuel 25:2–42)*

ABIHU A priest and second son of Aaron. He transgressed by burning incense in the Tabernacle and was burned to death with his elder brother. *(Exodus 6:23)*

ABIJAH Son of King Jeroboam of Israel who became critically ill and died after being cursed by the prophet Ahijah as recompense for the sins of his father. *(I Kings 14:1–17)*

ABIJAM (Abijah in *Chronicles*) Second King of Judah after the division of the kingdom, son of Rehoboam. He reigned for three years. The conflict with Israel that had begun in the reign of his father continued, and Abijam is recorded as having inflicted a significant defeat on Jeroboam. Abijam made an inspiring speech to his assembled army; the Israelites then attacked the rear of his army, but with God's help they were repulsed and crushed. Abijam was able to take control of the hills of Ephraim and the religious center of Bethel. *(I Kings 15, II Chronicles 13)*

ABIMELECH Ruler of Gerar at the time of Abraham. When Abraham settled in the Gerar area, he let it be known that his wife, Sarah, was his sister. Abimlech abducted her but was warned in a dream by God that he must not lay hands on her, for this was Abraham's wife. So Abimelech returned Sarah with gifts of livestock, slaves and silver as compensation. Relations between the two men seem to have been repaired by a great feast; and when there later arose a dispute about water rights, this was harmoniously resolved. *(Genesis 20, 21:22–32)*

ABIMELECH A subsequent ruler of Gerar, who, extraordinarily, experienced very similar incidents with Isaac. In this case, Abimelech did not abduct Rebekah but was informed that she was Isaac's wife, not his sister, when passers by observed them 'sporting' together. There appears to have been a good relationship between Abimelech and Isaac, however, as the easy resolution of a dispute over wells indicates. *(Genesis 26: 1–30)*

ABIMELECH Son of Gideon who set himself up as king. Abimelech put himself forward as

Abihu and his brother failed to follow the practice of worship set down by the Lord and were punished by death.

ABRAHAM

monarch and was accepted as such by the people of Sechem, who donated 70 pieces of silver to further his project. Abimelech then hired a band of villains and proceeded to force his way to power, in the process killing his brother and half-brothers (who numbered seventy). One survived, Jotham, and he placed a curse upon Abimelech and his followers before fleeing to Beer. For the next three years Abimelech held power, even suppressing a rebellion led by interlopers headed by a man called Gaal and punishing the city of Shechem. It was during fighting for Thebez that he met his fate. Having taken the city, he set the citadel on fire, from which a woman launched a millstone that dealt him a mortal blow. Ashamed for it to be said that he had been killed by a woman, Abimelech persuaded one of his henchmen to despatch him with his sword. The Jews would not be ruled again by a king until Saul. (*Judges 9*)

ABISHAG Concubine to King David in his old age and object of Adonijah's marriage intentions after David's death. She was a Shunammite (I Kings 1:1–4, 15, 2:13–25)

ABNER General of King Ishbosheth, whom as head of the army he had proclaimed king after the Battle of Mount Gilboa, and the death of Saul and his first three sons. He quareled with the King over Rizpah, a concubine of the late King, and deserted to Judah, where he arranged the return of David's wife, Michal (Saul's daughter) to him and set out to help rally the countryside to David. He was slain by David's general Joab in pursuance of a long-standing grievance, for he had killed Joab's youngest brother Asahel in battle. He was Saul's cousin. (*I Samuel 14:50, 17:55–8, 20:25, 26:13–16, II Samuel 2, I Chronicles 26:28, 27:20*)

ABRAHAM (Abram) 'The Father of Many Nations' (*Genesis 17:4*) was the first of the Hebrew Patriarchs and the founder figure of the Judaic, Christian and Mohammedan faiths. A sheep farmer, Abram was the youngest son of Terah, a citizen of Ur in the Chaldees, in lower Meso-

Abishag gave comfort to David in his extreme old age; but upon the succession of Solomon, his step-brother Adonijah asked for her hand.

Abram and his family move from Ur to Canaan.

13

potamia, 'the cradle of civilization'. The family
moved to Haran in Syria, and there God visited
him and told him to move with his wife Sarai to
Canaan, where he would become the progenitor
of a great nation.

In a series of visions and meetings, he
accepted a Covenant with God, just as Noah
had and Moses would. In a vision, God told
him that his descendants would number more
than the stars he could see in the night sky
above him. Abram was now to be known as
Abraham, and his wife as Sarah.

After a sojourn in Egypt as refugees during
a period of famine, Abraham and Sarah
prospered in Canaan, while his nephew, Lot,
moved to one of the coastal cities, Sodom,
from which Abraham had to rescue him when

*Above left: God tells
Abram that he is to be the
father of many descen-
dants.*

*Left: Abraham, knife in
hand, prepares to sacrifice
his son.*

*Right: Absalom becomes
entangled in the branch of
a tree while fleeing the
battlefield. He hung there
until Jael, with David's
troops, found him and
dispatched him.*

he became embroiled in a war between the cities. These cities became dens of vice and evil, and Abraham had later to ask for God's mercy to save Lot when the Lord destroyed Sodom and Gomorrah.

But neither Abraham nor Sarah were in the first flush of youth, and childbearing seemed unlikely, despite the Lord's reassurances. So Abraham's servant, Hagar, became his concubine and gave birth to a son, Ishmael. Only later did the now elderly Sarah miraculously bear him a son, who was named Isaac. Now Abraham cruelly sent Hagar and Ishmael away into the desert to fend for themselves, there to be saved by God. It would be through the line of Isaac that the Hebrew nation would emerge.

Abraham's faith and his adherence to the Covenant was tested terribly in one of the Bible's most dramatic episodes. God told him to take Isaac up into the mountains and there build an altar and sacrifice the child. Abraham obeyed, but God, seeing that the strength of his faith had been confirmed, stopped him before he could administer the fatal blow and directed him to a lamb caught in a thicket for sacrifice instead.

After a long life, Abraham was buried at a

place he had purchased from a Hittite, Machpelah, near Hebron. Here too were buried his wife and descendants, Isaac, Rebekah, Leah and Jacob. *(Genesis 11:26 to 25:19)*

ABSALOM was the third son of David by Maacah, a handsome, well-built young man with a commanding presence and persuasive eloquence. He was also his father's favorite but became the center of a dramatic internecine conflict.

When the violation of his sister, Tamar, by his half-brother Amnon went unpunished by the King, Absalom took the law into his own hands and had Amnon murdered. He then fled Jerusalem, returning three years later and coming face to face with his father another two years after that.

David's grief at the affair was profound, but there was no true reconciliation on the part of Absalom, who now had designs on the throne itself. The unresolved conflict between the king and the heir apparent culminated in a revolt, taking David so completely by surprise that he was forced to flee the city, leaving behind spies, chief of whom was Hushai, who persuaded Absalom to take the time concentrate his forces before pursuing his father. This gave David time to regroup. Meanwhile Ahitophel talked Absalom into lying with the ten concubines David had left in the city – which was seen as a deliberate public insult to his father, making reconciliation out of the question.

In the broken, wooded country of Ephraim the decisive battle took place. David was victorious; Absalom, fleeing through the trees, was trapped by his long hair in the branches of an oak and killed by David's men. Again David grieved. *(II Samuel 18:1, Psalms 42 and 43)*

ACHAN Looter of Jericho. When Joshua set out to capture Ai, his first assault failed, and God revealed that one of the Hebrews had broken His ban on looting during the conquest of Jericho: unless this were expiated, there could be no conquest of Ai. Joshua set forth an investigation, and Achan, of the tribe of Judah, confessed that he had taken 'a goodly Babylon-

15

Achan confronted with the evidence of his looting.

ian garment and two hundred shekels of silver, and a wedge of gold of fifty shekels weight'. For this he was stoned and his body burned, and a pile of stones set upon the remains; henceforth the place was known as the Valley of Achor. (*Joshua 7:1,18–26*)

ACHISH The king with whom David took refuge after fleeing from Saul, (*I Samuel 21:10–15*), called Abimelech in the superscription of *Psalms 34*. David a second time repaired to this same king at the head of a band of warriors. Achish assigned him Ziklag, whence he made war on the surrounding tribes. (*I Samuel 27:5–12*) Achish confided in David (*I Samuel 28:1, 2*), but to please his courtiers did not permit him to go to battle with the Philistines. (*I Samuel 29:2–11*) David remained with Achish a year and four months.

ACHISH Another king of Gath, to whom Shimei's two servants fled. Shimei went to Gath to seek them, thereby breaking an oath, and for this Solomon put him to death. (*I Kings 2:39–46*)

ADAM The first man, formed by God in His own likeness on the sixth day of Creation.

Placed in the Garden of Eden, an earthly Paradise, he was joined as helpmeet by Eve, the first woman. Both were created without sin, and they were instructed to be fruitful and multiply.

The animals were presented to Adam to

Adem and Eve: Top, as God intended; below, expelled from Eden into a harsh world.

name, and he was given dominion over them. In this state of naked innocence, the only condition imposed by God was that they should not eat the fruit of the tree of the knowledge of good and evil.

But the serpent's temptation of Eve ended this idyll; Adam and Eve ate the forbidden fruit and found shame in their nakedness. The purity of the relationship between God and Man was thus destroyed. They were expelled from Eden and forcibly prevented from re-entering by a ring of cherubim with flaming swords. Henceforth they would have to work to live, would face the dangers of a sometimes hostile world and be prone to disease and suffering; eventually they would die and their bodies return to the dust from which they had been created.

Eve bore Adam two sons, Cain and Abel; then, after Abel killed his brother and was condemned as an outcast by God, Eve bore another son, Seth, through whom the chosen line was to continue. (*Genesis 1–5*)

ADONIJAH Fourth son of David, by Haggith. Toward the end of David's reign, when he was very old, Adonijah saw himself as the heir-apparent to the throne; however, David had made a promise to Bathsheba that her son, Solomon, would succeed him. Adonijah conspired with Joab, David's nephew and leading general, and Abiathar, one of the High Priests, to remove David and seize the throne. He even gathered his brothers and a number of high officials for a fast at En-rogel in the Kidron valley to seal the agreement to proceed. But he did not include Solomon; and word of the plot reached the ears of Nathan, David's counsellor. He and Bathsheba urged David to act at once: Solomon was sent upon the King's mule to Gihon with Nathan, Zadok, the other High Priest, and Benaiah, captain of the king's bodyguard, and there he was anointed king. 'And they blew the trumpet; and all the people said, God save king Solomon. And all the people came up after him, and the people piped with pipes, and rejoiced with great joy, so that the earth rent with the sound

of them.' (*I Kings 1:39–40*) The conspirators were too late. David took no action against Adonijah, but after David's death Adonijah asked for the hand of Abishag, who had been David's last concubine. This Solomon interpreted as a move towards a usurpation attempt, and he ordered Benaiah to execute his older step-brother immediately. (*I Kings 2*)

ADONIRAM Minister of works to King Rehoboam of Judah, unpopular because of the use of forced labor for the great buildings erected by Solomon; he was stoned to death at Shechem after the breakaway of the ten northern tribes. (*I Kings 12:18, II Chronicles 10:18*)

AGAG A king of the Amelekites defeated and made prisoner by Saul, but not slain. The Israeli king was reproved by Samuel for letting him live, and this became the first incident to incur God's displeasure with Saul. Agag was killed by Samuel himself. (*I Samuel 7–33*)

AHAB Seventh king of Israel after the division of the kingdom, son of Omri. He reigned for 22 years and completed construction of his father's new capital, Samaria.

His father had pursued a policy of main-

Samuel shocks Saul by slaughtering the captured Amalekite king, Agag.

taining good relations with the Phoenician coastal cities, and it was there, at Sidon, that Omri found a wife for his son and heir. She was Jezebel, daughter of King Ethbaal. But with Jezebel came the worship of Baal, so Ahab built a temple in his new capital and worshipped the god himself – 'And Ahab the son of Omri did evil in the sight of the Lord above all that were before him.' (*I Kings 16:30*)

It was Ahab's misfortune to be on the throne of Israel at the time the formidable prophet Elijah was active, and he was constantly subjected to Elijah's tirades. Indeed, Ahab's reign is dominated by the activity of Elijah in condemning the King's turning away from God. Elijah prophesied a drought, which came and then ended in heavy rain just after his celebrated sacrificial contest, when the priests of Baal were humiliated by their inability to bring down fire on their altar at Mount Carmel. The priests of Baal were slaughtered as a result, and Jezebel vowed revenge on the prophet, who fled into the wilderness.

The story of Naboth's vineyard reflects

Samuel encounters Ahab and warns him about his conduct.

badly on the royal couple: the King's offer to buy the vineyard was rejected, and Jezebel had the poor man condemned on false charges of blasphemy. He was stoned to death. Elijah confronted the King, telling him he would pay for this crime. But Ahab repented, and Elijah told him that the end of his dynasty would be deferred until the next of his line.

During Ahab's reign, relations with Judah, which had begun to improve during his father's time, reached a point where they formed an alliance. This was sealed by the marriage of his daughter Athalia to King Jehoshaphat's son, Jehoram, which put a reunification of the original Jewish state in prospect. An attack by King Ben-hadad II of Damascus was repulsed and he was defeated decisively in a second battle; subsequently the two kings considered an attack to recover the city of Ramoth-gilead, and they put this to a panel of prophets whom they assembled at Samaria. The prophet

Naboth, owner of the vineyard coveted by Ahab, refuses to sell to the King.

Micaiah, who at first snubbed the invitation to attend, then revealed that God was putting lies into the mouths of the other prophets, deceiving Ahab into a battle that would bring about his death. Unheeding, and with Micaiah safely thrown into prison, the two kings took the field, and Ahab did indeed perish by an arrow that penetrated between the joints of his armor. At the end of the battle he was propped up in his chariot facing the enemy until at sunset he died. (*I Kings 16:29 to 22*) The prophet Micah later warned about the danger of following the evil practices of Ahab and his father. (*I Kings 6:16*)

AHAB False prophet named together with Zedekiah in *Jeremiah 29:21* – 'Thus saith the Lord of hosts, the God of Israel, of Ahab the son of Kolaiah, and of Zedekiah the son of Maaseiah, which prophesy a lie unto you in my name; Behold, I will deliver them into the hand of Nebuchadnezzar king of Babylon; and he shall slay them before your eyes.'

AHASUERUS Persian king and husband of Esther; possibly identical to Xerxes. (*The Book of Esther*)

AHAZ Eleventh king of Judah, son of Jotham, he ruled for sixteen years. Unlike his father and

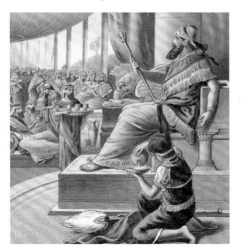

Ahasuerus was very nearly persuaded by the evil Haman to slaughter the Jewish community in his kingdom.

Ahaz ignores God and worships idols.

grandfather, Ahaz failed to place his faith and trust in God, instead taking up the idolatrous and pagan practices of the Assyrians. 'He sacrificed also and burnt incense in the high places, and on the hills, and under every green tree ... Moreover he burnt incense in the valley of the son of Hinnom, and burnt his children in the fire, after the abominations of the heathen whom the Lord had cast out before the children of Israel.' (*II Chronicles 28:3,4*)

The decisive event of his reign was the attack made on Judah by King Pekah of Israel and King Rezin of Syria. Their combined armies reached Jerusalem and inflicted a heavy defeat on Judah's forces, the King's son Maaseiah falling in battle to a mighty man of Ephrain named Zichri. The defenses of the city, which had been strengthened during previous reigns, held, but the invaders departed with many prisoners and a vast amount of booty. Worse, simultaneous with this incursion, the Edomites took the opportunity to rebel and seized Elath, while Philistines raided in the west. In this time of emergency, the prophet Isaiah urged the King to put his trust in God; instead he sent messengers to the Assyrian king, Tiglath-Pileser III, pleading for help and offering gold and silver in payment. In response, and seizing their opportunity, the Assyrians took the field, and captured Damascus. King Rezin was killed. Ahaz hastened there to greet his new ally.

Calling upon Assyria for help, he successfully redressed the military balance for a while, but it was dangerous. Almost as dangerous was the Assyrian altar that Ahaz found in Damascus; a copy was made and set up in proximity to the Temple in Jerusalem, and there Ahaz began to worship Baal with even greater enthusiasm. Despite the dire warnings of Isaiah, 'Ahaz gathered together the vessels of the house of God, and cut in pieces the vessels of the house of God, and shut up the doors of the house of the Lord, and he made him altars in every corner of Jerusalem. And in every several city of Judah he made high places to burn incense unto other gods, and provoked to anger the Lord God of his fathers.' (*II Chronicles 28:24–5*)

AHAZIAH Sixth king of Judah. As the son of Jehoram and Athaliah, his reign of just one year was no better than that of his father – 'Wherefore he did evil in the sight of the Lord like the house of Ahab: for they were his counsellers after the death of his father to his destruction.' (*II Chronicles 22:4*) He made common cause with his uncle, Jehoram of Israel, to fight King Hazael of Damascus, and at the Battle of Ramoth Jehoram was wounded. Both kings retired to Jezreel, where Jehoram was assassinated by the usurper Jehu. According to *II Kings*, Ahazia fled, but his pursuers wounded him in the chase, and he died at Megiddo; according to *II Chronicles*, he fled but was discovered hiding in Samaria and was put to the sword, as were his family. (*II Kings 8:25–9, 9:16–29, II Chronicles 22*)

AHAZIAH Eighth king of Israel after the division of the kingdom. Son of Ahab and grandson of Omri, he reigned for two years. According to the Bible, he followed the wicked example of his father and, like him, had the prophet Elijah to contend with. But it was his mother, Jezebel, who continued the feud with the prophet that had started under Ahab. The King suffered a serious accident – he fell from the balcony of his palace in Samaria – and sent word to the shrine of Baal-zebub of Ekron to discover whether he would survive. Elijah intercepted the messengers and sent back a message telling the King that he would indeed die. Troops sent to capture the elusive prophet were met with fire, brought down from the heavens. Two detachments of troops were despatched this way before the intimidated third could return to the palace with Elijah voluntarily, there to pass judgment on the failing King. It was during Ahaziah's reign that Elijah ascended to heaven in a whirlwind and Elisha took on his mantle. (*I Kings 22:51–3, II Kings 1*)

AHIJAH Prophet of Shiloh. He incited Jeroboam to rebel against Solomon, telling him how, because of the sins of Solomon in worshipping foreign gods, the nation would split asunder: 'And Ahijah caught the new garment that was on him, and rent it in twelve pieces: And he said to Jeroboam, Take thee ten pieces: for thus saith the Lord, the God of Israel, Behold, I will rend the kingdom out of the hand of Solomon, and will give ten tribes to thee.' (*I Kings 11:30–1*) Jeroboam did attempt to kill Solomon but failed, and Ahijah's prophecy only came true after Solomon's death. But Jeroboam was no improvement on Solomon, allowing the worship of foreign gods in his new kingdom. When the King's son, Abijah, was critically ill and the Queen came to Ahijah in disguise to ask for God's help, she was sent away with the message that the child would die and the house of Jeroboam would be cursed. (*I Kings 14:10*) This was fulfilled very soon: Jeroboam's son Nadab reigned for only two years before he was killed and his family wiped out by the usurper Baasha. (*I Kings 15:25–30*)

AHIMELECH Chief priest at Nob in the land of the Benjamites who perished in the massacre ordered by King Saul. He was visited by the fugitive David and gave him consecrated bread, since this was all he had. In such haste had David departed the King's court that he had no weapon, so Ahimelech gave him the only sword there – the sword of Goliath, whom David had killed. When this was reported to Saul by Doeg, the King ordered the execution of all the priests there. Eighty-four other priests died, but Ahimelech's son Abiathar escaped to serve under David. (*I Samuel 21:1–20*)

AMAZIAH Eighth king of Judah, son of Joash. Aged 25 at the time of his accession, Amaziah waited until he felt securely in power before executing the murderers of his father. While he worshipped the Lord, he did nothing to eliminate the idolatry that had once more spread through Judah. He reorganized the army, which had declined further during the latter years of his father's reign, and set out to reconquer the formerly vassal state of Edom. He defeated the Edomites in the Valley of Salt, the prisoners taken in battle being thrown over cliffs and dashed to pieces on the rocks below.

David in triumph over Goliath. The giant's sword was preserved at Nob until Ahimelech saw that David had need of it.

His military adventures, however, led him astray. Amaziah returned to Judah with the idols worshipped in Edom and set them up for worship; objections from the prophet received a haughty reply, and the prophet told him that God would destroy him. Before the Edom campaign, he had contracted a number of mercenary troops from Israel but was persuaded to send them away, since, as the prophet told him, they came from a country of sin. Amaziah lost the money he had paid them, and in their anger at his rejection the mercenaries rampaged through Judah looting and destroying.

After his successful reconquest of Edom, Amaziah became excessively ambitious and sent a message to King Jehoash of Israel challenging him to battle. Jehoash, his army fresh from victories against Syria, at first refused, seeing no point in such a war. But Amaziah persisted and was soundly defeated at the Battle of Beth-Shemesh. He was taken prisoner and forced to watch a 400-cubit stretch of his capital city's walls being demolished. Jehoash then returned to Samaria with all the gold and silver he could find in Jerusalem.

Thoroughly humiliated, Amaziah met the fate the prophet had foreseen: a plot against his life forced him to flee to Lachish, but his assassins followed him there and dispatched him. He had ruled Judah for 29 years and was succeeded by his son, Uzziah. (*II Kings 14–22, II Chronicles 25*)

AMON Fourteenth king of Judah, son of Manasseh. He fell back into the sinful ways of his father's early years and was assassinated in his palace after two years. (*II Kings 21:18–26, II Chronicles 33:21–4*)

AMOS Prophet from Tekoa, just south of Bethlehem in the Kingdom of Judah. He was active during the reigns of Uzziah in his native land and of Jeroboam II in Israel. However, he preached in Israel, particularly at Bethel, a place of worship established by Jeroboam I as the central shrine of the northern kingdom to rival the established place of worship in Jesusalem. As such it was seen as illegitimate and fell into corrupt practices and even idolatry.

But while Amos's contemporary, Hosea, preached against this worship of idols and false gods, Amos denounced the moral decline of the Hebrews. His time was one of prosperity and relative peace, and it was this that had led to social and moral corruption – prosperity, he said, was even more dangerous than poverty. His message, however, was seen as sedition by Amaziah, the local priest, who complained about him to King Jeraboam. Amos defended himself as just a sheep farmer and cultivator of fig trees who had been called by God to deliver this truth.

He continued to preach and was the first to point out that God was a universal deity, not just the god of the Hebrews but the god of all nations. However, God had made a Covenant with them, and they must respect it and act accordingly. God's chosen people had rejected Him and indulged in empty rituals; so God would reject them. He was also the first to predict the forthcoming time of troubles and the captivity of Israel; and indeed thirty years later

Amos preaching.

the Assyrians were to begin the destruction of the Hebrew kingdoms. (*The Book of Amos*)

ANTIOCHUS the name of several Syrian kings. Antiochus the Great, referred to in *Daniel 11:13–19*, was succeeded by his son, Seleucus Philopater (*Daniel 11:20*), who calls him 'a raiser of taxes'. Antiochus IV, surnamed 'Epiphanes'(Illustrious), succeeded his brother Seleucus (*Daniel 11:21–32*) and destroyed Jerusalem, putting multitudes of its inhabitants to a most cruel death. He compelled the Jews to conform to the worship of the Greeks, consecrated the Temple to Jupiter, and turned it into a scene of the foulest revelry, placing the statue of Jupiter on the altar. (*Daniel 11:31*) He died suddenly.

ARAUNAH (also called Oman in *Chronicles 21:15*) A Jebusite who dwelt in Jebus (Jerusalem) before the Israelite conquest. The threshing-floor belonging to Araunah was situated on Mount Moriah, and he made a free gift of it to David, together with the oxen and the threshing instruments. But the King insisted on purchasing it, paying its full price. (*II Samuel 24:24, I Chronicles 21:25*) It was on this spot that Solomon subsequently erected the Temple. (*II Samuel 24:16, II Chronicles 3:1*)

ARMONI one of the two sons of Saul and Rizpah. With his step-brothers he was delivered to the Gibeonites by David, who hanged them. (*II Samuel 21:8, 9*)

ARTAXERXES King of Persia who sent Ezra and Nehemiah to Jerusalem. (*The Book of Ezra, The Book of Nehemiah*)

ASA Third king of Judah after the division of the kingdom. The son of Abijam, his long reign of 41 years was a generally benign one in terms of both religious and military affairs.

The prophet Azariah assured him that if he was faithful to the Lord, all would be well; he should not be discouraged by setbacks. (*II Chronicles 15*) Thus encouraged, Asa tackled the pagan and alien cults that had been introduced to Judah during the reigns of his predecessors, expelling the male and female prostitutes from the pagan shrines and removing idols. The degree to which these foreign influences had penetrated Judah can be judged by his destruction of the obscene idol of a fertility god that his grandmother Maacah had erected. Asa did not succeed in removing all these foreign religious practices, but he remained loyal to God throughout his reign.

His military record was also a good one. When King Baasha of Israel invaded Judah and began to fortify an advanced base at Ramah, Asa made an alliance with King Ben-hadad of Damascus, sending him great treasure to encourage him to break his alliance with Israel. The combined forces dealt Baasha a heavy blow, and Asa was able to take control of the territory of Naphthali. (The prophet Hanani infuriated Asa by telling him that his

Artaxerxes listens sympathetically to Nehemiah's request to go to Jerusalem.

alliance with Damascus showed a lack of faith in God.) He also repulsed a raid by the Cushite King Zerah of Ethiopia.

In the last two years of his reign, Asa was afflicted by a disease of the feet (possibly dropsy), and he was criticized for consulting doctors instead of just placing his fate in the hands of the Lord. (*I Kings 15:9–24, II Chronicles 14–16*)

ASAHEL Youngest brother of Joab, David's general. He was killed by Abner in battle, leading Joab to pursue vengeance, which he obtained when Abner deserted Ishbosheth for the cause of David. (*II Samuel 2:18–23*)

ASENATH Wife of Joseph and mother of Manasseh and Ephraim. She was the daughter of Potipherah, priest of On. (*Genesis 41:50*)

ASHER Eighth son of Jacob, by Zilpah, Leah's handmaid. (*Genesis 30:13*) Anna the prophetess was of this tribe. (*Luke 2:36*)

ASHTORETH the moon goddess of the Phoenicians, who called her Astarte. She deified the passive principle in nature, and was their principal female god, called the 'queen of heaven' (*Jeremiah 44:25*), as Baal, the sun-god, was their chief male deity (*Judges 10:6, I Samuel 7:4, 12:10*). She was the Ishtar of the Accadians and the Artemis/Hecate of the Greeks. (*Jeremiah 44:17, I Kings 11:5, 33; II Kings 23:13*) Among the Philistines in the time of Saul there was a temple of this goddess. (*I Samuel. 31:10*) Solomon introduced her worship (*I Kings 11:33*); and Jezebel's 400 priests were probably employed in her service. (*I Kings 18:29*)

ATHALIAH Queen of Judah, daughter of King Ahab of Israel and wife to King Jehoram of Judah. When the usurper Jehu killed King Jehoram of Israel and wiped out the entire royal family there, he also executed Ahaziah of Judah and slaughtered most of his family. In Jerusalem, the Queen Mother, Athaliah, joined in the killing by ordering the death of all the members of the royal family of Judah and seized power. This mass slaughter of the two royal houses of the Jews left usurpers in both kingdoms. But in Judah, a child of Ahaziah survived the massacre, rescued by Ahaziah's half-sister Jehosheba. For six years he remained hidden in the Temple compound until Jehosheba's husband, the priest Jehoiada, decided that the time was ripe and staged a revolution – King Joash was anointed and crowned, and Athaliah was executed away from the Temple at the Horse Gate of the city. She was a worshipper of Baal. (*II Kings 11:1–16, II Chronicles 21:10–12, 23:1–15*)

AZARIAH See Uzziah.

AZARIAH Son of Oded and prophet of Judah during the reign of King Asa. He reassured the King that if he remained faithful to the Lord all would be well, but if he turned away then he would be abandoned. He invoked the history of the Jews and showed how, when the people had fallen away from the worship of God and trouble came, they could always find Him. The King should be strong and not demoralized by the problems that lay ahead. This encouraged the young King to purge Judah of the alien cults that had penetrated the land. (*II Chronicles 15*)

B

BAAL God of the Canaanites and Phoenicians and chief rival to the god of the Hebrews. Variously seen as the god of crops and fruitfulness, of storms and the weather, and of war, he was worshipped at shrines set on high places. Practices were said to include prophecy, fornication, self-mutilation and child sacrifice. Prophets in the two kingdoms of Israel and Judah were constantly warning against the cult of Baal, which tended to be imported when Jews married neighboring races. One such was Ahab, who married Jezebel and allowed the large-scale worship of Baal to invade Israel. (*I Kings 16:31–3*) Elijah's contest with the prophets of Baal as to which god could light a fire ended with total defeat for Baal. (*I Kings 18:18–28*) Other names or spellings for Baal include Bel, Belus, Baalim and Merodach. However, it is probable that the use of the word Baal in the Bible may be an all-embracing expression for various gods or cults, usually in the context of rivalry with the Jewish God. (*Judges 2:11, 6:25,*

The worship of Baal, a constant threat to the religion of the Hebrews.

10:10, II Kings 10:22, 17:16, Isaiah 46:1, Jeremiah 50:2, 51:44)

BAALBERITH The god worshipped in Shechem after the death of Gideon (*Judges 8:33, 9:4, 46*) as the god of the Covenant made by the Israelites with the Canaanites against the command of Jehovah. (*Exodus 34:12*)

BAALHANAN A king of Edom, son of Aebbor. (*Genesis 36:38, 39, I Chronicles 1:49, 50*)

BAALHANAN One of David's overseers of 'the olive trees and sycamore trees in the low plains'. (*I Chronicles 27:28*)

BAALIS King of the Ammonites, at the time of the Babylonian captivity. (*Jeremiah 40:14*) He hired Ishmael to slay Gedaliah, governor of the cities of Judah.

BAALPEOR An obscene god of Moab (*Numbers 25:3, 31:16 Joshua 22:17*) the Baal of Peor, (Mount Peor), where his worship was celebrated. The Israelites fell into this idolatry. (*Numbers 25:3, 18; Deuteronomy 4:3; Psalms 106:28; Hosea 9:10*)

BAANA Father of Zadok. (*Nehemiah 3:4*)

BAANAH A son of Rimmon the Beerothite, captain in Saul's army. He and his brother Rechab assassinated Ishbosheth, for which they were slain by David. (*II Samuel 4:2,5,6,12*)

BAASHA Third King of Israel after the division of the kingdom. He usurped the throne by killing King Nadab at the siege of Gibbethon and exterminated the house of Jeroboam I, as prophesied by Ahijah. This act and his continuation of his predecessor's religious policies, the prophet Jehu told him, condemned him in the eyes of the Lord: 'Forasmuch as I exalted thee out of the dust, and made thee prince over my people Israel; and thou hast walked in the way of Jeroboam, and hast made my people Israel to sin, to provoke me to anger with their sins; Behold, I will take away the posterity of Baasha, and the posterity of his house; and will make thy house like the house of Jeroboam the son of Nebat. Him that dieth of Baasha in the city shall the dogs eat; and him that dieth of his in the fields shall the fowls of the air eat ... So Baasha slept with his fathers, and was buried in Tirzah: and Elah his son reigned in his stead.' He also

Balaam: right, an angel confronts him as he goes to curse the Hebrews; below, he blesses them.

failed as a military leader, invading Judah but being then defeated by the combined armies of King Asa and Ben-hadad of Damascus. (*I Kings 16:2–6*)

BALAAM A mystic of Beor called upon for help by the King of Moab. En route to the Promised Land, the Hebrews needed to cross the Plain of Moab, and the King was naturally apprehensive of the approach of such a numerous migrating tribe. Balaam was asked to pronounce a curse upon the Hebrews, but God appeared to him in a dream telling him not to do so. The King's entreaties prevailed, however; then, as he rode out to make the curse, Balaam found his ass would not pass a certain point. When he beat it, the animal miraculously protested vocally, and at the same time Balaam saw what the donkey could see: an angel with a sword blocking the way. Balaam thereupon blessed the Hebrews and made sacrifices to God. (*Numbers 22–4, Deuteronomy 23:4*) He was later killed during the battle between the Hebrews and the Midianites. (*Numbers 31:8*)

BALADAN Father of the Babylonian king Merodach-baladan. (*II Kings 20:12; Isaiah 39:1*)

BALAK King of Moab (descendant of Moab, son of Lot), son of Zippor. He commissioned Balaam to curse the Hebrews as they approached his lands (see entry above).

BANI A Levite and reformer after the return from Babylon (*Nehemiah 8:7; 9:4, 5*). His son Rehum helped to rebuild the city wall. (*Nehemiah 3:17*)

BARACHEL The father of Elihu, one of Job's friends. (*Job 32:2, 6*)

BARACHIAH The father of Zechariah. (*Zechariah 1:1, 7 Matthew 23:35*)

BARAK Son of Abinoam and Deborah's general at the battle near Mount Tabor at which the Canaanite Sisera was defeated. (*Judges 4–5*)

BARIAH one of Shemaiah's five sons. Their father is counted along with them in *I Chronicles 3:22*.

BARZILLAI Gileadite who gave sustenance to David during his flight from Jerusalem during the usurpation of Absalom. He refused the King's offers of rewards, citing his great age, but sent his son, Chimham to David's court instead. (*II Samuel 20:31–40*)

BASHEMATH The daughter of Ishmael, one of Esau's three wives. (*Genesis 36:3, 4, 13*) She is also called Mahalath. (*Genesis 28:9*)

BASHEMATH A daughter of Solomon and wife of Ahimaaz, one of his officers. (*I Kings 4:15*)

BATHSHEBA Queen of Israel and David's eighth wife. A great beauty, she was originally the wife of Uriah, a Hittite. David saw her and was consumed with desire for her, marrying her after arranging the death of her husband. They were punished for this sin by the death of their

Barak at the Battle of Mount Tabor, with Deborah the judge urging the army onward.

Belshazzar's feast – the writing on the wall, which Daniel interprets as forecasting the doom of Babylon.

first born. (*II Samuel 11, 12:24*) Subsequently Bathsheba bore David four sons: Solomon, Shammua, Shobab and Nathan. (*I Chronicles 3:5*) On David's death, she ensured the succession went to Solomon. (*I Kings 1:11–31*) She was also mistakenly involved in the attempt of Adonijah to usurp the throne by marrying Abisgag. (*II Kings 2:13–25*)

BECHER The second son of Benjamin (*Genesis 46:21*), who went down to Egypt with Jacob. His descendants were classed with the tribe of Ephraim (*Numbers 26:35, I Chronicles 7:20, 21*) rather than among the descendants of Benjamin. (*Numbers 26:38*)

BELSHAZZAR Last King of Babylon. As joint ruler with his father, Nabonidus, a successor to Nebuchadnezzar, Belshazzar feasted at Babylon on the eve of its conquest by the Persian Cyrus. Writing on the wall of his palace – *MENE MENE TEKEL UPHARSIN* – was interpreted by Daniel as predicting his fall, God's vengeance for Belshazzar's impious use of the gold- and silverware looted from the Temple in Jerusalem. (*Daniel 5*)

BELTESHAZZAR The Babylonian name given to Daniel. (*Daniel 1:7*)

BENAIAH A priest who blew the trumpet when the Ark of the Covenant entered Jerusalem. (*I Chronicles 15:24; 16:6*)

BENAIAH The son of Jehoiada, High Priest (*I Chronicles 27:5*) and appointed by David over his bodyguard of Cherethites and Pelethites. (*II Sam. 8:18, I Kings 1:32; I Chronicles 18:57*) For his exploits see *2 Samuel 23:20, 21, 22* and *I Chronicles 11:22*. He served Solomon (*I Kings 1:8, 10, 26*), by whom he was made commander-in-chief in Joab's place after he had been put to death. (*I Kings 2:25,29,30,34,35, 4:4*)

BEN-HADAD I King of Aram in Syria, whose capital was at Damascus. He was seduced from his alliance with King Baasha of Israel by gifts from Asa of Judah; their combined armies defeated Baasha, whereupon both rulers made territorial gains, Ben-hadad taking much of northern and eastern Galilee. (*I Kings 15:18–20, II Chronicles 16:2–6*)

BEN-HADAD II King of Aram in Syria, son of Ben-hadad I. In league with 32 other rulers, Ben-hadad attacked Israel and besieged Samaria, but after negotiations had reached stalemate King Ahab's troops made a surprise sally against the besiegers, who fled. However, Ben-hadad soon returned, and in the ensuing battle was made prisoner by Ahab. Instead of killing him, Ahab treated him well and made a treaty with him whereby Ben-hadad returned to Israel the towns in Galilee taken by his father. Two years of peace followed, and then King Jehosphat persuaded Ahab to join forces against Ben-hadad at Ramoth-gilead. As retribution for breaking his treaty with Syria, Ahab became the focus of Ben-hadad's attack and was killed. Later, when Ben-hadad fell seriously ill, he heard that the prophet Elisha was in Damascus, so he ordered one of his officers, Hazael, to take gifts to Elisha and ask him if he would live. But when Elisha received

King Ben-hadad of Damascus.

Reuben pleads for Benjamin before Joseph, as yet unaware that he is their brother.

the Syrian officer, he told Hazael to lie to the King, for God had decreed that he, Hazael, would become king. This Hazael did, and the next day soaked a blanket with water and suffocated Ben-hadad. (*I Kings 20, II Kings 6:24, 8:7–15*)

BEN-HADAD III King of Aram in Syria, son of Hazael. The fortunes of Syria declined after his father's death. As prophesied by Elisha on his death-bed, King Jehoash of Israel defeated Ben-hadad three times and recovered much of the territory lost to his father. (*II Kings 13:14–25*)

BEN-AMMI The son of Lot's youngest daughter by her father (*Genesis 19:38*); also called Amman.

BENJAMIN Twelfth and youngest son of Jacob by Rachel, who died at his birth. His elder brother was Joseph. He went on the second visit of the sons to Egypt, and it was in his baggage that Joseph hid a silver cup then accused his brothers of theft. The tribe of Benjamin, the smallest at the time of the Exodus, was later almost eliminated during inter-tribal wars. It became part of the Kingdom of Judah when the nation divided upon the death of Solomon. (*Genesis 35:42–6, 49:4, Exodus 1:3, Deuteronomy 33:12–13, I Chronicles 2:2, 7:6*)

BERA King of Sodom at the time of the invasion under Chedorlaomer. (*Genesis 14:2, 17:21*)

BERIAH A son of Asher and father of Heber. (*Genesis 46:17*)

BERIAH A son of Ephraim, so named by his father 'because it went evil with his house' at that time. (*I Chronicles 7:20-23*)

BERIAH A Benjamite who, with his brother Shema, founded Ajalon and expelled the Gittites. (*I Chronicles 8:13*)

BERODACH-BALADAN The king of Babylon who sent a friendly ambassador to Hezekiah. (*II Kings 20:12*) In *Isaiah 39:1* his name is Merodach-baladan.

BETHUEL The son of Nahar and Milcah, nephew of Abraham, and father of Rebecca. (*Genesis 22:22, 23, 24:18,24,47*)

BEZALEEL The skilled artisan connected with the Tabernacle in the wilderness. His handiwork was chiefly works of metal, wood, and stone. He was the son of Uri, the grandson of Hur, of the tribe of Judah. In *Ezra 10:30* we read of another of the same name. (*Exodus 31:2, 35:30*)

BIGTHA A eunuch who served in the harem of Ahasuerus. (*Esther 1:10*)

BIGTHAN A eunuch who 'kept the door' in the palace of Ahasoerus, and who, with Teresh, conspired against the king. Through Mordecai they were detected and hanged. (*Esther 2:21–23, 6:1–3*)

BILDAD one of Job's visitors. (*Job 8:1, 18:5, 25:1*)

BILGAH A priest who returned from Babylon with Zerubbabel. (*Nehemiah 12:5, 18*)

BILHAH Concubine to Jacob, formerly maidservant to Rachel. In view of Rachel's apparent barrenness, she asked her husband to take Bilhah as a proxy, and she bore him two sons, Dan and Naphthali. She later had an affair with Reuben, to the great distress of Jacob. (*Genesis 29:29; 30:3–8; 35:22, 49:4*)

BILSHAN A man who returned from Babylon with Zerubabbel. (*Ezra 2:2, Nehemiah 7:7*)

BIRSHA King of Gomorrah. (*Genesis 14:2*)

BLASTUS A chamberlain of King Herod Agrippa I. (*Acts 12:20*)

BOAZ A rich farmer of Bethlehem in whose fields Ruth gleaned. Naomi, Ruth's mother-in-law, adopted a clever strategy to bring Ruth's identity as his close kinsman to Boaz' attention: 'And when Boaz had eaten and drunk, and his heart was merry, he went to lie down at the end of the heap of corn: and she came softly, and uncovered his feet, and laid her down. And it came to pass at midnight, that the man was afraid, and turned himself: and, behold, a woman lay at his feet. And he said, Who art thou? And she answered, I am Ruth thine handmaid: spread therefore thy skirt over thine handmaid; for thou art a near kinsman. And he said, Blessed be thou of the Lord, my daughter: for thou hast shewed more kindness in the latter end than at the beginning, inasmuch as thou followedst not young men, whether poor or rich. And now, my daughter, fear not; I will do to thee all that thou requirest: for all the city of my people doth know that thou art a virtuous woman. And now it is true that I am thy near kinsman.' She later became his wife and bore him a son, Obed, who was the grandfather of David. (*Ruth 2–4, I Chronicles 2:11–12*)

Boaz encounters Ruth, whom Naomi has sent to glean in his fields.

CAIN The first-born son of Adam and Eve, thus the first natural offspring of Man; also the first murderer. A tiller of the soil, he was outraged when his sacrifice of the fruits of the land was rejected by God, while that of his brother, Abel, a shepherd, was accepted. So he killed his brother, and when God asked him where Abel was, he replied, 'Am I my brother's keeper?' God punished him: he was cursed; he would fail as a farmer; and he would wander the earth as a fugitive. When Cain pointed out that he was likely to be slain, God put a mark on him as a sign that he was not to be killed; this may also be seen as redemptive. Cain moved to the land of Nod, where he built the first recorded city and founded the Kenite tribe. (*Genesis 4; Numbers 24:22; Hebrews 11:4; I John 3:12; Jude 11*)

CAINAN The fourth and antediluvian patriarch (*Genesis 5:9–14*), also called Kenan. (*I Chronicles 1:2*)

CAINAN The son of Arphaxad. (*Luke 3:35, 36*)

CALCOL Probably the same as Chalcol (*I Kings 4:31*), one of the four sages whom Solomon excelled in wisdom. (*I Chronicles 2:6*)

CALEB Of the tribe of Judah, he was one of the twelve spies sent by Moses to investigate the Promised Land. Only he and Joshua returned with positive news: 'And Caleb stilled the people before Moses, and said, Let us go up at once, and possess it; for we are well able to overcome it.' (*Numbers 13: 30*) But the others had been awed by the size of the task ahead of them in attempting to conquer such a land, and, for their lack of faith, God consigned the Hebrews to forty years of wandering before they could reach their destination. Only Caleb and Joshua, as reward for their faith, were permitted to live long enough to enter Canaan. Caleb had been promised the land he had seen during the mission, Hebron,

The first murder: Abel lies dead, but Cain cannot escape God's punishment.

Caleb and Joshua are the only two of the spies sent to Canaan who returned with good news.

and here he settled. (*Numbers 13, 14, Joshua 14:13*)

CHEDORLAOMER King of Elam. (*Genesis 14:17*)

CHILEAB David's second son by Abigai.l (*II Samuel 3:3*)

CHILION the younger son of Elimelech and Naomi, husband of Ruth's sister (*Ruth 1:2; 4:9*).

CHUSHAN-RISHATHAIM A king of Mesopotamia who oppressed Israel for eight years; conquered by Othniel. (*Judges 3:8, 10*)

COLHOZEH a worker under Nehemiah; father of Shallun and Baruch. (*Nehemiah 3:15, 11:5*)

CONIAH See Jehoiachin.

CONONIAH Supervisor of the offerings and tithes at the Temple during the reign of King Hezekiah of Judah. The King's reforms brought forth a great number of donations, which Cononiah and his brother Shimei were entrusted with taking in. The scale of the task was increased by Hezekiah's invitation to the people of the northern kingdom to participate in the Passover. (*II Chronicles 31:12–13*)

CONONIAH Another Levite, in the reign of Josiah, who carried out a similar role at the celebration of the rebuilt Temple.

CUSH Son of Ham and father of Nimrod. (*Genesis 10:8; I Chronicles 1:10*)

CYRUS II (the Great) King of Persia and conqueror of the Babylonian Empire. He proved a much more magnanimous and benign master to the captive Jews than the Babylon-

ians had; he even returned to them the precious treasures and sacred objects that had been looted from the Temple by Nebuchadnezzar. He sent Zerubbabel back to Jerusalem with a party of Jews and encouraged them to rebuild the Temple; Jewish exiles not returning were exhorted to donate funds for the expedition. (*II Chronicles 36:22-3; Ezra 1:1-8, 3:7, 4:3, 5, 6:3, 14; Daniel 1:21*)

Cyrus the Great.

D

DAGON A god of the Philistines, whose cult existed in Phoenicia and Canaan. It was in the temple to Dagon at Gaza that Samson pulled down the pillars and brought the building down (*Judges 16:23*); at the temple in Ashdod the Philistines placed the captured Ark of the Covenant, with the consequential destruction of the god's idol (*I Samuel 5:2*); and the armor and head of the slain Saul was put in the temple to Dagon at Beth-shan. (*I Chronicles 10:10*) Dagon possibly began as a fish-god, more probably as an agricultural god (dagon meaning 'grain' in Hebrew).

DALPHON The second of Haman's ten sons, all put to death by the Jews in Susa. (*Esther 9:7*)

DAN The fifth son of Jacob. (*Genesis 30:6, 49:16*)

DANIEL The greatest prophet during the period of the captivity, he was one of the Jews taken to Babylon as a child and was probably of royal blood or the nobility. With three companions (Shadrach, Meshach and Abed-nego) he was identified by the Babylonians as especially gifted and with the potential to become a high-level administrator for the Empire; as such, after being given special treatment and schooled for their future roles, they rose to positions of eminence. Daniel served four kings in two empires: Nebuchad-nezzar, Belshazzar, Cyrus (the conqueror of Babylon) and Darius.

It is as an interpreter and visionary that Daniel stands out. King Nebuchadnezzar had a disturbing dream of a giant effigy being destroyed by a rock striking its feet and the whole edifice crumbling to dust, while the rock grew to fill the world. Daniel consulted God and was able to interpret the dream as representing the rise and fall of empires, downwards from the golden head symbolizing Babylon through successive empires ending with that represented by the feet, which, made of composite materials, were weak; the rock represented God's eternal kingdom, which would outlast them all.

Daniel also interpreted another of Neb-uchadnezzar's dreams, this time of a huge tree suddenly cut down to a stump and a man re-duced to living like an animal without human consciousness. Royal experts failed to see the meaning: the tree represented the King in his glory, struck down and humbled until he should repent and acknowledge God. The Bible does not recount Nebuchadnezzar's reaction to this,

Dagon, god of the Philistines, depicted as a fish.

Left: Daniel demonstrates his God-given talent to interpret the dreams of the Babylonian King Nebuchadnezzar.

Right: Daniel survives a night in a den of lions.

but later he went mad, recovering only after seven years of torment.

Daniel was present at the fall of Babylon to the invading Persians during the reign of Nabonidus and Belshazzar, when he interpreted the inscription wrought by the terrifying specter of a hand upon the palace wall as saying that the King had been found wanting, and forecasting the demise of the kingdom. Daniel's prominent role in the administration was continued by the conqueror, but this provoked jealousy: when King Darius insisted that he be worshipped, Daniel had to refuse,

and for this he was put on trial. His punishment was to be placed in a den of lions, where instead of being mauled and eaten he was preserved from harm by the God in whom he placed his faith.

Daniel also experienced a number of personal visions and dreams, which were often far-seeing predictions of events into the time of the Seleucids (the rulers of the area after the fall of the Persian Empire) and included the coming of the Messiah. He lived a long life, characterized by public service, courage, wisdom and unwavering faith. (*The Book of Daniel*).

the captive communities in his empire, allowing the Temple in Jerusalem to be rebuilt (*Ezra 5–6*) and handing back to the Jews the gold and silver taken from the Temple by Nebuchadnezzar.

DARIUS THE MEDE Known only from the *Book of Daniel* (*5:31, 6*), and almost certainly a fictitious character. The author of *Daniel,*

Darius I returns the Temple gold and silver to the Jews.

DARIUS I Ruler at the time of the prophets Haggai and Zechariah. It was only after a struggle against rival claimants that he established himself on the throne, and he adopted a more benevolent attitude toward

writing some centuries after the event, received only confused traditions about the order of the Persian rulers and also supposed there to have been a Median Empire interposed between the Babylonian and Persian. Despite many attempts, it has not proved possible to identify this Darius with any known historical character.

DARKON An exile in Babylon; his children are listed among those who returned with Zerubbabel to Jerusalem. (*Ezra 2:56, Nehemiah 7:58*)

DATHAN A son of Eliab, a Reubenite, who joined Korab in his rebellion against Moses while the Hebrews were in the wilderness. (*Numbers 16:5, 26:9, Deuteronomy 11:6, Psalms 106:17*)

The writing on the wall for Babylon: Daniel explains the meaning of the mysterious words.

Above: Samuel anoints the shepherd boy David King of Israel in place of Saul, whom God has abandoned.

DAVID Shepherd, musician, warrior, bandit, adulterer, murderer and poet – David was both an ancestor of Christ and the greatest king of Israel, founder of a dynasty. His life forms a keystone in the broad narrative of the Old Testament.

His origins were seemingly humble: the eighth son of Jesse, a shepherd, and great-grandson of Boaz and Ruth. He was in the fields near the family home at Bethlehem when the prophet Samuel found him, directed by God, who had turned his back on King Saul and now chose a successor. David was summoned to the royal court at Gilboa, where his musical talents were much appreciated, especially when they soothed Saul's increasingly frequent bouts of melancholia. He was made the King's armor bearer and formed a close bond with the King's son, Jonathan.

David's encounter with the giant Philistine Goliath is one of the best-known stories in the Bible, an enduring metaphor for the victory of the underdog. It tells how, while bringing provisions to the Israeli camp on campaign, he heard of Goliath's challenge to individual combat. Despite Saul's offer of wealth and the hand of his daughter to whoever would defeat the Philistine, none in his army had come forward. Now David volunteered and killed the heavily armored giant, stunning him with a shot from his sling to his forehead, before cutting off his head.

Famous and popular in court, David's growing reputation was met with hostility by Saul, however – knowing that God had turned against him, he increasingly felt threatened by the popularity of this glamorous youngster and set him challenges on the battlefield that might have resulted in his death. Several attempts on David's life failed until he fled the court. Now he was a refugee and a traitor, and soon he became a bandit, dominating an area of the Judaean countryside from the cave of Adullam. Attempts by Saul's men to track him down and kill him failed, while David's own guile and audacity twice brought the King within his power – it is part of the legend of

Above: David kills the giant Goliath with a stone from his sling, despite his opponent's heavy armour.

Above: David carried the head of Goliath back to the Israelite army's lines in triumph.

Right: Saul's frustration and anger erupts, and David flees the court.

northern and southern parts of the Jewish homeland. Here David made his capital, ornamenting it with a palace built with the help of King Hiram of Lebanon. More than that, he brought from Kiriath-Jearim the Ark of the Covenant and housed it in a new tabernacle within the city walls. Jerusalem was thus the new heart of the Jewish religion, and in centuries to come 'the City of David' would become one of the world's most important religious centers.

This momentous event was followed by conquest, as David led armies against Israel's foes – to Syria, Moab, Edom and the land of the Ammonites – and the old enemy, the Philistines, were decisively defeated. A powerful and wealthy empire was created, dominating the region between the Nile and the Euphrates.

As a warrior, David excelled, but as a man he was subject to normal human weaknesses and temptations. Now a powerful monarch, he allowed himself to become an adulterer, stealing another man's wife and ruthlessly engineering the death of the husband. But Uriah's death did not go unpunished: his first-born son by Bathsheba died, and the grieving King acknowledged his guilt. Family tragedy

David that he forbore to kill Saul when the sleeping king was at his mercy. Later he offered his services to Achish, Philistine King of Gath, who made him governor of Ziklag.

Upon the death of Saul at the Battle of Gilboa, Saul's son Ishbosheth was elected king, but the southern tribe of Judah chose David, and civil war broke out. Ultimately Ishbosheth proved inept and was assassinated, and the elders of Israel came to David's capital at Hebron to anoint him king of a reunited kingdom.

A new era in the history of the Jews was beginning, for one of David's first acts was the conquest of Jerusalem, hitherto an independent Jebusite city sitting centrally between the

later brought David more heartbreak. He was father to nineteen children by his eight wives (and an unknown number of concubines), and when one of his sons, Amnon, raped his half-sister, Tamar, he failed to deal with the matter forcefully enough. Tamar's brother, Absalom, had Amnon killed, then fled; years passed before his return to Jerusalem, and the reconciliation between father and son was never complete. Absalom attempted to usurp

The City of David: left, the capture of Jerusalem from the Jebusites. David made it the capital of his kingdom and, above, brought the Ark of the Covenant there, so that the city became both the political and religious center of the kingdom. As the Ark entered the city, David danced before it, incurring the displeasure of his wife, Michal (Saul's daughter), who thought this unseemly. As a result, God made her barren.

the throne and David, now old and completely unprepared, was compelled to flee before returning to retake the city – but losing his son in the process.

During these man-made troubles, God sustained David, whose faith remained constant. When he displeased the Lord by taking a census of fighting men in his kingdom, Israel was punished with a plague that only abated when David, directed by God, made sacrifice at a specific location: the threshing floor of a man called Araunah. Here was later to be the nation's great temple and a permanent home for the Ark of the Covenant. But David would not build it: this was to be the role of his son and successor, Solomon, to whom David bequeathed a prosperous and mighty kingdom.

The character of David as portrayed in the Bible is complex – hero, statesman, but also a family man and a lover of music and poetry: *The Book of Psalms* is traditionally attributed to him. Most importantly, he is seen as Jesus' illustrious ancestor: *Matthew I:1–17* names Jesus 'the son of David', and there are other references of a similar nature in the New Testament. (*I Samuel 16–31, II Samuel, I Kings 1–2*)

DEBORAH Third of the Judges who ruled Israel between the conquest and the establishment of the kingdom. She is unique in the Old Testament as a female leader in her own right and is portrayed as dispensing justice while seated simply beneath a palm tree, somewhere between Bethel and Ramah. During her time the Israelites were almost constantly at war with the Canaanites, and

Above left: The grief of David at the death of Bathsheba's child. His counsellor, Nathan, explained that this was God's punishment for his connivance at the death of her first husband, Uriah.

Above: David leaves Jerusalem as his son Adonijah usurps the throne.

Right: The judge Deborah, beneath her customary palm tree, with her general, Barak.

God directed her to assemble an army to attack them in the Jezreel valley, which the enemy dominated. She had trouble in persuading the tribes to contribute men, but her faith and audacity on the battlefield overrode the caution of her general, Barak, and they won a decisive victory near Mount Tabor. The Canaanite general Sisera was killed seeking refuge in the tent of Jael, and forty years of relative peace ensued. (*Judges 4, 5*)

Left: Delilah eventually persuades Samson to tell her the secret of his phenomenal strength.

DELAIAH The head of a family of exiles who returned to Jerusalem under Zerubbabel. (*Ezra 2:60, Nehemiah 7:62*)

DELILAH The evil seductress responsible for the fall of Samson. A Philistine neighbor of the mighty judge, she was promised rich rewards for discovering the secret of Samson's great strength. By a mixture of seduction and harassment, she eventually discovered that the answer lay in his uncut hair, for he was a Nazarite; cutting his hair while he slept, she made him easy prey for the Philistine agents she had quietly admitted to their dwelling, and Samson was made captive. (*Judges 16*)

DIBLAIM Father of Gomer, Hosea's wife. (*Hosea 1:3*)

DINAH Daughter of the patriarch Jacob and his first wife, Leah, who was seduced or raped by the son of Hamor, ruler of the neighboring tribe at Shechem (Nablus). The son wanted her hand, and it was proposed that the two tribes should intermarry, which was agreed on condition that the men of Shechem be circumcised. However, Dinah's brothers were furious, and this was a ruse: as soon as the circumcisions had taken place, Simeon and Levi set upon the town, killing everyone and looting it. When Jacob suggested that this was possibly an excessive response, they replied: 'Should he deal with our sister as an harlot?' (*Genesis 34*)

DODAVAH Father of the prophet Eliezer. (*II Chronicles 20:37*)

DOEG Perpetrator of the massacre at Nob. He was one of King Saul's herdsmen who happened to be at the priestly city of Nob when David arrived, in flight from the royal court. He witnessed the chief priest, Ahimelech, giving David consecrated bread and also the sword of Goliath, which had been preserved there. When he reported this to Saul, the King ordered the execution of all the priests at Nob, but none of his men would comply, so Doeg volunteered and massacred 85 priests before destroying the place. (*I Samuel 21:7, 9–19*).

DUMAH Son of Ishmael (*Genesis 25:14, I Chronicles 1:30*)

E-F

EBAL Son of Joktan and grandson of Eber (*I Chronicles 1:22*) called also Obal. (*Genesis 10:28*)

EBAL Son of Shobal and grandson of Seir the Horite. (*Genesis 36:23*)

EBED The father of Gaal in whom the men of Shechem put confidence when he conspired against Abimelech before being expelled from Shechem. (*Judges 9:26–41*)

EBER The great grandson of Shem (*Genesis 10:24, 11:14*), considered to be the founder of the Hebrew race. (*10:21, Numbers 24:24*) In *Luke 3:35* he is called Heber.

EBER Head of one of the families of the Gadites. (*I Chronicles 5:13*)

EBER Head of one of the families of Benjamites in Jerusalem. (*I Chronicles 8:22*)

EBER Chief of the priestly family of Amok in the time of Joiakim. (*Nehemiah 12:20*)

Above: Eglon assassinated by Ehud.

EBIASAPH Son of Korah, a Levite (*I Chronicles 6:23, 37*), called Abiasaph in *Exodus 6:24*.

EGLAH One of David's wives, mother of his sixth son, Ithream. (*II Samuel 3:5, I Chronicles 3:3*)

EGLON King of Moab, who defeated the Israelites after the time of Othniel and exacted tribute from them for eighteen years. He was assassinated by Ehud, and Moab was then defeated by the Israelites. (*Judges 3*)

EHUD Second Judge of Israel, slayer of King Eglon the Moabite. After the death of the first judge, Othniel, the Israelites lapsed from their faith in God, and divine punishment followed – the tribes fell into the power of the Moabites. Ehud had a special double-edged dagger made and strapped this to his right thigh beneath his clothing. He then took the tribute to Eglon and told him that he had secret information to impart. When he and the King were alone, Ehud drew the dagger and plunged it into Eglon's fat belly before escaping from the palace. Rallying the Israelites, he inflicted a decisive defeat on the leaderless Moabites, and brought eighty years of peace. (*Judges 3*).

EKER Son of Ram, of the family of Judah. (*I Chronicles 2:27*)

ELADAH A descendant of Ephraim. (*I Chronicles 7:20*)

ELAH Fourth king of Israel after the division of the kingdom. The son of Baasha, who died violently, he reigned for just two years before he himself was assassinated by Zimri, one of his chariot corps commanders, while drunk at his steward's house. Zimri lasted but seven days before he was overthrown by Omri, who then proceeded to slaughter all the family and friends of the house of Baasha. (*I Kings 16:8–14*)

ELAH Second son of Caleb, the son of Jephunneh. (*I Chronicles 4:15*)

ELAH Father of Hoshea, the last king of Israel. (*2 Kings 17:1*)

ELAM Son of Shem. (*Genesis 10:22*)

ELAM Son of Shashak, a Benjamite. (*I Chronicles 8:24*)

ELASAH Son of Shaphan, sent by Zedekiah to Nebuchadnezzar. (*Jeremiah 29:3*)

ELASAH Son of Pashur, a priest who married a Gentile wife in the time of Ezra. (*10:22*)

ELDAD One of the seventy elders appointed to help Moses. (*Numbers 11:26,27*) He and Medad prophesied in the camp, but did not go to the Tabernacle with the others, as Moses had commanded:'And Moses went out, and told the people the words of the Lord, and gathered the seventy men of the elders of the people, and set them round about the tabernacle. And the Lord came down in a cloud, and spake unto him, and took of the spirit that was upon him, and gave it unto the seventy elders: and it came to pass, that, when the spirit rested upon them, they prophesied, and did not cease. But there remained two of the men in the camp, the name of the one was Eldad, and the name of the other Medad: and the spirit rested upon them; and they were of them that were written, but went not out unto the tabernacle: and they prophesied in the camp. And there ran a young man, and told Moses, and said, Eldad and Medad do prophesy in the camp. And Joshua the son of Nun, the servant of Moses, one of his young men, answered and said, My lord Moses, forbid them. And Moses said unto him, Enviest thou for my sake? would God that all the Lord's people were prophets, and that the Lord would put his spirit upon them!' (*Numbers. 11:24–29*; see also *Mark 9:38*)

ELDAAH A son of Midian. (*Genesis 25:4*)

ELEAD An Ephraimite slain by the men of Gath. (*I Chronicles 7:21*)

ELEAZAR Third son of Aaron and High Priest of the Israelites. On the death of his brothers Nadab and Abihu he took their place in assisting his father at the Tabernacle, and he also took a part in conducting Moses' census of the tribes. At Aaron's death on Mount Hor, he was invested with the high priesthood, and he participated in the allotting of the Promised Land to the twelve tribes. He was regarded as the ancestor of the high priests; he married Putiel who bore him a son, Phinehas, who was High Priest at the time of Joshua. (*Exodus 6:23,25; Numbers 3:2,4,32, 20:25–9, Joshua 14:1, 19:51, 24:33; Judges 20:28*)

Left: The camp of the Hebrews during their wandering in the wilderness, showing the location of the Tabernacle in the center, with the twelve tribes encamped about it.

ELEAZAR Son of Abinadab and guardian of the Ark of the Covenant at Kiriath-Jearim before its move to Jerusalem. (*I Samuel 7:1*)

ELEAZAR Son of Dodo the Ahohite, one of David's three veterans who broke through the Philistine army, camped in the plain of Rephaim, and brought him water from the well of Bethlehem: 'And the three brake through the host of the Philistines, and drew water out of the well of Bethlehem, that was by the gate, and took it, and brought it to David: but David would not drink of it, but poured it out to the Lord, And said, My God forbid it me, that I should do this thing: shall I drink the blood of these men that have put their lives in jeopardy? for with the jeopardy of their lives they brought it. Therefore he would not drink it. These things did these three mightiest.' (*I Chronicles, 11:12, 16–19*)

ELI High Priest and long-serving judge of Israel. His two sons, Hophni and Phinehas, were also priests but became increasingly corrupt and immoral, which Eli failed to arrest. God's punishment for this was confided to the young Samuel, then serving Eli, who was now very old and blind. When God first spoke to Samuel, he thought it was Eli calling him from his bed; the third time this happened, Eli realized that God was addressing Samuel and

Right: The young Samuel, woken by a voice, thinks Eli has been calling him.

sent him back to bed to await the word of the Lord. That word was that the sins of Eli's family would be punished by defeat on the battlefield and the loss of the Ark of the Covenant to the Philistines. When this catastrophic event was announced to Eli – together with news of the deaths of his two sons – the aged priest fell and broke his neck. (*I Samuel 1:9, 2, 3, 4:12–18*)

ELIAB A Reubenite, son of Pallu, and father of Dathan and Abiram. (*Numbers 16:1, 12, 26:8, 9; Deuteronomy 11:6*)

ELIAB Eldest son of Jesse, and brother of David (*I Samuel 16:6*), called Elihu in *I Chronicles 27:18.*

ELIAB One of the Gadites who joined David in Ziklag. (*I Chronicles 12:9*)

ELIADA One of David's sons, born in Jerusalem (*II Samuel 5:16*), called Beeliada in *I Chronicles 14:7.*

ELIADAH Father of Rezon, who was an adversary of Solomon. (*I Kings 11:23*)

ELIAKIM Son of Melea, and father of Jonan. (*Luke 3:30, 31*)

ELIAKIM Son of Hilkiah, governor of Hezekiah's palace (*II Kings 18:18, 19:2*)

ELIAKIM (Jehoiakim, King of Judah) His name was changed to Jehoiakim by Pharaoh Necho II. See Jehoiakim. (*II Kings 23:34*)

ELIAM The father of Bathsheba (*II Samuel 11:3*), called Ammiel in *I Chronicles 3:5.*

ELIASHIB The High Priest in the days of Ezra and Nehemiah, who helped to repair the walls. (*Nehemiah 12:22,23, 3:1*)

ELIATHAH Son of Heman and chief of the twentieth course of musicians. (*1 Chronicles 25:4, 27*).

ELIASAPH Son of Deuel (or Reul), prince of the tribe of Gad at the time of the census in the wilderness. (*Numbers 1:16*)

ELIASAPH Son of Lael, a Levite, and chief of the Gershonites. (*Numbers 3:24*)

ELIDAD Son of Chislon and prince of the tribe of Benjamin. (*Numbers 34:21*)

ELIEL A Gadite who joined David at Ziklag. (*I Chronicles 7:11*)

ELIEL An overseer of offerings in the time of Hezekiah. (*2 Chronicles 31:13*)

ELIENAI A son of Shimhi, a chief in the tribe of Benjamin. (*I Chronicles 8:20*)

ELIEZER Of Damascus, the steward of Abraham's house (*Genesis 15:2,3*) whom Abraham sent to Nahor to find a wife for Isaac. It was at a well that he first met Rebekah: 'Behold, I stand here by the well of water; and the daughters of the men of the city come out to draw water: And let it come to pass, that the damsel to whom I shall say, Let down thy pitcher, I pray thee, that I may drink; and she shall say, Drink, and I will give thy camels drink also: let the same be she that thou hast appointed for thy servant Isaac; and thereby shall I know that thou hast shewed kindness unto my master. And it came to pass, before he had done speaking, that, behold, Rebekah came out, who was born to Bethuel, son of Milcah, the wife of Nahor, Abraham's brother, with her pitcher upon her shoulder. And the damsel was very fair to look upon, a virgin, neither had any man known her: and she went down to the well, and filled her pitcher, and came up.' (Genesis 24:13–16) Eliezer introduced himself to her, met her family, and explained who he was, with the result that Rebekah was betrothed to Isaac.

ELIHU One of the captains who joined David at Ziklag. (*I Chronicles 12:20*)

Eliezer first encounters Rebekah at the well near Nahor.

ELIJAH The paramount prophet of the Old Testament, Elijah occupies a special place in the narrative of the Bible. Stern, forceful, a solitary figure, his image is akin to that of John the Baptist – a wild-looking man in leather loincloth and cloak of hair – and he appears to have been able to invoke miraculous powers: restoring the dead to life, parting the waters with his cloak and calling down fire from heaven. He is referred to as the Tishibite (possibly meaning he came from Thisbe, in Gilead), and his name meant 'My God is Yaweh (Jehovah)'.

Elijah's story begins in the reign of Ahab, King of Israel. There, under the influence of his Phoenician queen, Jezebel, the King had permitted the growth of Baal-worship in the kingdom to the great detriment of the Hebrew god, and in the capital, Samaria, a temple to the Phoenician god Baal had been established. We first hear of Elijah warning the King that such wickedness must bring retribution, but the royal court would not listen, and God sent a severe drought, with famine in its wake. Led by God into the wilderness, Elijah drank the waters of the Cherith brook and was miraculously brought food by ravens.

As the famine tightened its grip upon the country, the Lord guided Elijah's footsteps to the town of Zarephath, there to dwell with a widow who would sustain him, but she confessed that she and her child were on the verge of starvation. Their food supplies miraculously failed to run out, and they survived, but then her young child became sick and died. The widow bitterly repented taking in the prophet – had he come to slay her son? Elijah prayed and the child revived.

An even more spectacular miracle was about to happen. Elijah received another instruction from the Lord: he was to go to the King and propose a trial of strength between his god and the King's. Ahab and Jezebel took up the challenge, and the rival priests ascended Mount Carmel, there to build altars to their respective deities. Could they invoke their god to set the

Elijah confronts the sinner King Ahab.

Elijah, fed by ravens during the famine.

Elijah heals the woman of Zarephath's child.

offerings afire? The priests of Baal prayed in vain – nothing happened. And, to pile humiliation on their failure, Elijah had water poured on his altar and dug a trench around it to keep it wet. Then he prayed to God and, before the astonished and terrified crowds, fire fell from the sky upon the sacrificial pyre. It was an awesome demonstration, and the multitude was easily angered to ensure that not one of the Baalist priests survived.

Elijah calls down fire upon his sacrificial altar, setting the offering alight.

Right: Elijah races the King's chariot back from the site of the sacrifices to Jezreel as the tempest begins.

Below: The despairing Elijah on Mount Horeb, where the 'still, small voice of God' reassures him.

Now the drought was drawing to end: Elijah told the King that a torrent was about to descend, but the King would not believe him. Foreshadowed by 'a cloud the size of a man's hand' seen out to sea, the drought broke, and Elijah raced the royal chariot back to the palace at Jezreel.

But Elijah, like so many of the prophets who followed him, was now a hunted man as Jezebel sought revenge. Eluding her soldiers, Elijah fled to the wilderness of Judah, in growing despair and desolation – so hopeless did he become that he even begged God to let him die. As he took shelter in a cave on Mount Horeb, the wind rose, a mighty tempest howled, the rocks shook and fire raged in the air. There, in the tumult, he heard 'a still small voice' reassuring him.

Meanwhile Ahab and Jezebel remained unrepentantly corrupt. When the King coveted a nearby vineyard, his offers of purchase fell on deaf ears; his bullying failed to move the owner, Naboth; so Jezebel had him arrested on false charges of blasphemy, and before a court packed with false witnesses he was condemned to death by stoning. Elijah did not save Naboth from this terrible fate but confronted Ahab in the vineyard and told him that he would pay for what he had done.

Still Elijah's warnings failed to impress the King, and when he died his successor, Ahaziah, continued to ignore the Hebrew god: badly injured in an accident, he sent for help to the temple of Baal-zebub. Elijah intercepted the messengers and assured the King that he would certainly die, which he soon did, but not before troops had been sent out to find Elijah and make him prisoner. Again, the prophet invoked the power of the Lord, bringing down fire upon the soldiers.

Elijah's wandering role as prophet was a lonely one, but as he travelled through the Jordan valley he was guided to a youth who would become his disciple and successor, Elisha. This young man would also witness Elijah's departure from this world, as miraculous and dramatic as his life had been. Crossing the River Jordan, the aged prophet parted the waters with his cloak; then he was carried up to Heaven in a chariot of fire.

The importance of Elijah cannot be overstated: the books of the New Testament relate how both John the Baptist and Jesus himself were taken to be Elijah returned; and indeed, he is portrayed as an equal to Moses – at the Transfiguration of Jesus, the disciples saw Christ in conversation with both of these great figures. (*I Kings 17–19, 21; II Kings 1–3:11, 9:36–7*).

ELIMELECH A man of the tribe of Judah in the days of the judges. Famine drove him, his wife Naomi, and his two sons to seek a home in Moab, where he and his sons died. (*Ruth 1:23, 2:1, 3; 4:3, 9*) Naomi afterwards returned to Bethlehem with her daughter-in-law Ruth, whose story is told in *The Book of Ruth*.

ELIPHALET A son of David (*I Samuel 5:16*), also called Eliphelet in *I Chronicles 3:8*.

ELIPHAZ One of Job's three friends, or 'comforters'. (*Job 4:1, 12–21, 15:12–16*)

ELISHA Disciple and companion of Elijah, a prophet in the Kingdom of Israel. Under divine direction, Elijah discovered the young Elisha at work ploughing near his parents' home at Abelmeholah, in the valley of the Jordan south of the Sea of Galilee. Elijah threw his cloak over him, and Elisha at once understood, bade farewell to his parents and followed Elijah. He would spend the next sixty years as a prophet, first with Elijah, then on his own. He was at Elijah's translation into Heaven, picking up the old prophet's mantle and thereby his role. He was immediately accepted as Elijah's successor, for a group of holy men witnessed his recrossing of the River Jordan by parting the waters with Elijah's cloak, as the old prophet had done, and saw that Elijah's spirit rested with him.

While Elijah had been a forceful and unbending prophet, Elisha exhibited a more gentle nature and one less solitary – he spent some time living among a community of holy men at Gilgal on the Plain of Jericho. Many miracles are associated with him, generally less spectacular and on a smaller scale than those of his master – for example, the retrieval of an ax that had fallen into the river by throwing his staff into the water. They varied from endowing a barren woman with a child then (years later) bringing that youth back to life; curing a man of leprosy; providing for the debts of a widow with a never-ending supply of oil; to divining the presence of water for armies in the field and predicting the movements of Israel's enemies. The latter was dangerous: the Moabites, whom the Israelites were fighting, decided that somehow he was an untrustworthy and sent a party of men to capture him. He blinded them all, then took them before the King of Israel. When the King ordered their execution, Elisha persuaded him instead to entertain them with food and wine, then send them back, with the result that hostilities ceased. Elisha's relation-

Leaving Elisha with his mantle, Elijah ascends to heaven in a chariot of fire.

ship with the royal court appears to have been better than Elijah's.

Although his miracles were on more of a modest scale than those of his predecessor, he continued Elijah's battle with the cult of Phoenician gods in Israel and the punishment of corruption and evil. Of his appearance we know only that he was bald, for on one occasion he was mocked by a group of youths whom he repaid by invoking two bears to maul them. Even after death, he seems to have been able to work miracles – when a band of Moabites surprised a burial party, the body was thrown into Elisha's sepulcher, and as it touched the prophet's bones the man sprang back to life. (*II Kings 2–7, 8:7ff, 14:14–21*)

The Shunnamite woman, whose child lay dead, appeals to Elisha for help. 'And when she came to the man of God to the hill, she caught him by the feet ...Then she said, Did I desire a son of my lord? did I not say, Do not deceive me? ... And when Elisha was come into the house, behold, the child was dead, and laid upon his bed. He went in therefore, and shut the door upon them twain, and prayed unto the Lord. And he went up, and lay upon the child, and put his mouth upon his mouth, and his eyes upon his eyes, and his hands upon his hands: and he stretched himself upon the child; and the flesh of the child waxed warm. Then he returned, and walked in the house to and fro; and went up, and stretched himself upon him: and the child sneezed seven times, and the child opened his eyes. And he called Gehazi, and said, Call this Shunammite. So he called her. And when she was come in unto him, he said, Take up thy son.' (II Kings 4:27–36)

ELISHAH the oldest of the four sons of Javan. (*Genesis 10:4*)

ELISHAMA The name of one, perhaps two, of David's sons by concubines. (*II Samuel 5:16, I Chronicles 3:6*)

ELISHAMA A priest sent by Jehoshaphat to teach the people the law. (*II Chronicles 17:8*)

ELISHAPHAT One of the 'captains of hundreds' appointed to overthrow the usurpation of Athaliah. (*II Chronicles 23:1*)

ELISHEBA The daughter of Amminadab and wife of Aaron. (*Exodus 6:23*)

ELISHUA A son of David by one of his concubines (*II Samuel 5:15*), who may be the same as Elishama in *I Chronicles 3:6*.

ELKANAH Father of Samuel. A Levite residing in Ephraim, he had two wives, Peninnah and Hannah, whose relationship was poor. He seems to have loved Hannah, for when Samuel was born, after Hannah's prayer at Shiloh, he acquiesced in her plans for the child to become a Nazarite, perhaps seeing in this unexpected reversal of Hanah's barrenness that Samuel was destined for some great purpose. (*I Samuel 1–2*)

ELKANAH The second son of Korab. (*Exodus 6:24*)

ELNATHAN The father of Nehushta, the mother of King Jehoiachin. (*II Kings 24:8*)

ENOCH First-born of Cain, grandson of Adam and Eve. (*Genesis 4:17, 18*)

ENOCH Son of Jared, descendant of Seth and the father of Methuselah. Evidently a righteous and pious man, he is said to have 'walked with God'. Like Elijah after him, he did not die but was translated into Heaven. (*Genesis 5:18–24, I Chronicles 1:3*)

ELON A Hittite, father of Esau's wife. (*Genesis 26:34*)

ELON A son of Zebulun. (*Genesis 46:14*)

ELON The tenth Hebrew judge. (*Judges 12:11,12*)

ENOS Son of Seth and grandson of Adam. (*Genesis 5:6–11; Luke 3:38*)

EPHAH A son of Midian, and grandson of Abraham. (*Genesis 25:4*)

EPHRAIM Second son of Joseph by Asenath and founder of the tribe that bore his name. On Jacob's death, Joseph took his sons to be blessed by their grandfather, and Jacob unexpectedly placed his hand on Ephraim's head, telling him that his descendants would be more important than those of his brother, Manasseh. The two tribes founded by these boys joined the others – those of Jacob's sons – to make up the twelve tribes of Israel. Joshua was an Ephraimite, and the tribe was given a large, central position in the allocation of the

Enoch translated to Heaven. 'And Enoch walked with God: and he was not; for God took him.' (Genesis 5:24)

Promised Land. They were a powerful tribe, dominant in the northern kingdom from the reign of Jehoshaphat, who was of their number. (*Genesis 41:50–2, Chronicles 37*)

EPHRATAH The grandmother of Caleb, one of those sent to spy upon the Promised Land. (*I Chronicles 2:19, 50*)

EPHRON The son of Zohar, the owner of the field and cave of Machpelah, which Abraham bought as a family tomb for 400 shekels of silver. (*Genesis 23:8–17, 25:9, 44:29,30*)

ESARHADDON King of Assyria, son and successor of Sennacherib. (*II Kings 19:37, Isaiah 37:38*) Nothing is recorded of him in the Bible except that he settled certain colonists in Samaria. (*Ezra 4:2*)

ESAU Son of Isaac and Rebekah, cheated out of his birthright by his twin, Jacob; a hairy man, he was also called Edom, from his red hair. He was the ancestor of the Edomites.

He was first of the twins to emerge from the womb and was Isaac's favourite, destined to be his heir; but when he was cheated out of this by Jacob, his father felt he could not reverse his blessing, even though it had been given in error. Esau threatened to kill Jacob, who took refuge in Havan, returning to Canaan only thirty years later. On news of his coming, Esau

Jacob cheats Esau: 'and Esau came from the field, and he was faint: And Esau said to Jacob, Feed me, I pray thee, with that same red pottage; for I am faint: therefore was his name called Edom. And Jacob said, Sell me this day thy birthright. And Esau said, Behold, I am at the point to die: and what profit shall this birthright do to me? And Jacob said, Swear to me this day; and he sware unto him: and he sold his birthright unto Jacob. Then Jacob gave Esau bread and pottage of lentiles; and he did eat and drink, and rose up, and went his way: thus Esau despised his birthright.' (Genesis 25:29–34)

The reconciliation between Jacob and Esau. 'And Esau ran to meet him, and embraced him, and fell on his neck, and kissed him: and they wept.' (Genesis 33:4)

set out with four hundred armed men, evidently with violent intent; but he was mollified by gifts sent ahead by Jacob, and when the twins met they were tearfully reconciled.

Esau married three Hittite women and then the daughter of Ishmael, his father's half-brother. He settled at Seit, south of the Dead Sea. The lineage of Jesus Christ follows that of Jacob rather than Esau. (*Genesis 25–7, 32–3, 36*)

ESHBAAL See Ishbosheth.

ESHCOL An Amorite chief, brother of Mamre, who joined Abraham in the rescue of Lot from Chedorlaomer. (*Genesis 14:13, 24*)

ESHEK A descendant of Jonathan. (*I Chronicles 8:39*)

ESHTON Son of Mehir, of the tribe of Judah. (*I Chronicles 4:11, 12*)

ESROM (Hezron) Son of Phares in the genealogy of Christ. (*Matthew 1:3, Luke 3:33*)

ESTHER A heroine of the Babylonian captivity who saved the Jews from massacre. She was a Benjamite and an orphan, who became queen to the Persian King Ahasuerus, when he set aside his previous wife, Vashti, for disobedience.

Esther and King Ahasuerus.

Right: The disgrace of Haman.

Although the Persian regime was generally benign towards the Jews of Babylon, there were some who wished them harm. One such was Haman, the King's favorite. Offended by the lack of respect shown to him by Mordecai, Esther's cousin, he resolved to destroy not only this Jew but all the others. His method was to fabricate charges that these people, who were easy to suspect because they lived by their own different laws and religious practices, were plotting rebellion. And, as would happen many times in Jewish history down the ages, their persecution would allow the persecutors to seize their property. To this the King acquiesced, but fortunately for the Jews word of the impending purge reached Mordecai, who at once took the news to the Queen. Esther, over the course of two banquets, made it known to the King that Mordecai, far from plotting against him, had actually been responsible for thwarting an ealier assassination plot. Haman was unmasked and hanged; his wealth was transferred to Esther; and the Jews were given permission to carry arms for their own defence. These events are commemorated by Jews as the feast of Purim, and the story is told in the *Book of Esther* – the only book of the Bible without mention of the name of God.

ETHBAAL King of Sidon and father of Jezebel. (*I Kings 16:31*)

60

ETHIOPIAN WOMAN The second wife of Moses. (*Numbers 12:1*) This marriage gave great offence to Aaron and Miriam.

ETHNAN Son of Ashur, of the tribe of Judah. (*I Chronicles 4:7*)

ETHNI Son of Zerab, a Levite. (*I Chronicles 6:41*)

EVE The first woman. Eve was created after Adam and the other animals of the world from a rib of the sleeping Adam, being intended as 'an help meet for him'. She was seduced by the serpent into disobeying God's warning not to eat the fruit from the tree of the knowledge of good and evil, provoking the Fall – the expulsion from the Garden of Eden. Among the ills promised by the Lord, some of the worst were addressed to the woman: 'I will greatly multiply thy sorrow and thy conception; in sorrow thou shalt bring forth children; and thy desire shall be to thy husband, and he shall rule over thee ...' It is only at this point that the woman is actually given a name, Eve, 'the mother of all living'. She bore Adam three sons: Cain and Abel; and then Seth, as replacement for the murdered Abel. (*Genesis 1:27, 2:21–5, 3, 4:1*)

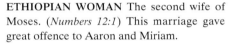

Above: Eve, created from Adam's rib and (below) expelled from the Garden of Eden.

EVI A prince of Midian slain by the Israelites. (*Numbers 31:8, Joshua 13:21*)

EVIL-MERODACH King of Babylon. He was Nebuchadnezzar's son and successor. (*II Kings 25:27, Jeremiah 52:31, 34*) He released Jehoiachin

Above: Ezekiel preaching. Above right: Ezekiel's vision of the valley of dry bones. (Ezekiel 37:1–27)

from prison, and 'spoke kindly to him'. He was murdered by his brother-in-law, Neriglissar, who succeeded him.

EZEKIEL One of the three major prophets of the Old Testament. He was a contemporary of Jeremiah, his life spanning the fall of Jerusalem and the early years of the Jewish exile in Babylon.

Priest, prophet and mystic, he was a member of one of the first parties to be deported from Jerusalem to Babylonia. *The Book of Ezekiel* is written entirely in the first person, being Ezekiels's experiences and visions, which are full of startling, vivid imagery, sometimes told in actions and mime, with parables and similes. Several great themes characterize the book. As with the prophets who preceded him, his early visions warn that the faithlessness of the people will bring about the doom of Jerusalem. These are followed by a series of invectives against the corrupt states surrounding Israel, particularly about Tyre and Egypt, but also Moab, Edom, Ammon, Philistia and Sidon. Next, and evidently written in a different situation, come messages of comfort for the exiles concerning the promise of God's return to Jerusalem together with his people, with details

of the restored city, the Temple and worship. Ezekiel experienced four great visions. The first was at his calling – God himself in a great chariot in the sky, telling him that he was to be His messenger to the people. Many times throughout the book, the Lord calls him 'son of Man'. In the second vision the Almighty showed him the idolatrous and corrupt practices to which the Jews had descended in the city and in the Temple. His third vision was of a valley of dry bones given life, symbolizing the promise of the return from exile; and the fourth, a vision that came to him fourteen years after the fall of Jerusalem, took the form of a survey of the city and the Temple, with an angel providing intricate detail, a virtual blueprint that included even dimensions of the new buildings.

There is thus in *Ezekiel* a dichotomy between the early visions, which are doom-laden and terrifying, and the later visions, which are optimistic and would have inspired those who returned. A key theme of *Ezekiel* is a stress upon the responsibility of the individual for morality and faith rather than collective guilt: 'the soul that sins shall die ... the wickedness of the wicked shall be upon himself.' (*Ezekiel 18:20*)

Above: Ezra and Nehemiah enter the ruins of Jerusalem. Above right: Ezra reads the Mosaic law to the people.

EZER A Gadite who joined David at Ziklag. *(II Chronicles 12:9)*

EZRA A priest and scribe who led the Jews returning from Babylon in the reign of Artaxerxes, and the writer of the book that bears his name. He was the son of Seraiah and descended from Phinchas, son of Aaron. In the seventh year of Artaxerxes, he obtained permission to go to Jerusalem and take with him a large party of exiles. The King gave him many gifts for the Temple. Ezra devoted himself to enforcing the observance of the law of Moses, and to collecting and correcting the sacred books. He induced many of the priests and Levites to put away the Gentile wives that they had taken; he cleansed the chambers of the Temple and reformed the priestly offices; and he enforced the observance of the Sabbath.

The Book of Ezra is a continuation of *II Chronicles* and brings the history down to the time of its writer, extending over a period of nearly eighty years. It provides an account of the first return of captives led by Zerubbabel and the rebuilding of the Temple; then, after an interval of nearly sixty years, there is an account of the second return under Ezra, and what he accomplished at Jerusalem after his return.

G

GAAL The son of Ebed. He led band of intruders who took control of Shechem and defied Abimelech: 'And Gaal the son of Ebed came with his brethren, and went over to Shechem: and the men of Shechem put their confidence in him. And they went out into the fields, and gathered their vineyards, and trode the grapes, and made merry, and went into the house of their god, and did eat and drink, and cursed Abimelech. And Gaal the son of Ebed said, Who is Abimelech, and who is Shechem, that we should serve him? ... And he said to Abimelech, Increase thine army, and come out.' But when Abimelech attacked, he routed Gaal and his brethren, who fled. Abimelech then too vengeance on the city of Shechem. (*Judges 9:26–46*)

GABRIEL Archangel who explained visions to Daniel. When he saw the vision of the ram and goat, Daniel heard Gabriel discussing it with another angel, who suggested that Gabriel interpret the vision for Daniel. Later, at the vision of the four beasts, Daniel reports that Gabriel flew to him and made it intelligible for him. (*Daniel 9:21–7*) See also entry for Gabriel in the New Testament.

GAHAR One of the chief of the Nethinim, whose descendants returned to Jerusalem with Zerubbabel. (*Ezra 2:47*)

GAMLIEL A chief of the tribe of Manasseh. (*Numbers 1:10; 2:20, 7:54, 59*)

GAMUL The leader of a priestly course. (*I Chronicles 24:5*)

GAREB One of David's warriors (*II Samuel 23:38*).

GEBER One of Solomon's purveyors. (*I Kings 4:19*)

GEDALIAH The son of Jeduthun. (*I Chronicles 25:3, 9*)

GEDALIAH The grandfather of Zephaniah and father of Cushi. (*Zephanaih 1:1*)

GEDALIAH Babylonian governor of Jerusalem after the Babylonian conquest. The prophet Jeremiah, in prison during the final stages of the siege of the city, was released by the Babylonians and entrusted to the care of Gedaliah, who was then appointed governor of the newly acquired province. Not all the Israelites had been marched off to Babylon, those remaining being among the poorest, and Gedaliah assured them that they would be allowed to stay in safety. However, some did not believe this; and nor did Gegdaliah believe it when he was told that they were planning to kill him. Led by an ex-officer in the army of Judah, a group of them killed the governor while he was dining at his home in Mizpah. (*Jeremiah 39:14, 40:5–16, 41:1–7*)

GEHAZI Elisha's servant. (*II Kings 4:31, 5:25, 8:4, 5*) Before King Jehoram he recounted the deeds of his master. (*II Kings 8:1–6*)

GEMARIAH The son of Shaphan, and a Levite of the temple. (*Jeremiah 36:10; 2 Kings 15:35; Jeremiah 36:11–20*)

GEMARIAH The son of Hilkiah, who was the bearer of a letter from Jeremiah to the Jews at Babylon. (*Jeremiah 29:3, 4*)

GENUBATH The son of Hadad, brought up in Pharaoh's household. His mother was a sister of the king of Egypt's wife (*I Kings 11:20*).

GERA The son of Bela and grandson of Benjamin. (*I Chronicles 8:3, 5, 7*)

GERA The father of Ehud (*Judges 3:15*)

GERA The father of Shimei. (*II Samuel 16:5, 19:16, 18*)

GERSHOM The elder of the two sons of

Right: Gidon chooses his men. 'So he brought down the people unto the water: and the Lord said unto Gideon, Every one that lappeth of the water with his tongue, as a dog lappeth, him shalt thou set by himself; likewise every one that boweth down upon his knees to drink. And the number of them that lapped, putting their hand to their mouth, were three hundred men: but all the rest of the people bowed down upon their knees to drink water. And the Lord said unto Gideon, By the three hundred men that lapped will I save you, and deliver the Midianites into thine hand: and let all the other people go every man unto his place.' (Judges 7:5–7)

Moses, born to him in Midian. (*Exodus 2:22, 18:4*)

GERSHOM The eldest son of Levi. (*I Chronicles 6:16, 17, 20, 43, 62, 71; 15;7*)

GESHEM (GASHMU) An enemy of the Jews after the return from Babylon. (*Nehemiah. 2:59; 6:1–2*)

GIDEON Fifth Judge of Israel and victor of a decisive battle against the Midianites. He was the son of Joash, of the tribe of Manasseh, living at Ophrah, between Shechem and the Jezreel valley.

Gideon was called to action by an angel, who appeared to him announcing that he had been commissioned by the Lord to rid Israel of the threat from the Midianites. He first destroyed the local shrine to Baal, whose worship many of the Jews had taken up. For the battle with the Midianites, he selected a band of elite warriors, chosen for their zeal and battlefield craft (demonstrated by the way they drank water from a stream with cupped hands so that they were constantly on the lookout, as against simply lapping the water head-down). At the first battle, fought in the darkness of night at the foot of Mount Gilboa, he divided his 300 warriors into three groups, arming each man with a trumpet and torch. The columns converged and encircled the enemy, alarming them by a deafening uproar that threw the Midianites into panic. Gideon's men pursued

GOLIATH The Philistine giant of Gath defeated and killed by David. He is described as some nine feet tall and wearing heavy bronze armor. When the army of Saul was confronting that of the Philistines across the Valley of Elah, Goliath paraded between the opposing camps each day challenging the Jews to single combat. None dared until David arrived and received his king's permission to make the attempt. With just the first of five smooth pebbles chosen carefully from a brook, he shot the giant, hitting him at his most vulnerable point, his forehead. Dashing forward, David cut off Goliath's head. (*1 Samuel 17:4–54*) The giant's sword was later preserved at the priestly city of Nob, wrapped in an ephod. It was presented by the chief priest there, Ahimelech, to David, who was fleeing from Saul's court. (*I Samuel 21:9–10*)

the fleeing enemy and surprised them again, eradicating the Midianite menace. On the way, the army had been refused succor at two Jewish towns, and Gabriel punished these as he returned.

As a result of his victory, Gideon was urged by the people to declare himself king, but he refused and returned to Ophrah. His ephod, made from captured gold, later became the object of idolatrous worship. (*Judges 6–8*)

GOG A Reubenite, the father of Shimei. (*I Chronicles 5:4*)

GOG The name of the leader of the hosts coming from the 'north country' and destroying the people of Israel. (*Ezekiel 38:39*)

GOMER The eldest son of Japheth, and father of Aslikenas, Riphath, and Togarmah. (*Genesis 10:2, 3*) He is regarded as the ancestor of the Celtic race.

Right: 'And the Philistine came on and drew near unto David; and the man that bare the shield went before him. And when the Philistine looked about, and saw David, he disdained him: for he was but a youth, and ruddy, and of a fair countenance.
And the Philistine said unto David, Am I a dog, that thou comest to me with staves? And the Philistine cursed David by his gods ... Then said David to the Philistine, Thou comest to me with a sword, and with a spear, and with a shield: but I come to thee in the name of the Lord of hosts, the God of the armies of Israel, whom thou hast defied.' I Samuel 17:41–5)

H

HABAKKUK Author of the 35th Book of the Bible, Habakkuk is the eighth among what are classified as the Minor Prophets. Nothing is known of him save his writing, but he evidently lived during the late pre-cataclysmic days in Judah. He saw the rising power of Babylon (which he called Chaldea) and demanded of God how he could allow such cruel and wicked people to flourish. This question was met with God's prophesy that the Babylonians would destroy the people of Judah but would themselves suffer in turn. His short book, which contains just three chapters, ends with a psalm praising the Lord. His words 'the just shall live by his faith' are quoted by Paul in *Romans 1:17* and in *Acts 13:42* and *Hebrews 10:38*. (*The Book of Habakkuk*)

HADAD A king of Edom who defeated the Midianites. (*Genesis 36:35, I Chronicles 1:46*)

HADAD Son of the King of Edom. He escaped to Egypt and married Pharaoh's sister-in-law before returning to Edom after the death of David. (*I Kings 11:14–22*).

HADAD A son of Ishmael (*I Chronicles 1:30*) called Hadar in *Genesis 25:15*.

HADADEZER (HADAREZER) Son of Rehob, king of Zobah. David defeated him when he went 'to stablish his dominion' by the Euphrates (*I Chronicles 18:3*) and took from him much gold and brass, which he dedicated to the service of the temple, and from which many of the gold and brass vessels for the Temple were made. Afterwards, Hanun, King of the Ammonites, hired his army to fight against David, but they were again totally routed at Helam. (*II Samuel 10:6, 17*) Thus the Ammonites and Syrians were completely subdued. (*II Samuel 10:15–19, I Chronicles 19:15–19*)

HADAR A son of Ishmael (*Genesis 25:15*) called Hadad in *I Chronicles 1:30*.

HADLAI A chief of Ephraim. (*II Chronicles 28:12*)

HADORAM Son of Tou, king of Hamath, sent to congratulate David. (*I Chronicles 18:10*) He is called Joram in *II Samuel 8:10*.

HADORAM Fifth son of Joktan. (*Genesis 10:27, I Chronicles 1:21*)

HADORAM Son of Abda. He was superintendent of taxes under David and Solomon

Above: The prophet Habakkuk.

Above: Sarah bids Hagar and her son Ishmael depart.

and was stoned during the revolt at Shechem. (*II Chronicles 10:18*) He is called Adorani in *II Samuel 20:24*, and Adoniram in *I Kings 4:6*.

HAGAR Egyptian slave-girl who was maid to Sarah and mother of Ishmael. Although God promised Sarah that she would bear Abraham a child, this seemed unlikely due to her age, and she remained barren. So they agreed that Abraham should take Hagar as a concubine, with whom he would father a child. When Hagar conceived, Sarah began mistreating her, and she ran off into the desert, there to be saved from dying of thirst by an angel, who sent her back. She duly gave birth to a child, Ishmael. Later Sarah, in accordance with the Lord's promise, gave birth to a boy, and in time hostilities grew between the two mothers, for Sarah's concern was that her son, Isaac, should be Abraham's heir, not Ishmael. Sarah told Abraham to send Hagar and Ishmael away, which, after consulting God, he did. Again, in the wilderness of Beersheba, Hagar ran out of water but was saved by a passing angel, who told her that through Ishmael she would have many descendants. (*Genesis 16, 21:9–21*)

HAGARENE 'Jaziz the Hagerite' had charge of King David's flocks. (*I Chronicles 27:31*) He was possibly a descendant of Hagar.

HAGGAI Post-exilic prophet, author of the 37th Book of the Bible and one of the twelve Minor Prophets. He returned to Jerusalem with the first of the Jews sent back from Babylon, his companions including the prophet Zechariah, the priest Joshua and the new Governor of Judah, Zerubbabel. His principal message to the people was that, while the Lord's house lay in ruins, they should spend less time building their own homes and instead concentrate upon constructing the Temple. When that was complete, prosperity would surely follow. He presented an image of the glory to come and encouraged the builders in their work; it is possible that he had seen Solomon's Temple before its destruction. He looked forward also to the Day of Judgement

Above: The propher Haggai.

Above: The news that the Jews may return to their homeland is greeted with joy by the exiles.

HAM Second son of Noah, and thus one of the three ancestors of the peoples of the world. He had four sons, Mizrain, Canaan, Cush and Put, from whom, according to *Genesis 10,* descend

and described Zerubbabel in messianic terms. (*The Book of Haggai*)

HAGGITH One of David's wives and the mother of Adonijah. (*II Samuel 3:4, I Kings 1:5, 11*)

HAKKOZ Head of the seventh course of priests under David. (*I Chronicles 24:10*) He is called Koz in *Ezra 2:61* and *Nehemiah 3:4, 21.*

Above: Ham and his brothers build an altar to make sacrifice after the deluge has passed.

the peoples of Egypt, Canaan, Ethiopia and Lydia. It was Ham who one day found his father stark naked and insensible from drink, which he called his brothers to see. They, in modesty, covered their father. When he recovered, Noah was angry with Ham and put a curse upon his son, Canaan: 'Cursed be Canaan; A servant of servants shall he be unto his brethren.' (*Genesis 9:25*) In due course, this curse was fulfilled when the Hebrews, the descendants of Shem, conquered the Promised Land, Canaan. (*Genesis 9, 10*)

HAMAN Villain of the tale of Esther, son of Hammedatha the Agagite (possibly Amalekite) and chief minister to the Persian king, Ahasueras. His arrogant pride led to his downfall at the hands of Queen Esther. When Esther's cousin, Mordecai, failed to bow to Haman, the King's favourite became angry and resolved to destroy not only Mordecai but all the Jews in Babylon. Alleging that the Jews within the empire, who lived by their own religious laws, constituted a dangerous alien minority, he persuaded the King to have them all slaughtered. He also made plans to hang Mordecai. Esther's ruse was to reveal Mordecai's part earlier in averting an assassination attempt on the King: the King consulted Haman about how Mordecai should be rewarded but does not seem to have mentioned that he was talking about Mordecai – the King's favorite thought he was talking about himself, and so recommended great honors. When Esther revealed herself to the King as a Jewess and publicly accused Haman of planning the slaughter of her people, Haman met the fate he had planned for Mordecai: hanging on a gallows fifty cubits high. (*The Book of Esther*)

HAMMEDATHA Father of Haman, the

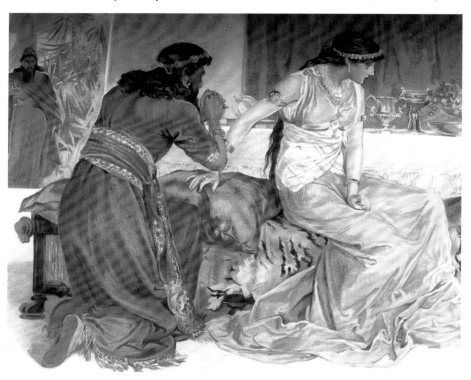

Above: The craven Haman begs for mercy from Queen Esther.

Agagite, whose story is related in the previus entry. (*Esther 3:1*)

HAMMOLEKETH Daughter of Machir and sister of Gilead and a granddaughter of Manasseh. (*I Chronicles 7:17, 18*)

HAMOR A Hivite from whom Jacob purchased a field (*Genesis 33:19*), where Joseph was afterwards buried (*Joshua 24:32*). Called 'Emmor' in *Acts 7:16*, he was slain by Simeon and Levi. (*Genesis 34:26*)

HAMUL A son of Pharez, son of Judah (*I Chronicles 2:5*). His posterity were called Hamulites (*Numbers 26:21*).

HAMUTAL Daughter of Jeremiah of Libnah, wife of King Josiah of Judah and mother of Jehoahaz (*II Kings 23:31*) and Zedekiah (*II Kings 24:18*).

HANAMEEL Son of Shallum and cousin of Jeremiah, to whom he sold his field Anathoth. (*Jeremiah 32:6,12*)

HANAN Son of Shashak, a Benjamite. (*I Chronicles 8:23*)

HANAN Son of Igdaliah. (*Jeremiah 35:4*)

HANAN Son of Azel a descedant of Saul. (*I Chronicles 8:38*)

HANAN One of the Nethinim. (*Ezra 2:46*)

HANAN A Levite who assisted Ezra. (*Nehemiah 8:7*)

HANAN Two of the chiefs who sealed the Covenant. (*Nehemiah 10:22, 26*)

HANAN A Levite who sealed the Covenant. (*Nehemiah 10:10*)

HANANI Son of Heman, head of the eighteenth course of temple musicians. (*I Chronicles 25:4, 25*)

HANANI A holy man of Judah during the reign of King Asa. When Asa allied with King Ben-hadad of Damascus in order to repel and then defeat the incursions of King Baasha of Israel, Hanani was critical. The King should not have made the alliance but placed his faith in God, just as he had done when the Cushite King Zerah invaded and was repulsed. This verdict exasperated the King, who threw Hanani into prison. Hanani was the father of the prophet Jehu. (*II Chronicles 16:7–10*)

HANANIAH A son of Shashak, a Benjamite. (*I Chronicles 8:24*)

HANANIAH Son of Heman, head of the sixteenth course of temple musicians (*I Chronicles 25:4, 23*)

HANANIAH One of Uzziah's chief captains. (*II Chronicles 26:11*)

HANANIAH One of Daniel's three companions in Babylon educated for high office and who were put into the fiery furnace by Nebuchadnezzar. Shadrack was his Babylonian name. (*Daniel 1:6–7,11–21, 3*)

HANANIAH Ruler of the palace under Nehemiah. (*Nehemiah 7:2*)

HANANIAH A false prophet in the days of Jeremiah. (*28:1–17*)

HANNAH Mother of Samuel and wife of Elkanah, a Levite living in Ephraim. Elkanah's other wife, Peninnah, had already born children and taunted Hannah's apparent barrenness, which vexed her greatly. On yearly pilgrimages to Shiloh (center of worship during the period of the Judges and location of the Ark of the Covenant), Hannah prayed for a child, eventually promising to God that if he would give her a son she would dedicate that child's life to His service. While making this earnest and heartfelt pledge, she was observed by the High Priest, Eli, who thought she must be drunk because although he could see her lips move he heard no voice (it was normal to pray aloud). When he learned the truth he blessed her. Before the next Passover, she gave birth to Samuel, and after he had been weaned took him to Eli to become a Nazarite, a sect who devoted their lives exclusively to the service of God (another such was Samson). Thereafter, when she and Elkanah visited Shiloh, she brought him a coat to wear over his ephod. Blessed again by the High Priest, she later gave birth to three sons and two daughters. Hannah's prayer, or song, of thanksgiving may be compared with that of the virgin Mary (*The Magnificat*) in the New Testament. (*I Samuel 1:1, 2:1–10,18–21*)

HANNIEL A prince of Manasseh. (*Numbers 34:23*)

HANNIEL A prince of Asher. (*I Chronicles 7:39*)

HANUM Son and successor to Nahash, King of Ammon. He insulted David's embassy and was in consequence fought against and defeated by Joab. (*II Samuel 10:1–14*)

HARAN Son of Torah, brother of Abraham and Nahor, and father of Lot, Milcah, and Iscah. He did not make the journey to Canaan and died in Ur of the Chaldees at an early age. (*Genesis 11:27–29*)

Left: Hannah presents Samuel to Eli. He was to become a Nazarite, the full implications of which are explained in Numbers 6:2–7: 'When either man or woman shall separate themselves to vow a vow of a Nazarite, to separate themselves unto the Lord: He shall separate himself from wine and strong drink ... All the days of his separation shall he eat nothing that is made of the vine tree, from the kernels even to the husk ... there shall no razor come upon his head: until the days be fulfilled, in the which he separateth himself unto the Lord, he shall be holy, and shall let the locks of the hair of his head grow ... he shall come at no dead body. He shall not make himself unclean for his father, or for his mother, for his brother, or for his sister, when they die: because the consecration of his God is upon his head.'

HARBONA One of the chamberlains of Ahasuerus. (*Esther 1, 10, 7:9*)

HARHUR One of the Nethinims. (*Ezra 2:51, Nehemiah 7:53*)

HARIM Head of the third course of priests. (*I Chronicles 24:8, Ezra 2:39, Nehemiah 7:42*)

HARNEPHER A prince of Asher. (*I Chronicles 7:36*)

HARSHA one of the Nethinims. (*Ezra 2:52, Nehemiah 7:54*)

HARUZ Father of Meshullemeth, wife of Manasseh and mother of Amon. (*II Kings 21:18, 19*)

HASADIAH A son or grandson of Jerubbabel. (*I Chronicles 3:20*)

HASENUAH A Benjamite. (*I Chronicles 9:7*)

HASHABIAH Son of Jeduthun. (*25:3, 19*)

HASHABIAH Son of Kemuel. (*27:17*)

HASHABIAH A chief priest in the time of Ezra. (*Ezra 8:24*)

HASHABNIAH A Levite in the time of Nehemiah. (*Nehemiah 9:5*)

HASHBADANA One who stood on Ezra's left when he read the law. (*Nehemiah 8:4*)

HASHUB A Merarite Levite. (*I Chronicles 9:14, Nehemiah 11:15*)

HASHUBAH A son or grandson of Zerubbabel. (*I Chronicles 3:20*)

HASHUM One who stood on Ezra's left when he read the law. (*Nehemiah 8:4*)

HASRAH Grandfather of Shallum, the husband of Huldah (*II Chronicles 34:22*); he is called Harhas in *II Kings 22:14*.

HASUPHA One of the Nethinim. (*Ezra 11:43 Nehemiah 7:46*)

HATACH One of the chamberlains of Ahasuerus. (*Esther 4:5–10*)

HATHATH Son of Othniel. (*I Chronicles 4:13*)

HATIPHA One of the Nethinim. (*Ezra 2:54*)

HATITA One of the temple doorkeepers who returned with Zerubbabel to Jerusalem. (*Ezra 2:42*)

HATTUSH A priest who returned with Zerubbabel (*Nehemiah 10:4; 12:2*)

HATTUSH A descendant of David (*I Chronicles 3:22, Ezra 8:2*)

HAZAEL King of Aram in Syria, a usurper. It was through Elisha that Hazael came to the Syrian throne: when King Ben-hadad II was seriously ill, he sent Hazael with forty camels laden with the finest products of Damascus to ask Elisha to consult God about his fate. Elisha told him to lie, but that Hazael would become king; when Elisha then began to weep, Hazael asked him why: 'And he answered, Because I know the evil that thou wilt do unto the children of Israel: their strong holds wilt thou set on fire, and their young men wilt thou slay with the sword, and wilt dash their children, and rip up their women with child.' (*II Kings 8:12*) Hazael returned to the palace and told the King he would live; next day he suffocated him with a wet blanket and seized the throne. Syria now rose to be the dominant power in the region. In the time of King Jehu of Israel (himself a usurper), Hazael recovered all the land east of the Jordan lost by his predecessor. (*II Kings 10:32–3*) During the reign of Joash of Judah, Hazael conquered Gath and attacked Jerusalem, exacting a high price to withdraw. (*II Kings 12:17–18*) And *II Kings 13:3–5, 22–4* relates how God caused Hazael to defeat King Jehoahaz of Israel many times until at last He relented. On the death of Hazael, his son, Ben-hadad III became king.

HAZAR-MAVETH The third son of Joktan. (*Genesis 10:26, I Chronicles 1:20*) (It is also the district in southern Arabia where his descendants settled.)

HAZO A son of Nahor by Milcah. (*Genesis 22:22*)

HEBER Son of Beriab and grandson of Asher. (*Genesis 46:17. I Chronicles 7:31, 32*)

HEBER A Kenite caught up in the conflict between Jabin of Hazor and the Jews at the time of Deborah. He gave shelter to the defeated and exhausted general, Sisera, inviting him into his tent, where his wife, Jael, heroically killed him with a tent peg as he slept. (*Judges 4:11, 17–22*)

HEGAI A eunuch in the harem of Ahasuerus. (*Esther 2:3*)

HELAH Wife of Ashur. (*I Chronicles 4:5,7*)

HELDAI One of David's captains (*I Chronicles 27:15*); called also Heleb in *II Samuel 23:29*.

HELDAI One who returned from Babylon. (*Zechariah 6:10*)

Above: Hezekiah praying.

HEMAN Grandson of Samuel. (*I Chronicles 6:33, 15:17*) He was one of the 'seers'. (*II Chronicles 29:14, 30*)

HEMATH A Kenite, ancestor of Rechab. (*I Chronicles 2:55*)

HENADAD The name of a Levite after the captivity. (*Ezra 3:9*)

HEPHER Youngest son of Gilead. (*Numbers 26:32, 27:1*)

HEPHER Second son of Asher (*I Chronicles 4:6*)

HEPHZIBAH Wife of Hezekiah and mother of Manasseh. (*II Kings 21:1*)

HEZEKIAH Twelfth king of Judah, reigning for 29 years. His father was Ahab, his successor Manasseh; thus his reign stands between those of two disastrous kings. In contrast, Hezekiah was a reformer, who attempted to bring his kingdom back to the Hebrew God. He was fortunate to reign at the time of the great prophet and statesman Isaiah, whose wise advice he generally heeded.

During the rule of his father, Assyrian influence had brought idolatry and the worship of other gods to Judah, and an alien altar defiled the Temple courtyard. Even the brazen serpent, still in existence after its worship in the wilderness, was an object of veneration. Inspired by Isaiah, the King swept these away, re-instituted the Passover and began to bring Judah back upon a godly path. He also strengthened the defenses of Jerusalem and constructed a long tunnel to bring water from Gihon to a reservoir called the Pool of Siloam. The administration of the country was thoroughly reorganized and silos for grain, oil and wine were constructed.

It was during his reign, however, that the northern Hebrew state, now a mere rump, was wholly absorbed by the Assyrian Empire, to whom Judah had to pay tribute. Hezekiah attempted to avoid payment – and made alliance with the Egyptians, despite the warning of Isaiah – but this brought down the wrath of the Assyrian king, who rapidly overcame the fortified cities of Judah, including Lachish, before displaying his mighty army before Jerusalem. 'And Hezekiah gave him all the silver that was found in the house of the Lord, and in the treasures of the king's house. At that time did Hezekiah cut off the gold from the doors of the temple of the Lord, and from the pillars which Hezekiah king of Judah had overlaid, and gave it to the king of Assyria.' (*II Kings 18:15–16*) With Jerusalem besieged, and the Assyrians attempting to intimidate the Jews, the city walls alone defied the enemy while Hezekiah and Isaiah prayed for deliverance. God responded to their trust by sending an angel of death upon the Assyrian host, and Jerusalem was saved.

Hezekiah later fell seriously ill. Isaiah visited him, prayed and prescribed a fig poultice, which healed the ulcerated King. God had granted him another fifteen years of life. But it was during these years that he received an ambassador from Babylon, to whom he showed the riches of the city. Hearing of this, Isaiah warned him that Babylon would be the kingdom's nemesis. Upon Hezekiah's death, he was succeeded by Manasseh, who reversed his father's religious policy and increased Judah's involvement with Babylon. (*II Kings 18–20, II Chronicles 29–32*)

HEZION Father of Tabrimon and grandfather of Ben-hadad, King of Syria. (*I Kings 15:18*)

HEZIR One who sealed Nehemiah's Covenant. (*Nehemiah 10:20*)

HEZRO A Carmelite, one of David warriors. (*I Chronicles 11:37*)

HEZRON A son of Reuben. (*Genesis 46:9, Exodus 6:14*)

HEZRON The elder son of Pharez. (*Genesis 46:12*)

HILKIAH Father of Jeremiah. (*Jeremiah 1:1*)

HILKIAH High Priest of Jerusalem during the reign of Josiah, who discovered the Book of the Law. This inspired a religious revival when it became evident that the Laws of Moses were being neglected. (*II Kings 22:4–14, 23:4, 24, I Chronicles 6:13, 9:11, II Chronicles 34:9–22*)

HILLEL A Pirathonite, father of Abdon. (*Judges 12:13, 15*)

HIRAM One of the sons of Bela. (*I Chronicles 8:5*)

HIRAM (Hurram in *Chronicles*) King of Tyre, whose reign overlapped with those of David and Solomon. He was friendly with David and sent Lebanese cedar wood, firs, carpenters and masons to help build his palace in Jerusalem. Solomon also made use of Lebanese cedars and expertise in the construction of the Temple, importing 'sixscore talents of gold'. The Jewish king supplied Hiram's workers with 20,000 measures of wheat and 20 measures of oil each year during the building work. At the end of the construction Solomon made over twenty settlements in Galilee to Hiram, but the King of Tyre was apparently displeased with them. However, the two kings remained close allies,

Above: Isaiah visits the sick King Hezekiah.

and joint trading ventures included a fleet of merchantmen based at Tarshish and regular voyages to Ophir, bringing back gold, silver, precious stones, ivory, apes and peacocks. (*I Kings 5:1–18, 9:11–14,26–8, 10:11,22, I Chronicles 14:1, II Chronicles 8:2, 9:21, II Samuel 5:11*)

HOBAB A Kenite, probably the son of Jethro and brother-in-law of Moses. (*Number 10:29*) He accompanied the Hebrews to Canaan (*Numbers 10:29–32, Judges 1:16*) and settled in the south of Arad.

HOD Son of Zophab, an Asherite. (*I Chronicles 7:36, 37*)

HOGLAH A daughter of Zelophehad the Gileadite. (*Numbers 26:33, 37:1, 36:11*)

HOHAM King of Hebron defeated by Joshua. (*Joshua 10:3–27*)

HOMAM One of the descendants of Esau (*I Chronicles 1:39*), called Hemam in *Genesis 36:22*.

HOPHNI One of the sons of Eli, the High Priest who 'made themselves vile', and were slain by the Philistines in battle. The shock of hearing this news, and the capture of the Ark of the Covenant, killed his father. (*I Samuel 1:3, 2:34, 3:13, 4:11*)

HOSAH A Merarite Levite, doorkeeper for the Ark. (*I Chronicles 16:38, 26:10*)

HOSEA First of the Minor Prophets, Hosea was a native of the northern kingdom of Israel, a contemporary of Amos (who began preaching a little before Hosea), Joel, Isaiah and Micah. His time was a troubled one, as the fall of Israel approached, and he sought to persuade his fellow countrymen that their fate was in their own hands. His subject was the decline of the kingdom into idolatry and faithlessness, condemning the encroachment of Canaanite beliefs and the presence of golden calves at the shrines in Bethel and Dan. He denounced the corrupt practices of the priests, who failed

Above: The prophet Hosea.

to set the correct example to the people. The book that bears his name uses the story of his own disastrous marriage – his wife, Gomer, was adulterous and in the end left him – to convey the simile of the unfaithfulness of Israel to a fallen woman. (He gave his three children names of rejection, believing that they were not his own.) But his message ends with the assurance that God's love for his people would not fail them, just as he himself sought out Gomer, who had become the slave concubine of another man, and rescued her. Jesus quotes *Hosea 6:6* several times in the New Testament: 'For I desired mercy, and not sacrifice.' (*Matthew 9:13, 12:7*) (*The Book of Hosea*).

HOSHEA Nineteenth and last king of Israel after the division of the kingdom. Having assassinated his predecessor, Pekah, Hoshea reigned over a shrunken kingdom for nine years. During his reign, the oppression of Assyria intensified, and Israel paid annual tribute until Hoshea decided to try and throw off the Assyrian yoke with the help of the Egyptians. But this failed. The Assyrian King Shalmaneser V besieged Samaria, and after a three-year siege the city fell. Shalmaneser died during the siege, so it was his successor, Sargon II, who entered the city. The last of the northern Jews were deported and other peoples from the Assyrian dominions introduced in their stead. The Bible makes no mention of Hoshea's fate. (*II Kings 15:30, 17*)

HOSHAIAH Father of Jezaniah or Azariah. (*Jeremiah 43:1, 43:2*)

HOSHAMA One of the Royal House of Judah. (*I Chronicles 3:18*)

HOTHAM Son of Heber, an Asherite. (*I Chronicles 7:32*)

HOTHAM An Asherite. (*I Chronicles 11:44*)

HOTHIR Head of the twenty-first course of temple musicians. (*I Chronicles 25:4, 28*)

HUL Second son of Aram and grandson of Shem. (*Genesis 10:23, I Chronicles 1:17*)

HULDAH Prophetess during the reign of King Josiah of Judah. When the High Priest, Hilkiah, discovered the Book of the Law while the Temple was being renovated, the prophetess was consulted and concluded that God was about to punish Jerusalem and its people, as written in the Book, for they had rejected Him and offered up sacrifices to other gods. But punishment would not come until after Josiah's death. (*II Kings 22:14–20, II Chronicles 34:22–28*)

HUPHAM Son or descendant of Benjamin (*Numbers 26:39*); called Huppim in *Genesis 46:21* and in *I Chronicles 7:12,15*. His descendants were called Huphamites.

HUR A son of Caleb, the son of Hezron. (*I Chronicles 2:19, 50, 4:1, 4*)

HUR One who shared with Aaron the charge of the people in the absence of Moses on Sinai. (*Exodus 17:10; 24:14*) He may have been the husband of Miriam and grandfather of Bezaleel. (*Exodus 31:2; 35:30, I Chronicles 2:19*)

HUR A Midianite prince slain by Phinehas. (*Numbers 31:8*)

HUR Father of Rephaiah, the ruler of half of Jerusalem. (*Nehemiah 3:9*)

HUN A Gadite (*I Chronicles 5:14*)

HUSHAH Son of Ezer, of the tribe of Judah. (*I Chronicles 4:4*). His descendants were called Hushathites. (*II Samuel 21:18, 23:27*)

HUSHAI The 'Archite' and 'the king's companion' in *I Chronicles 22:33*. When Absalom rebelled and David fled from Jerusalem, Hushai joined his party in order to defeat the counsel of Ahithophel. (*II Samuel 15:32–37, 16:16–18, 17–14*) His son Baanah was one of Solomon's commissariat officers. (*I Kings 4:16*)

HUSHAM A king of Edom. (*Genesis 36:34*)

HUSHIM Son of Dan. (*Genesis 46:23*) He is called Shuham in *Numbers 26:42*, and his descendants were called Shuhamites.

HUSHIM Son of Aher, a Benjamite. (*I Chronicles 7:12*)

HUSHIM Wife of Shaharaim, a Benjamite. (*I Chronicles 8:8*)

HUZ The eldest son of Nahor, Abraham's brother. (*Genesis 22:21*)

I

IBHAR One of David's sons, born in Jerusalem to one of his concubines. (*II Samuel 5:15*)

IBNEIAH The son of Jeroham, a Benjamite. (*I Chronicles 9:8*)

IBNIJAH A Benjamite, the father of Reuel. (*I Chronicles 9:8*)

IBRI The son of Jaaziah, a Merarite Levite. (*I Chronicles 24:27*)

IBZAN Ninth judge of Israel, succeeding Jephthah. (*Judges 12:8–10*) He was a native of Bethlehem, of the tribe of Zebulun.

ICHADAD Son of Phinehas, born at the time when the news came that the Ark of the Covenant had been captured by the Philstines. (*I Samuel 4:19–22*) His mother named him 'Ichahod', saying, 'The glory is departed from Israel.'

IDBASH Brother of Jezreel, of the tribe of Judah. (*I Chronicles 4:3*)

IDDO A Gershonite Levite (*I Chronicles 6:21*); called Adaiah in *I Chronicles 6:41*.

IDDO Father of Ahinadab, one of Solomon's officers. (*I Kings 4:14*)

IDDO The son of Zechariah, a prince of Manasseh in David's time. (*I Chronicles 27:21*)

IDDO A prophet of Judah, who wrote the history of Rehoboam and Abijah. (*II Chronicles 12:15; 13:22*)

IDDO A priest, grandfather of Zechariah the prophet. (*Zechariah 1:1, 7*) He returned to Jerusalem from Babylon with Zerubbabel. (*Nehemiah 12:4*)

IDDO A Nethinim, one of the Temple assistants, in the time of Ezra. (*Ezra 8:17*)

IGAL One of the spies sent by Moses to investigate the Promised Land, of the tribe of Issachar. (*Numbers 13:7*)

IGDALIAH Father of Hanan. (*Jeremiah 35:4*)

IKKESH A Tekoite, father of Ira, one of David's warriors. (*II Samuel 23:26, I Chronicles 27:9*)

ILAI An Ahohite, one of David's warriors (*I Chronicles 11:29*); he is called Zalmon in *II Samuel 23:28*.

IMLAH (IMLA) Father of the prophet Micaiah. (*I Kings 22:8,9, II Chronicles 18:7,8*)

IMMANUEL Name given to the child prophesied in *Isaiah 7:14–15*: 'Therefore the Lord himself shall give you a sign; Behold, a virgin shall conceive, and bear a son, and shall call his name Immanuel. Butter and honey shall he eat, that he may know to refuse the evil, and choose the good.' The birth of Jesus was seen as fulfillment of this prophesy. (Also in *Matthew 1:23*, where the spelling is Emmanuel).

IMUA Son of Helem, an Asherite. (*I Chronicles 7:35*)

IMNAH The eldest son of Asher (*I Chronicles 7:30*); called Jimnah in *Genesis 46:17*.

IMRAH Son of Zophah, a prince of the Asherites. (*I Chronicles 7:36*)

IMRI Son of Bani a descendant of Judah. (*I Chronicles 9:4*)

IPHEDEIAH Son of Sahshak, a chief of the tribe of Benjamin. (*I Chronicles 8:25*)

IR A Benjamite (*I Chronicles 7:12*); he is called Iri in *I Chronicles 7:7*.

IRA A Tekoite, son of Ikkesh, one of David's heroes (*II Samuel 23:26, I Chronicles 11:28*) and

Above: Isaac on the altar, as his father prepares to sacrifice him to God. But God did not require human sacrifice.

captain of the army on duty in the sixth month. (*I Chronicles 27:9*)

IRA An Ithrite, one of David's heroes. (*II Samuel 23:38; I Chronicles 11:40*)

IRA A Jafrite, one of David's chief rulers. (*II Samuel 20:26*).

IRAD Grandson of Cain. (*Genesis 4:18*)

IRIJAH A captain in *Jeremiah 37:13, 14.*

IRU Eldest son of Caleb the spy. (*I Chronicles 4:15*)

ISAAC Son of Abraham and Sarah, father of Esau and Jacob. The second of the patriarchs, Isaac is presented as a passive man, one to whom things happened rather than being an instigator of great events. He was Abraham's second son but inherited all his father's estate;

his half-brother Ishmael had by then departed with his mother, Hagar, and the six sons of his other wife, Keturah, were despatched to the east.

In his youth Isaac was central to one of the most dramatic and disturbing events in the Bible, when his father was commanded by God to sacrifice him but then relented when he saw the strength of Abraham's faith. By the age of forty, Isaac had not taken a wife, so his father sent his servant to his kinsmen in Haman to look for a suitable match. He returned with Rebekah, who, after much prayer, bore Isaac twin sons, Esau and Jacob.

In his dotage, aged and dim of sight, Isaac was also the victim of a great deception, when Jacob (abetted by Rebekah) misled the old man into giving him his blessing as his heir, to be head of the family when he died. When the subterfuge was revealed by the return of Esau, Isaac judged that the blessing could not be revoked. (*Genesis 21, 22, 24, 25:5,9,11,19–33, 26, 27, 28:1–6, 35:27–9*)

Above: Isaac is deceived into giving Jacob his blessing.

Left: Isaiah's vision at his calling. 'Then flew one of the seraphims unto me, having a live coal in his hand, which he had taken with the tongs from off the altar: And he laid it upon my mouth, and said, Lo, this hath touched thy lips; and thine iniquity is taken away, and thy sin purged.' (Isaiah 6:6–7)

ISAIAH One of the greatest of the prophets, whose work over some forty years embraced the reigns of four monarchs of Judah: Uzziah, Jotham, Ahaz and Hezekiah. Reformer, theologian, statesman, teacher of kings, he is often called 'the evangelical prophet'.

Isaiah was the son of a man called Amoz, possibly high-born, and thus well-connected and at ease within the royal court, making his relationship with King Hezekiah in particular one of familiarity; late in this king's reign, Isaiah saved him from a critical illness. His calling to the service of God, during the last year of Uzziah's reign, was a dramatic vision of the Lord on his throne, a seraphim placing hot coals to Isaiah's lips to purge him of his sin.

The 66-chapter book that bears his name is the 23rd and longest book of the Bible. It has some of the most beautiful poetry in the Bible, with many phrases familiar, including: 'And he shall judge among the nations, and shall rebuke many people: and they shall beat their swords into plowshares, and their spears into pruning hooks: nation shall not lift up sword against na-

Above: Isaiah witnesses the vice and folly of Jerusalem.

Right: As the Assyrians surround the city, Isaiah reassures the frightened people of Jerusalem that the Lord will come to their aid.

tion, neither shall they learn war any more.' (*Isaiah 2:4*)

Isaiah attacked the ostentation, false pride and moral corruption of the people, who had forsaken the way of the Lord and fallen prey to idolatry and evil practices; he warned them that their sinful ways would bring disaster upon their heads: retribution was on the way. But then there would be the hope of a new beginning. Only in the reign of Hezekiah were his words heeded, and the King was inspired to revive the true religion of the Jews and to destroy the alien shrines that had appeared during the reign of his predecessor.

He lived at a crucial time in the narrative of the Jews, with the northern kingdom falling to the might of Assyria and the resurgent ambi-

tion of Egypt pressing from the south. King Ahaz attempted appeasement and diplomatic maneuvers between the two – against which Isaiah protested in vain – but could not avoid the eventual confrontation with Sennacherib. At this desperate hour, it was Isaiah's steadying hand and powerful faith that came to Hezekiah and Judah's rescue. Isaiah later correctly identified Babylon as the greatest danger to Jerusalem.

The Book of Isaiah found considerable resonance in the books of the New Testament, which call him 'Esias'. It is in *7:19* that he writes of 'Immanuel', and many verses are quoted in the four Gospels. In *Luke 4:17–19* Jesus reads from *Isaiah* in Nazareth, while *Matthew 8:17* mentions Jesus' healing miracles as 'which was spoken by Esias the prophet' and writes of the fulfillment of other verses in *3:1–3* and *12:17–21*.

A dubious tradition has Isaiah martyred in the reign of the monstrous King Manasseh, during which time the nation once again lapsed into corruption and sin, by being sawn in half. (*The Book of Isaiah, II Kings 19–20*)

ISCAH Daughter of Haran and sister of Lot. (*Genesis 11:29, 31*)

ISHBAH A descendant of Judah. (*I Chronicles 4:17*)

ISHBAK A Son of Abraham by Keturah. (*Genesis 25:2*)

ISHBIBENOB A Philistine giant, 'the weight of whose spear weighed three hundred shekels of brass in weight', slain by Ahisbai. (*II Samuel 21:16, 17*)

ISHBOSHETH (Ishbaal) Fourth son of Saul and his successor as King of Israel. When Saul and three of his sons were killed at the Battle of Mount Gilboa, Ishbosheth was proclaimed king by the army, led by Abner. But he was a weakling, not suited for the role and was at once in conflict with David, who was proclaimed king in Judah. Abner deserted Ishbosheth following a quarrel over one of

Saul's concubines, Rizpah, and without him Ishbosheth's reign did not prove successful, evidently indicative that God's favor had also deserted the line of Saul. He was assassinated as he slept by two of his officers, Baanah and Rechab, who hacked off his head and presented it to the rival king at Hebron. David, however, was not pleased and had them executed, while the head of his enemy was buried at Hebron. (*II Samuel 2:8–10, 3:1, 4:1–12, I Chronicles 8:33, 9:39*)

ISHMAEL First son of Abraham by Hagar and half-brother of Isaac. Ishmael's mother was Hagar, Sarah's maid and then Abraham's concubine after he and his wife had accepted that they could not have children together. Friction between the two women resulted in the pregnant Hagar fleeing into the desert, there to be rescued by an angel who assured her that her descendants would be many: although they would be cast out by Abraham and Sarah, they would not be outcasts in the eyes of the Lord. But the angel also forecast that Ishmael would be 'a wild man; his hand will be against every man, and every man's hand against him'. (*Genesis 16:12*)

After the birth of Isaac to Sarah, the two step-brothers were quarrelsome, while their mothers enjoyed a mutual hostility, Sarah concerned to ensure that Isaac would be heir to the Covenant. Eventually Abraham was persuaded to expel Hagar and Ishmael, and they settled in the Sinai desert of Paran. Ishmael married an Egyptian and became a noted archer; his twelve sons became the tribes of the Ishmaelites, traditionally held to be the ancestors of the Arab nomads (and in Islam Ishmael is one of the prophets who, with Abraham [Ibrahim] built the Ka'ba in Mecca). Ishmael joined his half-brother in seeing their father to his burial at Machpelah, near Hebron, where Isaac, Rebekah, Leah and Jacob would also be entombed. (*Genesis 16, 17, 25, 36:3, I Chronicles 1:28–31*)

ISHMAIAH Son of Obadiah and prince of Zebulun. (*I Chronicles 27:19*)

ISHOD A descendant of Manasseh. (*I Chronicles 7:18*)

ISHUAH A son of Asher (*Genesis 46:17*); he is called Isuah in *I Chronicles 7:30*.

ISHUAI a son of Asher (*I Chronicles 7:30*); called Isui in *Genesis 46:17*, and Jesui in *Numbers 26:44*. His descendants were called Jesuites (*Numbers 26:44*).

ISHUI the second son of Saul (*I Samuel 14:49*) he was slain with his father. (*I Samuel 31:6*)

ISRAEL See Jacob.

ISSACHAR Jacob's ninth son and Leah's fifth (*Genesis 30:17*). He had four sons at the time that Jacob went into Egypt. (*Genesis 46:13*)

ITHAMAR The youngest son of Aaron (*Exodus 6:23*). He was consecrated to the priesthood with his brothers. Then, after Nadab and Ahihu died in punishment by God for incorrect sacrificial practises, he and Eleazar retained the office. (*Exodus 28:1; Leviticus 10:6, 12; Numbers 3:4*) He superintended the Gershonite bearers of the tabernacle during the journey through the wilderness. (*Numbers 4:21–28*) The first High Priest among his descendants was Eli.

ITHREAM Sixth son of David, by Eglah. (*II Samuel 3:5*)

Right: Ishmael and his mother, Hagar, are sent away by Abraham, at the behest of Sarah.

J

JABIN King of Hazor, who raised a coalition against the army of Joshua but was defeated in a great battle by the River Merom. Joshua slew Jabin himself. (*Joshua 11:1–14*)

JABIN King of Hazor, defeated by the judge Deborah and her general Barak. His army was completely annihilated and its general, Sisera, met a gruesome fate at the hands of the Kennite, Jael. (*Judges 4*)

JACOB Third of the Patriarchs, younger twin son of Isaac and Rebekah. His long story is a crucial phase in the narrative of the Jews and the passing on of the Covenant, for his sons were to be the progenitors of the twelve tribes of the Exodus and of the occupation of Canaan.

Jacob's life is marked by several key deceptions: cheating Esau out of his father's blessing; with Laban over their sheep; while he himself was deceived by Laban at his wedding

Above: Jacob's reunion with Esau.

Above: Jacob deceives his father into giving him the blessing for the firstborn.

to (as he thought) Rachel, and by his sons about the fate of Joseph.

As a young man he tricked his elder brother into giving up his inheritance and then, with the connivance of his mother, deceived his father into giving him his blessing instead of Esau, the deception made easier by Isaac's failing sight and kid-skin over Jacob's hands and neck to impersonate his hairier brother. To avoid family strife, Jacob was sent to distant Haran, to live with Rebekah's brother Laban and there find a wife. This proved deceptively easy: he encountered Rachel, Laban's younger daughter, at a well close to Laban's land, and he asked for her hand immediately. Only after seven years working with Laban was the marriage allowed to take place: but it was customary for daughters to wed in the order of their age, so Laban tricked him into marriage with the elder daughter, Leah. Then (in this age of polygamy) marriage to Rachel followed soon after.

For some twenty years Jacob worked for Laban, earning growing flocks of animals as grasped him and refused to let go until he had been blessed, for he realized he had been struggling with the Lord himself. He had seen the face of God, who told him that henceforth his name would be Israel. But years before, as he journeyed to Haran, Jacob had first encountered the divine. As he rested at a place he later called Bethel, he dreamt he saw a stairway reaching up to Heaven, with angels ascending and descending; and there was God, who gave him the message he had given his father and his grandfather: that his descendants would be many, and that the Lord would always be with him. The Covenant was thus passed to a new generation.

Jacob settled his family near Sechem (now Nablus, in the hills of Samaria), then moved towards his father's lands near Hebron. In time, Isaac died, and Esau joined Jacob in putting him to rest in the tomb of Abraham, Sarah and Rebekah.

On their journey between Bethel and Ephrath, Rachel had given birth to a son,

Above: Jacob's vision of a ladder to Heaven.

payment despite his father-in-law's attempt to cheat him out of the better animals. Relations between the two men deteriorated, and when the time was ripe, and Laban was away sheep-shearing, Jacob set out to return to his family home – taking large flocks of sheep, goats and cattle, together with a burgeoning family. An angry Laban came in pursuit, but the two were reconciled and separated in peace. There was to be a second encounter on this long migration. On the way he met Esau, warned of Jacob's approach and surrounded by many followers – the confrontation looked set to be violent. But Jacob sent ahead a fulsome peace offering of cattle, sheep and goats, and Esau, mollified, was reconciled to his wayward brother.

By a ford across the River Jordan, Jacob found himself alone one night – the main caravan had crossed, and he remained for a while on the east bank. Just before daybreak, a stranger came and wrestled with him; and when he wanted to break off the fight, he struck Jacob, dislocating his hip. Still Jacob

Above: Jacob wrestles with God.

Above: Jacob's dismay and grief at Joseph's apparent death.

Above: The reunion of Joseph with his father, Jacob.

whom they named Benjamin, but Rachel died in childbirth. Her first son, Joseph, was Jacob's favourite, and the old man doted on him, giving him presents that included a coat of many colors. This favoritism, and Joseph's own character, turned his brothers (the sons of Leah) against him, and eventually, when they were all out looking after the animals, they seized him and sold him to passing merchants bound for Egypt. Once more, Jacob was deceived: they brought home Joseph's distinctive coat, stained with animal blood, and claimed that he had been set upon by wild beasts and killed. It was years before father and son were reunited. Joseph's spectacular career in Egypt, his rise to power in Pharaoh's court and then his meeting with his brothers, seeking help in a time of famine, at last brought about their meeting; it was an emotional reunion, and at an audience with Pharaoh it was agreed that he and his family should settle in Goshen.

Shortly before he died, Jacob blessed Joseph's two sons, Manasseh and Ephraim, whose descendants would join those of the other sons to become the twelve tribes of Israel.(The descendants of Levi became priests.)

Both Jacob's wives had preceded him to the grave, and his body was embalmed in Egypt, then taken with much ceremony to join those of his father and grandfather at Hebron. (*Genesis 25–50*)

JAEL Killer of Sisera. When the judge Deborah and her general, Barak, defeated the army of Jabin of Hazor in battle, the defeated commander, Sisera, fled the field. The

Above: Jael nails Sisera's head to the ground.

pursuing Jews lost him, and he sought refuge in the tent of Heber, a Kennite who was on friendly terms with Hazor. Jael, his wife, gave Sisera food and drink, and then he lay down exhausted to sleep, whereupon Jael took a tent peg and a mallet and drove it through the sleeping man's temples, pinning his head to the ground. (*Judges 4:11,17–22, 5:24–7*)

JAIR The eighth judge of Israel who ruled 22 years. His 30 sons had possession of 30 cities, forming Havoth-jair. (*Judges 10:35*)

JAPHETH One of the sons of Noah, and so one of the three ancestors of the peoples of the world, having survived the Flood on board the ark. He had seven sons, Gomer, Magog, Madai, Javan, Tubal, Meshech and Tiras, from whom according to *Genesis* descend the Russians, Gauls, Germans, Britons, Scythians, Medes, Greeks, Iberians, Muscovites and Thracians. When Ham discovered Noah in an alcoholic stupor, he and his brother Ham covered their father's drunken nakedness and discretely left the tent. When he had sobered up, Noah laid a curse upon Ham, but said that 'God shall enlarge Japheth, and he shall dwell in the tents of Shem; and Canaan shall be his servant'. (*Genesis 5:32, 9, 10*)

JEHOAHAZ Eleventh king of Israel after the division of the kingdom, son of Jehu. The suppression of idolatry during his father's reign ceased, and Israel began to sin again, so God permitted King Hazael of Syria to inflict many defeats on Israel, until Jehoada prayed for deliverance, and the Lord gave him respite from the oppression. Nevertheless, the state remained weak, and the army was a shadow of its former self. Jehoahaz ruled for seventeen years and was succeeded by his son, Jehoash. (*II Kings 13*)

JEHOAHAZ Sixteenth king of Judah, son of Josiah. Succeeding his father at the age of 23, Jehoahaz reigned for only three months before Pharaoh Necho II, vanquisher of Josiah, made him prisoner and placed his brother Eliakim

(Jehoiakim) on the throne. Temporarily, with the eclipse of Assyria, Judah was under Egyptian control, and Jehoahaz died in Egypt. (*II Kings 23:30–4, II Chronicles 36:1–4*)

JEHOASH Twelfth king of Israel after the division of the kingdom, son of Jehoahaz. In general he followed the wicked example of his idolatrous forebears, but he did find time to visit the deathbed of the prophet Elisha, who prophesied his victories against Syria. He made the King shoot an arrow through the window that faced north-east, towards Syria. This, he told him, symbolized his defeat of the Syrians. Then he told the King to strike the other arrows on the floor, and he tapped three times, which made the old man angry. Those three taps symbolized three defeats for the Syrians – had the King struck the floor five or six times he would have won a complete victory. It was after the death of King Hazael of Damascus that Jehoash took the field and, as the prophet had foretold, he won three

Above: Jehoash and the arrow shots. The dying Elisha predicts the King's success against the Syrians.

victories and recovered much of the territory the Syrians had previously taken.

This resurgence of Israel's military fortunes was evidently lost on King Amaziah of Judah, who foolishly challenged his neighbor to battle and was disastrously defeated at Beth-Shemesh. Amaziah was made prisoner, and Jehoash advanced to Jerusalem, where he pulled down a 400-cubit length of the city wall before departing for Samaria, his carts laden with booty. The remainder of Jehoash's sixteen-year reign was peaceful, and when he died he was succeeded by his son, Jeroboam II. (*II Kings 13:10–13, II Chronicles 25:17–25*)

JEHOIACHIN (Coniah) Eighteenth king of Judah, son of Jehoiakim, who was abducted by the Babylonians. The state that Jehoiachin inherited was nearing its end, and his reign lasted only three months and ten days. King Nebuchadnezzar of Babylon besieged Jerusalem and forced its surrender, Jehoiachin following his father as a prisoner to Babylon, where he was imprisoned for a time before being released and treated with kindness. Since Jerusalem had surrendered rather than having been taken by storm, the Temple was spared, but its treasures and the royal palace were looted. Nebuchadnezzar also took to Babylon the nobles, leading men and skilled artisans of Jerusalem. Only the poor remained. (*II Kings 24:8–17, II Chronicles 36:9–10*) He is called Coniah in *Jeremiah 22:24.*

JEHOIADA High Priest in Jerusalem who brought about the accession of King Joash. He was a godly influence on the young king and was instrumental in finding wives for him. He oversaw repairs to the Temple with the King. He lived a long life; after his death his son, Zechariah, witnessed Judah's return to idolatry and spoke out about it, only to be stoned on the orders of the King. (*II Kings 11:4–21, 12:2,7,9, II Chronicles 22:11, 23, 24:3,6,14–17*)

JEHOIAKIM (Eliakim) Seventeenth king of Judah, brother of Jehoahaz. When Pharaoh Necho II carried off Jehoahaz to Egypt, he placed Eliakim on the throne, changing his name to Jehoiakim. Immense tribute had to be paid to Egypt, imposing a heavy tax burden on Judah, which was now fixed unhappily between the two great empires of Egypt and Babylon. The power of the Babylonians was in the ascendant, and it was not long before they had imposed their rule on Judah. When, after three years, Jehoiakim rebelled he was carried off to Babylon in chains with many of his countrymen; it is probable that Daniel was one of these. Judah was largely reduced to a no-man's land, ravaged by bands of Babylonians, Syrians, Moabites and Ammonites: this, reports *Kings* was God's vengeance for all the innocent blood that Manasseh had shed. (*II Kings 23:35 to 24:6, II Chronicles 36:58*)

JEHONADAB Son of Shimeah, and nephew of David, also the wicked adviser of Amnon. (*II Samuel 13:3–6*)

JEHONADAB Son of Rechab the founder of a tribe who abjured wine. (*Jeremiah 35:6, 19*)

JEHORAM Fifth king of Judah, son of Jehoshaphat. He had six younger brothers, and upon his accession to the throne he killed them all, setting the scene for a thoroughly unpleasant eight-year reign. He was married to Athaliah, daughter of King Ahab of Israel, and as a result was greatly influenced by deviant Israeli religious practices – in contrast to his father's reign, Judah found itself invaded by shrines to Baal and other pagan gods. A letter from Elijah set forth his doom: 'Thus saith the Lord God of David thy father, Because thou hast not walked in the ways of Jehoshaphat thy father, nor in the ways of Asa king of Judah, But hast walked in the way of the kings of Israel, and hast made Judah and the inhabitants of Jerusalem to go a whoring, like to the whoredoms of the house of Ahab, and also hast slain thy brethren of thy father's house, which were better than thyself: Behold, with a great plague will the Lord smite thy people, and thy children, and thy wives, and all thy goods: And thou shalt have great sickness by disease of thy bowels, until thy bowels fall out by reason of the sickness day by day.' *(II Kings 21:12–15)* His illness gave him two years of agony, and so unpopular was he that they buried him in Jerusalem but not in the royal tombs. During his reign he also seems to have neglected the defenses of the kingdom; Edom rebelled and frustrated Jehoram's attempt at reconquest at Zair, when the army of Judah was surrounded and escaped with difficulty. Later on, raiders penetrated to the walls of Jerusalem and killed all of Jehoram's sons save the youngest, Ahaziah. *(II Kings 8:16–23, II Chronicles 21:1–10)*

JEHORAM Ninth king of Israel after the division of the kingdom, and last of the dynasty of Omri. His parents were Ahab and Jezebel, and he succeeded to the throne on the death of his brother Ahaziah, who died after falling from a balcony in the royal palace at Samaria. He reigned for twelve years.

The Bible records him as sinning against the Lord but does not hold him in such low esteem as his father and mother; indeed, he pulled down the image of Baal that his father had worshipped before. The prophet Elisha was active during his reign and showed him scant respect. With Jehoshaphat, Jehoram put down a rebellion by

Above: King Jehoshaphat sending forth teachers to spread the word of God among his people.

the vassal King of Moab, and it was during this campaign that the prophet Elisha guided the thirsty armies to water; but he did this, he told Jehoram, out of respect for the godly Jehoshaphat rather than the sinner Jehoram.

Jehoram's death came shortly after the battle at Ramoth-gilead against Syria that he fought in alliance with King Ahaziah of Judah. Wounded, he withdrew to Jezreel, where Ahaziah accompanied him. It was here that the usurper Jehu killed him with an arrow through Jehoram's heart. The body was thrown into the field that had belonged to Naboth, fulfilling the Lord's promise to avenge his previous crime. *(II Kings 3, 9:14–26)*

JEHOSHAPHAT Fourth king of Judah, son of Asa. He continued the reforms began by his father, destroying places of pagan worship. The Bible gives a warm account of him as a godly king, sending out teachers to all parts of the kingdom to spread the word of God and traveling widely himself.

His 25-year reign was mainly a peaceful one, and his reputation among the neighboring kingdoms was high: he became wealthy and honored and even made peace with the northern kingdom, marrying his son, Jehoram (Joram) to Princess Athaliah, daughter of King Ahab and Queen Jezebel of Israel. Jehoshaphat reigned during the latter years of King Ahab in Israel, the brief reign of his son, Ahaziah, and for most of the reign of his grandson, Jehoram.

He planned to emulate Solomon and send a fleet to Ophir in search of riches and began construction of an ocean-going fleet, but the expedition never sailed, being destroyed by a storm at Eziongeber. A subsequent proposal from King Ahaziah for a joint venture was not taken up. *(I Kings 22:48–9)*

He significantly improved the defences of the kingdom and repulsed an invasion of Ammonites, Moabites and Edomites. At an assembly in Jerusalem, Jahaziel, son of Zechariah, provided the priestly inspiration for putting their trust in God and striking the invaders at the pass of Ziz. This resulted in a complete rout for the intruders, who are reported as turning on each other, so that none survived.

With King Ahab of Israel, Jehoshaphat attacked the Syrians at Ramoth-gilead, and it was during this battle that Ahab died, having been warned at Samaria by the prophet Micaiah. After the campaign, the prophet Jehu, son of Hanani, reproved him for going to war beside such a sinner as Ahab.

He allied with Jehoram of Israel and the vassal King of Edom to attack Moab. It was during this campaign that the combined armies found themselves without water and called upon the prophet Elisha for help: he success-fully predicted where there was water, and the armies were saved. *(I Kings 22:41–50, II Chronicles 17 to 21:3)*

JEHOSHEBA (Jehoshabeath) Daughter of King Jehoram of Judah, half-sister of Ahaziah and wife to the High Priest Jehoiada. When Queen Athaliah massacred the royal family of Jerusalem, Jehosheba hid the young Joash for six years until Jehoiada staged a revolution overturning Athaliah and anointing Joash king. *(II Kings 11:2–3, II Chronicles 22:11-12)*

JEHOZABAD Son of Shomer, one of the conspirators who put King Joash to death. *(II Kings 12:21)*

JEHU Prophet during the reigns of King Baashi of Israel and Jehoshaphat of Judah, son of Hanani. He told Baashi, usurper of the throne of Israel, that God, having raised him up to the leadership of Israel, had condemned

Left: Jehu, the usurper, espies Queen Jezebel at a window in Samaria and shouts for her eunuchs to throw her out. He and Queen Athaliah in Jerusalem practically wiped out the royal families of the Jews.

Right: The tragic story of Jephthah's daughter.

him for his sins. (*I Kings 16:1–7*) He later met King Jehoshaphat upon the King's return from battle with the Syrians, which he had fought in alliance with King Ahab of Israel. Jehu criticized Jehosophat for making himself an ally of such wicked and ungodly people as the Israelis; but he conceded that the King's actions in removing pagan idols indicated that he was trying to follow the will of God. (*II Chronicles 19:1–3*)

JEHU Tenth king of Israel after the division of the kingdom, usurper and founder of the longest-lasting dynasty of the Kingdom of Israel. A high-ranking officer in the army, he was chosen by God as his instrument in destroying the House of Omri, which had led the kingdom away from the Lord into idolatry and paganism.

At this time the frontline of war between the allied armies of Israel and Judah and the opposing Syrians lay at Ramoth-gilead, east of the Jordan. Here Jehu was visited by a disciple of the prophet Elisha, who anointed him King of Israel and instructed him to kill not only Jehoram but all the royal family as punishment for their sins, including Jezebel, who was not to be buried but her body left to be eaten by dogs. On hearing of this, his fellow officers acclaimed him and went with him to Jezreel,

where they found Jehoram and put him to death. At Samaria there were 70 descendants of Ahab (Jehoram's father) and Jehu sent word to the city that they were to be put to the sword. The heads of the victims were put in baskets and sent to Jehu, who then proceeded to slaughter every other member of the House of Omri. He also despatched a number of the royal house of Judah; most of those remaining were slain by Athaliah.

Jehu began the task of ridding Israel of Baal-worship by a trick, assembling priests and worshippers together and then setting his troops upon them. The temple, statues and images of Baal were destroyed. While Israel returned to God, however, the fortunes of the kingdom declined: the power of Syria became ascendant, King Hazael of Damascus conquering all the land east of the Jordan. Jehu ruled for 28 years and was succeeded by his son, Jehoahaz. (*II Kings 9–10, II Chronicles 22:7–9*)

JEPHTHAH Eighth Judge of Israel, who led Israel for six years between the conquest of the Promised Land and the establishment of the kingdom. Born in Gilead of a man also called Gilead, Jephthah's mother was a harlot, and his half-brothers drove him away. He took refuge in the land of Tob and in time became the leader of a bandit gang. His reputation as a warrior so impressed the elders of Gilead that when war broke out with the neighboring Ammonites they came to him for leadership. He made a peaceful approach to the Ammonites at first, but their reply was truculent: they claimed yet more of the disputed territory. A battle ensued in which Jephthah led the men of Gilead to victory.

But before the battle, Jephthah had vowed to God that, if he were granted victory on the field of battle, he would sacrifice whoever first came from his home to greet his return. To his horror, that person was his daughter! He granted her a stay of execution, 'And he sent her away for two months: and she went with her companions, and bewailed her virginity upon the mountains.' When she returned, Jephthah carried out his vow.

A subsequent campaign was fought against Ephraim: Jephthah attacked and trapped the enemy on the River Jordan. As the defeated army attempted to pass through the Israelite lines, they took advantage of Ephraimite pronunciation; however, 'when those Ephraimites which were escaped said, Let me go over; that the men of Gilead said unto him, Art thou an Ephraimite? If he said, Nay; Then said they unto him, Say now Shibboleth: and he said Sibboleth: for he could not frame to pronounce it right. Then they took him, and slew him at the passages of Jordan …' (*Judges 11,12, I Samuel 12:11*)

JEREMIAH Prophet at the time of the fall of Jerusalem. The son of a Benjamite priest of Anathoth, just north of Jerusalem, Jeremiah is regarded as one of the major prophets. He lived through a dramatic era that saw the destruction of the last Jewish kingdom, the razing of Jerusalem and the deportation of its inhabitants. His ministry began in the reign of King Josiah and continued through those of Jehoahaz, Jehoiakim, Jehoiachin and Zedekiah.

His name has become associated with unremitting pessimism, but this is unjustified: in fact, he saw the tribulations to come and through which he lived as a necessary stage in the journey to a new beginning and a restoration of God's Law and a new Covenant. Because of the seemingly negative nature of his message, he was never popular and, indeed, suffered persecution from the authorities.

He began his work in the thirteenth year of the reign of King Josiah, who had come to the throne at the age of eight, and was a significant factor in motivating the religious reforms made in this king's reign. However, these reforms were not entirely to Jeremiah's liking, for they relied, he felt, on excessive centralization of worship at the Temple; indeed, he managed to antagonize the Temple authorities to such an extent that he was scourged on the orders of the Temple overseer, Pashur and then set in the stocks.

Even during the reign of this benign monarch, Jeremiah was warning of the troubles that were soon to strike Judah. Earlier prophets had warned about the way in which God's anger would be excited by their disloyalty, corruption and espousal of alien cults; now Jeremiah told the people that the warnings were all about to come true. As the

Above and right: The trials of Jeremiah. Above, he sits in the stocks; right, he is thrown into a cistern (but later released on the orders of King Zedekiah).

When the Babylonians entered Jerusalem, they released Jeremiah and placed him in the care of the Babylonian governor of Judah, Gedaliah, in Mizpah. Later Gedaliah was assassinated by a band of Jews led by Ishmael, who then fled to Egypt, followed by others fearing Babylonian vengeance. Among those taken to Egypt was Jeremiah, now a very old man, who told them that this was against the wishes of the Lord and that he would destroy them all; but they failed to heed his words and continued worshipping their idols.

The Book of Jeremiah describes the prophet's calling, the prophecies he made during the reigns of Josiah, Jehoahaz, Jehoiakim, Jehoiachin and Zedekiah, the events of his life and the fall of Jerusalem. There are also references to the coming of a Messiah in *23:1–8*, and *33:14–16*. Traditionally *The Book of Lamentations*, which bewails the desolation of Jerusalem after the coming of the Babylonians, has been ascribed also to Jeremiah. He is mentioned in the *Gospel of Matthew* as 'Jeremy' (*2:17*) and 'Jeremias' (*15:14*) and also in *Chronicles*, *Ezra* and *Daniel*.

Above: The King destroys Jeremiah's sermons.

menace from Egypt and Babylonia replaced that of Assyria, the priests said that God would protect Jerusalem; but, replied Jeremiah, only by surrendering to the Babylonians would the Lord's purpose be served. He foresaw the exile but looked beyond that to the time when they would return and make a new beginning.

Jeremiah's prophesies made him unpopular, and later during the siege of Jerusalem he was even accused of deserting to the enemy. During the reign of Jehoiakim, he was put on trial as an enemy of Judah, but he defended himself successfully; later God commanded him to write down his prophecies, which he did, using Baruch as a scribe. By this time, Jeremiah was no longer permitted to enter the Temple, so to Baruch fell the task of reading the scroll of prophesies in public. When the King heard about this he sent for the scroll and cut it up before throwing it on the fire. Undeterred, Jeremiah and Baruch rewrote it.

The persecution of Jeremiah continued even as the city came under siege, and he was thrown into prison. This did not stop the King seeking his advice; but all Jeremiah could do was tell him the unpalatable truth – that the city would fall, and the King and his subjects would be taken off to Babylon. Zedekiah ordered him to tell no one else about their conversation.

JEROBOAM I First king of Israel after the death of Solomon and the partition of his kingdom, and 'who made Israel to sin'. (*I Kings 14:16*) Jeroboam was not of the line of David and Solomon. His origins lay in Ephraim, and during Solomon's reign he was overseer of the labor force from his tribe working on the King's grand construction projects. He became involved in a plot against Solomon, encouraged by a prophecy by Ahijah of Shiloh, who had turned against the King following his worship of foreign gods. The coup attempt failed, and Jeroboam sought refuge with Pharaoh Sishak in Egypt. (*I Kings 11:28–40*)

Upon the death of Solomon, Ahijah's prediction that the ten northern tribes would break away came true. Resentful of the high taxes and forced labor that Solomon had imposed, the northerners were also jealous of Judah and Jerusalem. So when Rehoboam acceded to his father's throne, they seceded and elected Jeroboam king.

Above: Jeroboam I worships the Golden Calf.

Jeroboam feared that the religious dominance of Jerusalem would lead to defections to Judah, so he set up new shrines at Bethel and Dan with golden calves similar to that which Aaron had made in the wilderness. The priests and Levites objected, and Jeroboam banned them from the Temple: so they left for Judah, and Jeroboam instituted a new, and illegitimate, priesthood.

For this he received the condemnation of Ahijah. When the King's son, Abijah, fell seriously ill and Ahijah was consulted, he replied that Jeroboam had 'done evil above all that were before thee: for thou hast gone and made thee other gods, and molten images, to provoke me to anger, and hast cast me behind thy back: Therefore, behold, I will bring evil upon the house of Jeroboam, and will cut off from Jeroboam him that pisseth against the wall, and him that is shut up and left in Israel, and will take away the remnant of the house of Jeroboam, as a man taketh away dung, till it be all gone. Him that dieth of Jeroboam in the city shall the dogs eat; and him that dieth in the field shall the fowls of the air eat: for the Lord hath spoken it. Arise thou therefore, get thee to thine own house: and when thy feet enter into the city, the child shall die.' *(I Kings 14:9–12)*

Hostilities between the two kingdoms did not abate, and late in his reign Jeroboam was defeated in battle by King Abijam of Judah. *(I Kings 11–14, II Chronicles 10–13)*

JEROBOAM II Thirteenth king of Israel after the division of the kingdom. Son of Jehoash, he inherited a strong and peaceful kingdom, whose prosperity reached a zenith during his long reign of 41 years. But that very prosperity was the subject of warnings by the prophet Amos, who denounced the moral decline of the Jews – the luxury, the corruption of justice, and the increasing division between rich and poor. Wealth could be more dangerous even than poverty. He warned that troubles lay ahead and predicted the captivity of Israel.

Israeli arms were meanwhile also at their zenith, as Jeroboam expanded the frontiers of the state to both north and south, even capturing Damascus. But when he died, disaster was approaching fast. The kingdom his son Zechariah inherited would last no more than a quarter of a century. *(II Kings 14:23–9)*

JESSE Father of David, second king of Israel, grandson of Boaz and Ruth. Jesse was a man of substance living in Bethlehem, whom Samuel visited in his search for a successor to Saul. When three of his eight sons, Eliab, Abinadab and Shammah, were serving in Saul's army facing the Philistines, he sent David, the youngest: 'Take now for thy brethren an ephah of this parched corn, and these ten loaves, and run to the camp to thy brethren; And carry these ten cheeses unto the captain of their thousand, and look how thy brethren fare, and take their pledge.' That historic visit led to David defeating the giant Goliath and entering Saul's court. Later, when the King turned against David and he fled, David sent Jesse and his mother to the King of Moab for safety. *Isaiah 11:1,10* predicted that there would 'come forth a rod out of the stem of Jesse, and a Branch shall grow out of his roots … 'And in that day there shall be a root of Jesse, which shall stand for an ensign of the people; to it shall the Gentiles seek: and his rest shall be glorious.' *(I Samuel 17, 18, 20, 22:3, Ruth 4:17, 22, Isaiah 11:1, 10, Matthew 1:5, 6, Luke 3:32)*

JETHRO (Reuel) Father-in-law of Moses, a priest of Midian. When Moses fled Egypt after killing an Egyptian and took refuge in the desert of Moab, he married Jethro's daughter Zipporah and tended their sheep. It was while he was here that he beheld the burning bush and received his calling. Jethro did not accompany Moses when he led the Hebrews out of Egypt but made a visit to their camp, where he saw the burden that Moses was carrying and wisely advised him to delegate some of his responsibilities. *(Exodus 2:18–21, 3:1, 4:18, 18:1–24) Exodus 3:18* calls him Reuel.

Above: 'Throw her down!' Jezebel falls to her death.

Above: Jethro with Moses in the wilderness.

JEZEBEL Queen to King Ahab of Israel, whose name has become synonymous with female wickedness. Daughter of King Ethbaal of Sidon, she converted Ahab to the worship of Baal, provoking the fury of the prophet Elijah, and they became mortal enemies. His victory in the contest with the priests of Baal to bring down fire on a sacrificial offering at Mount Carmel aroused her vow for vengeance when her priests were all slain: 'Then Jezebel sent a messenger unto Elijah, saying, So let the gods do to me, and more also, if I make not thy life as the life of one of them by to morrow about this time.' *(I Kings 19:2)* She was behind the plot to take Naboth's vineyard and arranged his judicial murder. Elijah's response was swift: 'And of Jezebel also spake the Lord, saying, The dogs shall eat Jezebel by the wall of Jezreel. *(I Kings 21:23)* The prophesy was fulfilled. When the usurper Jehu killed her son Jehoram at Jezreel, Jezebel was also in the city. As Jehu came through the gate in the city, she shouted out from an upstairs window that he

was a traitor and an assassin. Jehu called up to the eunuchs by her side: 'Throw her down. So they threw her down: and some of her blood was sprinkled on the wall, and on the horses: and he trode her under foot. And when he was come in, he did eat and drink, and said, Go, see now this cursed woman, and bury her: for she is a king's daughter. And they went to bury her: but they found no more of her than the skull, and the feet, and the palms of her hands. Wherefore they came again, and told him. And he said, This is the word of the Lord, which he spake by his servant Elijah the Tishbite, saying, In the portion of Jezreel shall dogs eat the flesh of Jezebel: And the carcase of Jezebel shall be as dung upon the face of the field in the portion of Jezreel; so that they shall not say, This is Jezebel.' *(I Kings 16:31, 18:4,13,19, 19:1,2 21:5–25, II Kings 9:22,30–37)*

JOAB Nephew of King David and commander of his army. He was the son of David's elder half-sister Zeruiah. An early supporter of

David after the future king fled Saul's court, Joab fought for David during his bandit days. At the Pool of Gibeon, Jael led David's force against that of Abner with the army of Ishbosheth, who had been proclaimed King of Israel after the death of Saul. A trial of strength between a dozen men of each side preceded a battle in which Abner's men were defeated. *(II Samuel 13–19)* In the rout, Abner killed Joab's brother, Asahel, and Joab vowed vengeance. When, after prolonged hostilities, Abner changed sides, Joab found an opportunity to exact revenge: he tricked Abner into meeting him and then 'Joab took him aside in the gate to speak with him quietly, and smote him there under the fifth rib, that he died, for the blood of Asahel his brother'. *(II Samuel 3:27)*

During David's conquest of Jerusalem, Joab distinguished himself *(I Chronicles 11:6)*, and he subsequently led David's forces in wars with the Syrians, defeating the army of King Hanun of Ammon and the following year destroying the city of Rabbah *(I Chronicles 19–20, II Samuel 10:7–14, 11ff, 12:26–31)* before fighting campaigns against the Philistines and Gath. It was during the fighting at Rabbah that David arranged the death of the husband of Bathsheba. He sent Joab a secret message: 'And he wrote in the letter, saying, Set ye Uriah in the forefront of the hottest battle, and retire ye from him, that he may be smitten, and die. And it came to pass, when Joab observed the city, that he assigned Uriah unto a place where he knew that valiant men were. And the men of the city went out, and fought with Joab: and there fell some of the people of the servants of David; and Uriah the Hittite died also.' *(2 Samuel 11:14–17)*

When David's son Absalom murdered his half-brother Amnon, Joab intervened and effected a reconciliation between father and son. In the later rebellion of Absalom, Jael fled Jerusalem with David, regrouped the Kings's forces and defeated Absalom in the woods of Ephraim. It was Joab who dealt Absalom his death blow when the fleeing usurper was caught up in the branches of an oak. *(II Samuel*

Above: top, the young Joash proclaimed king of Judah; below, the fund-raising collection box in the Temple.

18–19) David did not forgive Joab for killing his son, even though he was a traitor, and Joab lost his command to Amasa. But during the rebellion of Sheba, Joab took the opportunity to kill Amasa; he then pursued Sheba and returned to Jerusalem with the rebel's head.

Toward the end of David's reign, his son Adonijah began planning to seize the throne, but David took pre-emptive action by having

Solomon anointed king, and when it was known that Joab had been a party to Adonijah's plan, David counseled Solomon to execute him. *(I Kings 2:5–6)* Joab's demise was as violent as had been his career. On succeeding to the throne, Solomon followed David's advice and Joab, forewarned, took sanctuary in the tabernacle, clinging to the horns of the altar; but Benaiah, Solomon's general, followed Solomon's orders and dispatched him. *(I Kings 2:28–34)*

JOASH Seventh king of Judah, son of Ahaziah, whose accession restored the House of David to the throne of Judah. When Jehu killed both the kings of Israel and Judah, Joash's grandmother, Athaliah, seized power in Jerusalem and the baby Joash was preserved from the slaughter of his family by his aunt Jehosheba. When he was seven, the priest Jehoiada set in train a revolution: Joash was crowned king and his evil grandmother put to death.

Joash ruled for 40 years, for much of this time in a good and godly way. The temple of Baal, erected by Athaliah, was pulled down, and plans were laid for the repairs to the Temple, which had been damaged during her reign. Work was slow to begin, since the funds contributed at sacrifices somehow tended not to reach those who needed paying for work. Joash urged the priests to proceed, but not until the 23rd year of his reign was work started. This was aided by the simple expedient of a collection box in the Temple, and the proper administration of funds. Masonry and decorative work were the first priority, with utensils, bowls and cups made only when the structure was fully sound.

However, towards the end of his reign, Joash lost his religious mentor, and when Jehoiada died (at a very considerable age) both the King and Judah began to stray: idolatry reappeared. Jehoiada's son criticized this relapse, warning that God would abandon them, and with the connivance of the King he was stoned to death in the Temple grounds. But he was right: the power of Syria had grown during the reign of Jehu; now King Hazael took Gath and an army penetrated to the walls of Jerusalem, defeating Judah's larger army. Joash paid him off with the Temple treasure, but there remained a greater price to pay – to God. Badly wounded in the battle with Hazael, Joash was murdered in his bed by two conspirators (named in *Kings* as Jozacar and Jehozabad, in *Chronicles* as Zabad and Jehozabad) in revenge for the stoning of Zechariah. His son Amaziah succeeded him. *(II Kings 11–12, II Chronicles 22:11–12, 23, 24)*

JOB An inhabitant of Uz during the early patriarchal epoch and subject of the first of the five poetical books of the Bible. Job himself may not have been a historical figure, for the book may be seen as a treatise on the nature of faith. To test Job's righteousness, God gave Satan control of all this wealthy, pious man's possessions and family, but not his soul or person. A series of calamities followed: his oxen were stolen, his sheep and servants struck by lightning, his camels were also stolen, his home burned down and his children were dashed to their death by a storm. To this Job philosophically commented: 'Naked came I out of my mother's womb, and naked shall I return thither: the Lord gave, and the Lord hath taken away; blessed be the name of the Lord. *(Job 1:21)* He was then plagued by boils.

His friends Eliphaz, Bildad and Zophar came to comfort him, as Job cursed the day he was born. You must be being punished for some sin, suggested his friends. Job said he did not deserve this punishment, for he had been good and righteous; he could not understand why God was doing this to him. Job nevertheless declared his acceptance of the all-powerful nature of God, although wondering about his justice, and was confident that he would in the end be reconciled with God; but he wanted to speak with Him. Hearing this discourse, a fourth friend, Elihu suggested that God sent such disasters to prove people or to purge them, and that though Job was righteous yet he was not perfect.

Then God spoke to Job in a whirlwind, showing him his glory, and Job's bitterness

Above: The comforters of Job.

was replaced by awe and a sense of wonder. 'Then Job answered the Lord, and said, I know that thou canst do every thing, and that no thought can be withholden from thee. Who is he that hideth counsel without knowledge? therefore have I uttered that I understood not; things too wonderful for me, which I knew not. Hear, I beseech thee, and I will speak: I will demand of thee, and declare thou unto me. I have heard of thee by the hearing of the ear: but now mine eye seeth thee. Wherefore I abhor myself, and repent in dust and ashes.' *(Job 42:1–6)*

God finally declared his anger at the intervention of Job's friends and restored to Job double of all that he had lost. *(The Book of Job)*

JOEL Samuel's eldest son, a dishonest judge (*I Samuel 8:2*), called Vashni in *I Chronicles 6:28*.

JOEL A minor prophet, son of Pethuel. *(The Book of Joel)*

Above: Jonah – the storm at sea.

JONAH Prophet during the reign of King Jeroboam II of Israel and a contemporary of Amos. His story, which includes being swallowed by a great fish, is one of the most famous in the Bible, and his name became a byword for one whose presence brings bad luck.

Commanded by God to go to Nineveh, capital of the Assyrian Empire, to announce God's judgment upon their wickedness, Jonah rebelled and took ship instead for the Iberian

Above: Jonah preaches – to great effect – in Nineveh.

port of Tarshish (Tartessus). During the voyage a great storm arose, and when the sailors despaired of reaching safety they began to believe that someone on board had offended God. Jonah realized that he was the guilty man and graciously agreed to be thrown overboard. The storm abated, but instead of drowning Jonah was swallowed by a great fish, in whose belly he remained for three days and nights. Eventually his prayers were heard, 'And the Lord spake unto the fish, and it vomited out Jonah upon the dry land'. (*Jonah 2:10*)

God now insisted that he go to Nineveh, where he found his audience more ready to listen than he had imagined – even the King heard his message and decreed that his people should turn from their wicked ways. Jonah was less than overjoyed at this, for he believed it

Above: Jonathan the archer, brave and skilled in battle.

was the Assyrians' destiny to continue in sin so that the Lord would punish them.

As he sat outside the city walls in the heat of the sun, a castor-oil plant grew to shade him; but next day God sent a worm to eat the plant, leaving Jonah once more in the merciless heat of the sun. Then God told him his lesson: if Jonah was concerned at the wellbeing of a plant, how much more must God care for the great city? If they were taught, the Gentiles would repent. Salvation was not for the Jews alone.

The Book of Jonah is the fourth of the Minor Prophets, and Jonah is referred to by Christ in the *Gospel of Matthew*, calling him 'Jonas'. (*Matthew 12:40*)

JONATHAN Eldest son of Saul, by Ahinoam, whose friendship with David became legendary – 'the soul of Jonathan was knit with the soul of David, and Jonathan loved him as his own soul'. (*I Samuel 18:1*) A skilled archer, Jonathan was a dashing young leader in the army of King Saul, whose exploits at the Battle of Michash saved the Israelite army from destruction. However, during that battle Saul had decreed that no man should eat until evening; but

Jonathan, not having heard this command, tasted some honey they found in a wood, and so was condemned to death. When they heard this, the people petitioned Saul and the King relented.

Jonathan first met David after he had defeated the giant, Goliath, and gave him his own armor, sword and bow. They became not only brothers-in-law but firm friends. When Saul turned against David, Jonathan attempted a recon-ciliation between his father and his friend, but Jonathan eventually warned David to flee; when he remonstrated with Saul the King even threw a javelin at his son. David was eventually forced to escape the court. (*I Samuel 19, 20*)

Jonathan died with his father and two of his brothers at the Battle of Mount Gilboa (*I Samuel 31*) The loss of Jonathan grieved David greatly: 'How are the mighty fallen in the midst of the battle! O Jonathan, thou was slain in thine high places. I am distressed for thee, my brother Jonathan: very pleasant hast thou been unto me: thy love to me was wonderful, passing the

Above: Joseph in his coat of many colors.

Below: Having cast him in a well to die, Joseph's half-brothers change their minds and sell him as a slave to a party of traders on their way to Egypt.

love of women. How are the mighty fallen, and the weapons of war perished!' (*II Samuel 1:5–27*)

His only son Mephibosheth, then five years old and 'lame of his feet', was afterwards befriended by David. (*II Samuel 4:4, I Chronicles 8:34*)

JORAM See Jehoram.

JOSEPH Eleventh son of Jacob, by Rachel. His colorful story is one of the Bible's most famous, and it links the Jews with Egypt, setting the scene for Moses and the Exodus. Joseph's talents at interpreting dreams was to be his fortune, together with undoubted administrative talents and not a little self-confidence, for he rose to a position of high rank in Egypt.

First-born of Jacob's first love, and brought into the world when Jacob was old, Joseph was a spoilt child, and the favoritism shown by his father towards him irritated his siblings. He made matters worse by what they saw as his pretensions, interpreting two dreams as predicting that all his brothers would one day bow down to him.

Exasperated with his behaviour, the brothers eventually decided that they had had enough of him and determined to rid themselves of him. When the brothers were in the fields one day, tending their sheep, Joseph was sent to them on an errand, and they saw their opportunity. Laying hands upon him, they were only dissuaded from killing him by the eldest, Reuben, who suggested throwing him down a well instead (for secretly he planned to return later and save him). This they did, divesting him of the decorated coat his father had given him; they smeared it with blood, so that they could deceive Jacob into believing that he had been attacked and killed by wild beasts. Then there happened by a group of Midianite merchants on their way to Egypt, so they hauled Joseph from the well and sold him for twenty pieces of silver.

In Egypt, Joseph was sold to Potiphar, captain of Pharaoh's guard, and soon became his personal servant and then head of his

Above: Joseph in his splendor as Pharaoh's chief minister responsible for averting the effects of the famine and keeping Egypt fed.

household. In time, dangerous temptation appeared in the form of Potiphar's bored wife, who attempted to seduce Joseph. He would have none of it, and the frustrated matron vengefully alleged that he had insulted her. Joseph was thrown into prison. He found himself incarcerated with Pharaoh's chief butler, who was awaiting judgement on charges involving the chief baker; both dreamt strange dreams, which Joseph interpreted as indicating their fates. The chief butler was released but did not forget Joseph, for when Pharaoh himself was perplexed by a series of mysterious dreams, he told the king of Joseph's talents.

The dreams, of seven fat cows followed by seven lean ones, indicated seven good years followed by seven years of famine. But, said Joseph, if crops could be saved and stored aplenty during the good years, the nation would weather the bad years. His explanation was accepted, and his record as chief of Potiphar's household doubtless prompted his appointment to make the necessary arrangements, which he did with much success.

During the famine, which evidently affected Canaan too, the family of Jacob began to suffer,

Left: Jacob's sons before their now mighty half-brother, whom they do not recognize. But Joseph knows who they are.

so he sent Joseph's elder brothers to Egypt for relief. When they appeared before Joseph, they did not realise who he was, and he spoke with them in Egyptian through an interpreter; but Joseph recognized them. After several visits, during which he accused them of theft, Joseph revealed his identity to them and, with Pharaoh's blessing, invited all Jacob's family to move to the safety of Egypt, where they were well provided for. Reunited with Jacob and his family, Joseph lived out the rest of his years in peace, predicting to his brothers that one day their descendants would return to the land of their forefathers. *(Genesis 37–50)*

JOSHUA Conqueror of the Promised Land. Son of Nun, of the tribe of Ephraim, Joshua was one of only two men born in Egypt who lived through the entire Exodus journey and entered Canaan.

Joshua was prominent at the Battle of Rephadim when the Hebrews defeated the Alamekites *(Exodus 17:8–16)*. He is mentioned as being with Moses in the Tabernacle *(Exodus 33:11)* as his 'servant' and as his 'minister' in *Exodus 24:13*. He became the Hebrew leader's closest companion during the many years in the wilderness.

Chosen from his tribe as one of the twelve spies sent to investigate the Promised Land, with Caleb he returned enthusiastic. Their companions, however, came back with tales of great cities with massive walls; such an air of pessimism set in among the people that God

Right: The Battle of Rephidim, where Joshua distinguished himself in combat against the Amalekites.

Below right: The Hebrews cross the River Jordan and begin their conquest of the Promised Land under Joshua's leadership.

condemned the Hebrews to forty years of wandering before they would be allowed to enter Canaan. This lack of faith did not include Caleb or Joshua, and their reward was that they would both cross into the Promised Land. *(Numbers 13:8, 14:6–9)*

Moses did not live to enter Canaan, and God told him that Joshua would be his successor: 'And Moses called unto Joshua, and said unto him in the sight of all Israel, Be strong and of a good courage: for thou must go with this people unto the land which the Lord hath sworn unto their fathers to give them; and thou shalt cause them to inherit it. And the Lord, he it is that doth go before thee; he will be with thee, he will not fail thee, neither forsake thee: fear not, neither be dismayed.' *(Deuteronomy 31:7–8; also Deuteronomy 31:14,23, Numbers 13:8,16)*

At last the Hebrews entered the Promised Land, crossing the River Jordan miraculously, for the river was in flood. As the priests entered the river, the waters dried up, allowing the passage to take place. *(Joshua 3:14–17)* Another miracle brought the walls of the city of Jericho crashing down. God instructed Joshua to send his army around the city for six days; on the seventh they let loose a huge blast of sound from their trumpets and the walls fell. Jericho was destroyed. *(Joshua 6)* But one man failed to obey God's directive that there should be no

looting, and the consequence was that they could not capture the next city, Ai, until the sin was expiated by the stoning of the culprit, Achan. *(Joshua 7:1,18–26)*

The Gibeonites were the next tribe to face the invasion, but by a clever ruse they persuaded the Hebrews to make a treaty with them rather than attacking them. *(Joshua 9)* Seeing this, the King of Jerusalem, Adoni-zedek, gathered a

Left: The parade around the walls of Jericho.

Below: The sun stands still at the Battle of Gibeon.

coalition of Amorite tribes to attack the city of Gibeon – Hoham, King of Hebron, Piram, King of Jarmuth, Japhia, King of Lachish, and Debir, King of Eglon. Gathering their forces, they began to lay siege to Gibeon, but not before word of the attack had been sent to Joshua with the main Hebrew army at Gilgal. At once he ordered a forced march through the night and took the enemy by surprise, shattering the Amorites and pursuing them as a great hailstorm fell. But night was now closing in, and the Lord caused time to stand still to allow the complete destruction of the Amorites – 'And the sun stood still, and the moon stayed, until the people had avenged themselves upon their enemies. *(Joshua 10:13)* Nor did the five kings escape; sheltering in a cave, they were trapped and later brought out to be symbolically humiliated before the army before being slain. *(Joshua 10)*

More victories followed, including the defeat of Jabin of Hazor at the Battle of the River Merom, whom Joshua personally put to the sword *(Joshua 11)*, King Sinon, Amorite king of Heshbon, and then King Og of Bashan. In sum, 31 kings fell to the Hebrews *(Joshua 12:7–24, 24:11)*, and they had carved out a significant area of Canaan before God told Joshua to pause and allocate the conquered lands to the tribes. Further conquests would follow but not under Joshua's leadership, for he was now very old. Before he died he made a farewell address to the people, both renewing the Covenant and advising the Hebrews against intermarriage with the

people whose lands they had conquered (which was ignored, with the result that many alien religions became familiar in Israel; this would be the subject of many sermons from the prophets of the kingdom in later years).

In historical terms Joshua must be accounted one of the great commanders: under his leadership the wandering tribe of the Hebrews became a settled nation, which, after years of triumphs and vicissitudes, would find its greatest expression in the Kingdom of David and Solomon. *(The Book of Joshua)*

Above: The young Josiah crowned King of Judah.

JOSIAH Fifteenth king of Judah, who reformed the nation's religion and rebuilt the Temple. Aged eight at his accession, Josiah followed two bad kings on the throne of Judah; his father had lasted but two years before his staff assassinated him. It was in the thirteenth year of Josiah's reign that Jeremiah began his work, and the prophet had a positive effect on the young king, helping to inspire the religious reforms and revival that took place during his reign. He began to purge Judah of the corrupt and alien religious practices that had been adopted in the kingdom during the reigns of his predecessors. Pagan cults were suppressed, idols thrown down and false gods condemned. He also renovated the Temple, which had fallen into decay, and during this process the High Priest Hilkiah discovered the 'Book of the Law'. *(II Kings 22:8)* It thus became starkly clear that the Mosaic Laws had been neglected, and that Judah must turn back to its native faith. When Josiah consulted the prophetess Huldah about the book, she echoed Jeremiah's doom-laden predictions that God would punish the nation that had rejected him; but that reckoning would be made after Josiah's death.

It was during Josiah's reign the mighty empire of Assyria fell, but it was only to be replaced by the rising power of Babylon, while to the south Egypt saw the opportunity to expand. Josiah harbored ambitions to bring the lost northern kingdom back into the fold, but the whole area now became a battleground between Egypt and Babylon. When Pharaoh Necho II advanced to Megiddo, Josiah fought him, despite the Pharaoh's message that his quarrel was not with Judah. Mortally wounded by Egyptian arrows, Josiah was taken back to Jerusalem and died there after a reign of 31 years. *(II Kings 22–23, II Chronicles 34–5)*

JOTHAM Tenth king of Judah, son of the leper Uzzaiah, for whom he was regent during the last years of his father's reign. His sixteen-year reign was relatively peaceful but, while he kept faith with God, pagan temples were still tolerated and his people continued to worship idols: 'And he did that which was right in the sight of the Lord … And the people did yet corruptly.' *(II Chronicles 27:2)* He carried out

Above: Pulling down the idols during Josiah's great reforms.

much construction work, including work on the North Gate of the Temple, the city walls, and built settlements and fortified places in the mountains of Judah. His military campaigns included an engagement with the Ammorites, whom he forced to pay tribute for three years. (*Kings 15:37* also mentions that Judah was attacked by Kings Rezin of Syria and Pekah of Israel during his reign, but this may have been merely a preliminary raid, because the main attack came during the reign of his successor, Ahaz.) It was during the year that Jotham succeeded to the throne that the prophet Isaiah began his work. *(II Kings 15:32–8, II Chronicles 27:1–9)*

JUDAH Fourth son of Jacob and Leah, and founder of the Hebrew tribe of that name. When Jacob's sons were disposing of their brother Joseph, it was Judah who saved him from death in the well in which they had cast him: 'What profit is it if we slay our brother, and conceal his blood?' he asked. 'Come, and let us sell him to the Ishmeelites, and let not our hand be upon him; for he is our brother and our flesh.' (*Genesis 37:26–7*)

Later Judah went to Adullam and found a Canaanite wife, Shuah, who bore him a son, Er, and married him to Tamar. But Er 'was wicked in the sight of the Lord; and the Lord slew him', so Judah decided that it was the duty of his second son, Onan, to take her and have children 'raise up seed to thy brother. And Onan knew that the seed should not be his; and it came to pass, when he went in unto his brother's wife, that he spilled it on the ground, lest that he should give seed to his brother. And the thing which he did displeased the Lord: wherefore he slew him also.' (*Genesis 38:1–10*) According to custom, Tamar should then have been married to Judah's third son, Shelah, but Judah made no move to do this when the boy came of age. So Tamar, disguised as a harlot, seduced Judah and bore twin sons by him. (*Genesis 38:11–30*)

When famine struck the land, Judah was one of the brothers who went to Egypt to buy corn and was deceived by their half-brother

Above: Judah pleads for Benjamin before Joseph.

Joseph. When they needed more corn, Judah explained to their father that Joseph would not meet them unless Benjamin (Joseph's brother) were among the party. Judah promised Jacob that he would look after his young half-brother and was the spokesman for the brothers at their next interview with Joseph, pleading for Benjamin after Joseph planted a precious cup in Benjamin's baggage and accused him of theft. After Joseph revealed his identity, it was Judah who returned to Canaan to bring Jacob into Goshen. (*Genesis 42–6*)

As Jacob approached his death, he blessed his sons, with a special blessing for Judah, which foretold the prominence of the tribe of Judah in the Promised Land: 'Judah, thou art he whom thy brethren shall praise: thy hand shall be in the neck of thine enemies; thy father's children shall bow down before thee. Judah is a lion's whelp: from the prey, my son, thou art gone up: he stooped down, he couched as a lion, and as an old lion; who shall rouse him up? The sceptre shall not depart from Judah, nor a lawgiver from between his feet, until Shiloh come; and unto him shall the gathering of the people be.' (*Genesis 49:8–12*)

KADMIEL A Levite who returned with Zerubbabel. (*Nehemiah 9:4, 5, 10:9; 12:8, 24*; see also *Ezra 2:40, 3:9*)

KAREAH Father of Johanan and Jonathan, adherents of Gedaliah (*Jeremiah 40:8*); he is called Careah in *II Kings 25:23*.

KEDAR Second son of Ishmael. (*Genesis 25:13*)

KEDEMAH Youngest son of Ishmael. (*Genesis 25:15*)

KELITA A Levite in the time of Ezra who had taken a Gentile wife (*Ezra 10:23, Nehemiah 8:7, 10:10*); he is also called Kelaiah.

KEMUEL Third son of Nahor. (*Genesis 22:21*)

KEMUEL Son of Shiphtan, an Ephraimite prince. (*Numbers 34:24*)

KEMUEL A Levite. (*I Chronicles 27:17*)

KENAZ A son of Eliphaz, and one of the 'dukes' of Edom. (*Genesis 36:11,15,42*)

KENAZ Caleb's younger brother, the father of Othniel. (*Joshua 15:17, Judges 1:13*)

KENAZ Caleb's grandson. (*I Chronicles 4:15*)

KEREN-HAPPUCH Job's youngest daughter. (*Job 42:14*)

KETURAH Abraham's wife after Sarah's death (*Genesis 25:1–6*), by whom he had six sons. Called 'Abraham's concubine' in *I Chronicles 1:32*.

KEZIA The second of Job's daughters born after his return to prosperity. (*Job 42:54*)

KISH Father of Saul, son of Abiel, a Benjamite. God used the disappearance of Kish's asses as a means of bringing Saul to Samuel, who would anoint him king of Israel. Kish sent Saul and a servant to find the missing animals, and eventually they found themselves in the land of Zulph, where they decided to seek out the local seer, or holy man, for help. That man was Samuel. (*I Samuel 9*)

KISH Son of Jehiel, and brother of Ner. (*I Chronicles 9:35, 36*)

KISH A Merarite Levite in the days of Hezekiah. (*II Chronicles 29:12*)

KISH A Benjamite, an ancestor of Mordecai. (*Esther 2:5*)

KITTIM A grandson of Japheth. (*Genesis 10:4*)

KOA Named among the enemies of Jerusalem in *Ezekiel 23:23*.

KOHATH Second son of Levi and grandfather of Moses. (*Genesis 46:11*)

KOLAIAH Father of a false prophet named together with Zedekiah in *Jeremiah 29:21* – 'Thus saith the Lord of hosts, the God of Israel, of Ahab the son of Kolaiah, and of

Above: Kish the warrior.

Zedekiah the son of Maaseiah, which prophesy a lie unto you in my name; Behold, I will deliver them into the hand of Nebuchadrezzar king of Babylon; and he shall slay them before your eyes.'

KORAH Third son of Esau and Aholibamab. (*Genesis 36:14, I Chronicles 1:35*)

KORAH A Levite who led a revolt against Moses. After God had sentenced the Hebrews to an extra forty years of wandering, there was unrest among the Hebrews. With Daran and Abiram (both Levites) and On (a Reubenite), Korah led a revolt against Moses in the wilderness, 'And they gathered themselves together against Moses and against Aaron, and said unto them, Ye take too much upon you, seeing all the congregation are holy, every one of them, and the Lord is among them: wherefore then lift ye up yourselves above the congregation of the Lord?' An angry Moses appealed to God to demonstrate His will that he remain leader. God commanded that the 250 present themselves before the Tent of the Tabernacle and warned the other people to stand well clear of them. Then He appeared as a dazzling light and 'the earth opened her mouth, and swallowed them up, and their houses, and all the men that appertained unto Korah, and all their goods. They, and all that appertained to them, went down alive into the pit, and the earth closed upon them: and they perished from among the congregation.' This mass slaughter unnerved the people: 'on the morrow all the congregation of the children of Israel murmured against Moses and against Aaron, saying, Ye have killed the people of the Lord.' So God sent a plague upon them. (*Numbers 16*)

KORE A Korahite Levite, son of Ebiasaph, and father of Shallum and Meshelemiab. (*I Chronicles 9:19, 26:1*)

KORE A Levite, temple doorkeeper in the time of Hezekiah. (*II Chronicles 31:14*)

L

LAADAH A grandson of Jodah. (*I Chronicles 4:21*)

LAADAN Son of Gershon, a Levite (*I Chronicles 23:7–9*); called Libni in *Exodus 6:17* and *I Chronicles 6:57*

LAADAN An ancestor of Joshua. (*I Chronicles 7:26, 27*)

LABAN Father of Leah and Rachel, father-in-law to Jacob and brother of Rebekah. Isaac sent Jacob to find a wife among the daughters of Laban at Padanaram, and Jacob chose Rachel, with whom he had fallen in love. Laban made Jacob wait seven years before the wedding could take place. But Laban deceived Jacob: 'And it came to pass, that in the morning, behold, it was Leah: and he said to Laban, What is this thou hast done unto me? did not I serve with thee for Rachel? wherefore then hast thou beguiled me? And Laban said, It must not be so done in our country, to give the younger before the firstborn. Fulfill her week, and we will give thee this also for the service which thou shalt serve with me yet seven other years. And Jacob did so, and fulfilled her week: and he gave him Rachel his daughter to wife also. (*Genesis 29:25–8*)

Laban attempted deception again when Jacob wanted to return to the land of his parents: Laban was loath to let him go, since he valued his work, but Jacob wanted recompense for the years of service he had contributed to Laban's estate. It was decided that they would divide the flocks and herds between the two of them, but Laban tried to ensure he took the best for himself. Jacob circumvented this, but the relationship between the two men was not as before, so Laban consented to Jacob's departure for Canaan. So bad was the relationship now that Jacob left without telling Laban, who pursued them. Before setting out, Rachel had stolen Laban's images of the household gods, and Laban searched in vain for them among the tents of his daughters. Eventually, however, Laban and Jacob were reconciled; they came to an understanding and parted in friendship. (*Genesis 24:29, 29–31*)

LAHMI Brother of Goliath, slain by Elbanan. (*I Chronicles 20:5*)

LAISH Father of Phaltiel, who married Michal, David's wife. (*II Samuel 3:15*)

LAMECH A rather violent antediluvian, son of Methusael. 'And Lamech said unto his wives, Adah and Zillah, Hear my voice; ye wives of Lamech, hearken unto my speech: for I have slain a man to my wounding, and a young man to my hurt. If Cain shall be avenged sevenfold, truly Lamech seventy and sevenfold.' (*Genesis 4:23–4*)

LAMECH Son of Methuselah and father of Noah. (*Genesis 5:25–31*)

LAPIDOTH The husband of Deborah the judge and prophetess. (*Judges 4:4*)

Above: The wrath of Lamech.

LEAH First wife of Jacob, sister of Rachel: 'Leah was tender eyed; but Rachel was beautiful and well favoured.' (*Genesis 29:17*) When Jacob asked for Rachel's hand in marriage, her father Laban deceived Jacob into marrying Leah instead, for it was the custom in that land that daughters should be married in the order of their birth. Rachel was permitted to marry Jacob a week later. (*Genesis 29:25–8*) Leah bore Jacob five sons and a daughter: Reuben, Simeon, Levi, Judah, Issachar, Zebulun, and Dinah (*Genesis 29:32, 30:21*) She died in Canaan and was buried in the cave of Machpelah. (*Genesis 49:31*)

LEMUEL A king taught wisdom by his mother. (*Proverbs 31:1–9*)

LEVI Third son of Jacob and Leah. At his birth Leah said, 'This time will my husband be joined unto me.' (*Genesis 29:34*) He and Simeon took a cruel revenge on Shechem for the wrong to their sister Dinah. (*34:25–31*) He had three sons. (*Exodus 6:16*)

LIBNI Son of Gershon, the son of Levi. (*Exodus 6:17; Numbers 3:21*) His descendants were called Libnites.

LIBNI Grandson of Merari, the son of Levi, (*I Chronicles 6:29*)

LIKHI Son of Shemidah, a descendant of Manasseh. (*I Chronicles 7:19*)

LORUHAMAH Daughter of Hosea. (*Hosea 1:6*) The name, which means 'not pitied', was given as a warning to the Jews. (*Hosea 1:6,10, 2:1–23*)

LOT Nephew of Abraham, son of Haran. (*Genesis 11:27,31, 12:5*) When God called Abram (later named Abraham) out of Ur of the Chaldees, Lot went with him into Canaan, and they prospered, their herds and flocks growing in size to the point where the land they had settled would not support both, and indeed 'there was a strife between the herd-

Above: Lot accompanies Abram and his family from Ur to Canaan.

men of Abram's cattle and the herdmen of Lot's cattle'. (*Genesis 13:7*) So Lot moved to the plain of Jordan, near Sodom. When a raid by kings from the north struck the coastal cities, among the prisoners taken away were Lot and his family. Abram heard this and armed his 318 servants, then pursued the raiders and rescued Lot, his family and the property that had been carried off. (*Genesis 14*)

Some while later, two angels visited Sodom, and while they were there Lot entertained them with food and drink. A mob gathered, but Lot protected them, and next morning they warned him that during the night God would destroy the city, together with Gomorrah, for the wickedness therein. Lot and his family were eventually persuaded to flee – but not to look back. 'Then the Lord rained upon Sodom and upon Gomorrah brimstone and fire from the Lord out of heaven; And he overthrew those cities, and all the plain, and all the inhabitants of the cities, and that which grew upon the ground. But his wife looked back from behind him, and she became a pillar of salt.'

Lot went up into the mountains with his two daughters, who believed that the end of mankind had come about and that they were

Right: Lot and Abram agree on the locations for their herds, so that strife between their herdsmen will end.

Below: Lot settled near Sodom, and when that city was destroyed by the Lord, Lot's wife ignored the injunction upon looking behind at the devastation. She was turned into a pillar of salt.

the only ones left alive. So they plied their father with wine on two successive nights and when he was drunk seduced him, so that they both bore children by him. The firstborn, a son, was called Moab, and from him descended the Moabites; from the second, Benammi, descended the Ammonites. (*Genesis 19*)

LOTAN Son of Seir, and one of the Horite 'dukes'. (*Genesis 36:20,29*)

LUD Fourth son of Shem. (*Genesis 10:22, I Chronicles 1:17*)

M

MAACAH Queen of King Rehoboam of Judah. Her action in worshipping a fertility goddess (probably the Canaanite Ashtaroth) epitomizes the perennial problem of the ancient Jewish kingdoms – the espousal of foreign cults, especially by persons of significance, who thus set a bad example to the ordinary people. When her grandson Asa began his religious reforms, he destroyed the naked statue she had set up, chopping it into little pieces and burning it in the Valley of Kidron. (*I Kings 15:2, 13, II Chronicles 15:16*)

MAATH An ancestor of Jesus Christ. (*Luke 3:26*)

MAHLON Son of Elimelech and Naomi, the husband of Orpah He died and Orpah returned to her family. (*The Book of Ruth 1:1–5*)

MALACHI *The Book of Malachi* is the last of the nine minor prophets, and may be seen as a bridge between the Old and New Testaments. It is unclear whether the name 'Malachi' refers to a particular person or is the Hebrew word for 'my messenger'. The book dates from the period after the return from exile, when Zechariah set in motion the rebuilding of the Temple, but before the reforms of Nehemiah and Ezra. Its principal subject is the corruption of the practices of worship, the sacrifice of poor or unhealthy animals, the slackness and moral erosion of the Jews, their failure to pay their tithes to the Temple and the widespread taking of foreign, pagan wives. 'Behold, I will send my messenger, and he shall prepare the way before me: and the Lord, whom ye seek, shall suddenly come to this temple … And I will come near to you to judgment; and I will be a swift witness against the sorcerers, and against the adulterers, and against false swearers … For I am the Lord, I change not … Even from the days of your fathers ye are gone away from mine ordinances, and have not kept them. Return unto me, and I will return unto you, saith the Lord of hosts.' (*Malachi 3:1–7*)

The Lord's patience was exhausted, and the day of judgement was near.

MANASSEH Elder son of Jacob and founder of the tribe that bore his name. (*Genesis 41:50–2*) When, shortly before his death, Jacob blessed them, he reversed the customary bestowal of the rights of the firstborn by placing his hand upon Manasseh's brother, Ephraim. The tribe of Manasseh was split into two parts when the Promised Land was settled: 'Them did Moses the servant of the Lord and the children of Israel smite: and Moses the servant of the Lord gave it for a possession unto the Reubenites, and the Gadites, and the half tribe of Manasseh.' (*Joshua 12:6*)

MANASSEH Father of a Gershom. (*Judges 18:30*)

MANASSEH Thirteenth king of Judah, son of Hezekiah, he came to the throne at the age of twelve and reigned for 55 years. He was a ruler who sinned against the Lord on a grand scale, taking up idolatry and other pagan practices – restoring the shrines broken down by his father, using divination, magic, fortune-telling and mediums, with pagan idols in the Temple. 'And he built altars for all the host of heaven in the two courts of the house of the Lord and he caused his children to pass through the fire in the valley of the son of Hinnom: also he observed times, and used enchantments, and used witchcraft, and dealt with a familiar spirit, and with wizards: he wrought much evil in the sight of the Lord, to provoke him to anger.' (*II Kings 33:5–6*) Many innocent people died during this king's reign, punishment for which would come in Jehoiakim's reign.

But *II Kings 33:10–17* describes a dramatic reversal in Manasseh's character towards the end of his reign. Once again the Assyrians invaded Judah, and they took Manasseh captive, hauling him away in chains. Desperately repentant, Manasseh prayed to God; the Assyrians released him and he returned to

Jerusalem a changed man. (*II Kings 21–18, II Chronicles 33:1–20*) He is referred to as Manasses in *Matthew 1:10*.

MATTAN A priest of Baal slain before the altar. (*II Kings 11:18*)

MATTAN Father of Shephatiah in the time of Jeremiah. (*Jeremiah 38:1*)

MATTANIAH See Zedekiah.

MELCHI The name of two of the ancestors of Christ. (*Luke 3:24,28*)

MENAHEM Sixteenth king of Israel after the division of the kingdom, who assassinated his predecessor, Shallum, himself a usurper. He was evidently a vicious character: on his way to Samaria from Tirzah, where he had killed the King, Menahem found that the city of Tiphsah would not surrender to him, so he destroyed it and the surrounding area, committing many atrocities. By now the rising power of Assyria, to the north, was beginning to impinge upon the territories of the Jews, and King Tiglath-Pileser III appeared with his army to demand tribute. This was but a beginning to the threat to the Jewish kingdoms. Menahem paid, having raised the money forcibly from the nobility of Israel. He reigned for ten years and was succeeded by his son, Pekahiah. (*II Kings 15:14–22*)

MEPHIBOSHETH Son of Saul by his concubine Rizpah, hanged by the Gibeonites. *(II Samuel 21:8-10)*

MEPHIBOSHETH Son of Jonathan and grandson of Saul. (*II Samuel 4:4*) He was lame, his nurse having dropped him when escaping after Saul's death. He took refuge with Machir at Lodebar, in Gilead, and remained there until David invited him to Jerusalem and restored to him the property of Saul. (*II Samuel 9:4–13*) When David fled from Absalom, Meshibosheth's servant Ziba lied to David about his master's loyalty and treacherously obtained from David a grant of all that

Above: David and Mephibosheth.

belonged to Mephibosheth. But on David's return to Jerusalem, Mephiboshoth explained how the King had been deceived, and David restored half of his land to him. (*II Samuel 16:1–4, 19:24–30*) He is called Merib-baal in *I Chronicles 8:34, 9:40*.

METHUSAEL Son of Mehujael and father of the violent Lamech. (*Genesis 4:18*)

MESHACH (Original Jewish name Mishael) A companion of Daniel in Babylon, one of the Jewish nobles educated by the Babylonians for senior positions in their administration. When confronted by Nebuchadnezzar's golden idol, they refused to worship it and were thrown into a fiery furnace but miraculously emerged unburnt. Nebuchadnezzar, impressed by the power of their god, promoted them. (*Daniel 1:6–7,11–21, 3*)

METHUSELAH Son of Enoch and father of Lamech. He is notable as being the longest-lived of any of the dwellers of antiquity, his age being given as 969 years. (*Genesis 5:21–27*)

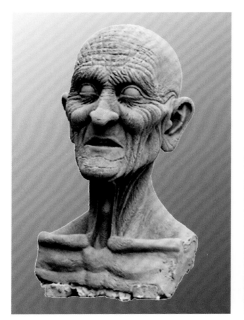

Above: The ancient Methuselah.

Above: The prophet Micah

MICAH Son of Mephibosheth. (*I Chronicles 8:34, 35*) He is called Micha in *II Samuel 9:12*.

MICAH An Ephraimite who stole silver from his mother but returned it when she cursed him. She then gave him 200 pieces of silver to make an image to worship, and Micah took in a wandering Levite to act as priest. When a band of the tribe of Dan came by, they stole his religious goods – 'an ephod, and teraphim, and a graven image, and a molten image'. (*Judges 18:14*) They conquered the city of Laish, renamed it Dan and set up Micah's idol there. (*Judges 17, 18*)

MICAH One of the Minor Prophets, Micah came from the country town of Moresheth in southern Judaea. He was a contemporary of Isaiah. A prophet for the poor, he damned the oppressors and the establishment, citing the cities as dens of iniquity, with their corruption and wickedness. Faith, he held, was manifested in the heart rather than in showy religious practices. He predicted the destruction of Jerusalem (*Jeremiah 26:18*), but that the city

would one day rise again to be the religious center of the world. He was also one of those who predicted the coming of a Messiah: 'But thou, Bethlehem Ephratah, though thou be little among the thousands of Judah, yet out of thee shall he come forth unto me that is to be ruler in Israel.' (*Micah 5:2*) He was stoned to death. (*The Book of Micah*)

MICAHIAH A prophet, the son of Imlah in the days of Ahab. (*I Kings 22:8–28*)

MICAIAH Prophet of Israel during the reign of King Ahab. When Ahab and King Jehoshaphat of Judah planned an expedition against King Ben-hadad II of Syria, they convened a meeting of prophets to consult the Lord about whether such an attack would be successful. The prophets answered positively, but Ahab called for Micaiah, who had disdained to attend, for he and the King did not enjoy an easy relationship – Ahab complained that he always predicted bad things. This time was no exception: the other prophets, he said, were not telling the whole truth, which was God's way of enticing the King into disaster. This did not please Ahab, who threw Micaiah into prison. But his prediction was accurate, and Ahab was killed. (*I Kings 22:8–28*)

MIRIAM Sister of Moses and Aaron, daughter of Amran and Jochebed. When the baby Moses was set afloat in the river to be found by the daughter of the Pharaoh, Miriam was keeping watch in the bulrushes. As the princess contemplated the future of the child, Miriam was able to volunteer her mother – Moses' mother – as nurse for the child, ensuring that Jochebed did not lose the boy.

Miriam accompanied her brothers on the Hebrews' epic trek into the wilderness and, as sister of Moses, she naturally adopted a leadership role among the Hebrews. *Exodus 15–20–1* records her leading the celebrations after the Egyptian army perished in the waters of the Red Sea: 'And Miriam the prophetess, the sister of Aaron, took a timbrel in her hand; and all the women went out after her with timbrels and with dances. And Miriam answered them, Sing ye to the Lord, for he hath triumphed gloriously; the horse and his rider hath he thrown into the sea.' Later in the wilderness she was at the heart of a family row

Right: Miriam awaits her moment to volunteer her mother as wet nurse, as Pharaoh's daughter discovers Moses afloat upon the banks of the Nile.

with Moses, criticizing him for taking an Ethiopian women to wife and questioning his leadership and whether God only spoke through him. 'And the Lord came down in the pillar of the cloud, and stood in the door of the tabernacle, and called Aaron and Miriam: and they both came forth. And he said, Hear now my words: If there be a prophet among you, I the Lord will make myself known unto him in a vision, and will speak unto him in a dream. My servant Moses is not so, who is faithful in all mine house. With him will I speak mouth to mouth, even apparently, and not in dark speeches; and the similitude of the Lord shall he behold: wherefore then were ye not afraid to speak against my servant Moses? And the anger of the Lord was kindled against them; and he departed.' (*Numbers 12:5–9*) He gave Miriam leprosy for seven days as punishment.

MITHREDATH Treasurer to King Cyrus of Persia, mentioned when the King returned to the Jews the gold and silver taken from the Temple. (*Ezra 1:8*)

MOAB Elder son of Lot, from whom the Moabites descended. (*Genesis 19*)

MORDECAI Cousin of Esther, son of Jair, a Benjamite. His great-grandfather, Kish, was among the Jewish captives taken to Babylon with Jehoiachin. He offended King Ahasuerus' favorite, Haman, by refusing to bow to him.

Left: The triumph of Mordecai.

Consequently the furious Haman resolved to destroy all the Jews living in Babylonia. However, when the King discovered that Mordecai had averted an attempt upon his life, he was rewarded and Haman condemned. (*The Book of Esther*)

MOSES Hebrew leader, prophet and lawgiver, son of Amram and Jochebed. Moses is the dominating figure in the first half of the Old Testament and occupies a special status in the Christian faith. He played a central role in the epic story of the Jews that took the Hebrews from slavery in Egypt to nationhood in Canaan – but with many vicissitudes, which his faith overcame.

Born during a time of persecution by the Egyptians, Moses survived the Pharaoh's decree that all new-born male Hebrews be drowned. His mother set him in a basket on the river, where he was found by the Pharaoh's daughter, who adopted the boy. His Hebrew roots were not affected, however, for he was nursed by his mother until he was old enough to stay at the palace and be treated as a prince. (*Exodus 2:1–10*) As a young man, he became aware of the burdens being born by his people and the harsh treatment being meted out by the Egyptians. So when he saw an Egyptian beating a Hebrew, he was enraged, killed the perpetrator and hid his body – but next day discovered that his crime had been witnessed. Fearing for his life, he fled Pharaoh's men to the land of Midian, where he married Zipporah, a daughter of Jethro (also known as Reuel), a priest. (*Exodus 2:11–25*) Later, in the wilderness, he also married an Ethiopian woman. (*Numbers 12:1*)

Moses' calling by God took place when he was in the fields, near Horeb, tending his father-in-law's flock. A voice from a burning bush told him, 'I am the God of thy father, the God of Abraham, the God of Isaac, and the God of Jacob ... I have surely seen the affliction of my people which are in Egypt ... And I am come down to deliver them out of the hand of the Egyptians, and to bring them up out of that land unto a good land and a large, unto a land flowing with milk and honey ... Come now therefore,

Above: God speaks to Moses from a bush that burns yet is not consumed.

and I will send thee unto Pharaoh, that thou mayest bring forth my people the children of Israel out of Egypt.' (*Exodus 3:6–10*)

Before Pharaoh, with his brother Aaron as his spokesman, Moses demanded that the

Above: Moses and Aaron before Pharaoh.

Four of the ten plagues with which God punished Egypt. Top left: 'And Moses and Aaron ... smote the waters ... and all the waters that were in the river were turned to blood.' (Exodus 7:20) Top right: 'and there came a grievous swarm of flies.' (Exodus 8:24) Middle left: 'And they took ashes of the furnace ... and Moses sprinkled it up toward heaven; and it became a boil ... upon all the Egyptians.' (Exodus 9:10–11) Middle right: 'and when it was morning, the east wind brought the locusts ... over all the land of Egypt.' (Exodus 10:13–15) Right: But only with the death of the firstborn, including that of Pharaoh himself, would Pharaoh set the Hebrews free.

Above: The parting of the Red Sea, enabling the Hebrews to cross in safety.

Below: When water ran out, God guided Moses to a rock, and when he tapped it a spring flowed forth.

Hebrews be set free, but this only made their oppression worse. Miracles wrought with Aaron's staff failed to convince Pharaoh of the power of God, so a series of ten plagues was brought down upon Egypt, culminating in the death of the firstborn – including Pharaoh's own son. At last the Hebrews were set free, and Moses led the Hebrew migration east, across the Red Sea and into Sinai, guided by God in a great pillar of cloud. Henceforward Moses' faith would be put to the test time and again. (*Exodus 5–14*)

Food and water were scarce in the deserts they crossed, but God provided manna and quail (*Numbers 11:7*), and when they were attacked by Amalekites at Rephidim (*Exodus 17:8–16*) they repulsed their assailants. Upon Mount Sinai came the dramatic moment when Moses climbed the mountain and returned with tablets of stone (*Exodus 9ff*) inscribed with the Laws of the Covenant including the Ten Commandments between God and His people that would dominate the story of the Jews from this time onward. (Deuteronomy 5) And at the Lord's direction a tented tabernacle was constructed (*Exodus 26ff*), within which the Ark of the Covenant progressed as the Hebrews marched onward. (*Exodus 13:17ff*)

119

Above left: Finding that the people have fashioned a golden calf while he is on Mount Sinai, Moses destroys the original tablets bearing the Ten Commandments.

Above right: The Ark of the Covenant carried by the priests in advance of the Hebrews throughout their wandering.

Left: At one stage, God punished the grumbling people by sending poisonous serpents among them, and they cried for mercy. 'And the Lord said unto Moses, Make thee a fiery serpent, and set it upon a pole: and it shall come to pass, that every one that is bitten, when he looketh upon it, shall live. And Moses made a serpent of brass, and put it upon a pole, and it came to pass, that if a serpent had bitten any man, when he beheld the serpent of brass, he lived.' (Numbers 21:8–9) The 'brazen serpent was preserved in the Temple in Jerusalem until Hezekiah's time.

Right: Moses gazes upon the Promised Land from the heights of Mount Nebo. 'And Moses went up from the plains of Moab unto the mountain of Nebo, to the top of Pisgah, that is over against Jericho. And the Lord shewed him all the land ... And the Lord said unto him, This is the land which I sware unto Abraham, unto Isaac, and unto Jacob, saying, I will give it unto thy seed: I have caused thee to see it with thine eyes, but thou shalt not go over thither. So Moses the servant of the Lord died there in the land of Moab, according to the word of the Lord. And he buried him in a valley in the land of Moab, over against Beth-peor: but no man knoweth of his sepulchre unto this day.' (Deuteronomy 34:1–6)

During the long years in the wilderness – made forty years longer as a result of the Hebrews' lack of faith – Moses had to confront opposition and despair among his people. When he was on Mount Sinai with God, they built a golden calf to worship (*Exodus 32*); when an expedition into the Promised Land returned with pessimistic reports (*Deuteronomy 1:19–46, Numbers 12–14*), he was almost stoned to death; an outright revolt against him was led by three Levites and their families (*Numbers 16*); and even his sister Miriam questioned his leadership. (*Numbers 12*) At every turn, however, Moses maintained his faith, asking for God's help and surmounting the obstacle.

Moses saw the Promised Land, but God did not permit him to enter. (*Deuteronomy 3:23–8*) His great role in leading the Jews from Egypt was over, and he died on Mount Nebo in the land of Moab. (*Deuteronomy 34*) It would be Joshua who would lead the conquest of Canaan. (*Exodus, Deuteronomy, Numbers*)

Moses and Zipporah had two sons, Gershom and Eliezer. (*Exodus 18:3–4*) In the New Testament, Moses is one of the two Old Testament figures whom the disciples of Christ witnessed in conversation with Jesus at the Transfiguration (the other being the prophet Elijah, referred to as Elias). (*Matthew 17:1–13, Mark 9:2–13, Luke 9:28–36*)

N

NAAMAN Fifth son of Benjamin. (*Genesis. 46:21*)

NAAMAN Commander-in-chief of the Syrian army in the days of Elisha. A good man honorable man, he was stricken with leprosy and through the suggestion of a 'little maid of the land of Israel', was induced to visit Elisha, who cured him. (*II Kings 5*)

NABOTH Owner of a vineyard coveted by King Ahab of Israel, close to Ahab's palace at Jezreel. Ahab wished to buy it from him, but he refused to part with it. Ahab was vexed; and Jezebel, his queen, taunted him for submitting to such an affront to his royal authority. By false witness she procured Naboth's condemnation on a charge of blasphemy, and he and his sons were stoned. She then told Ahab to take possession of the vineyard; but, while he was looking at it, Elijah met him and denounced his crime. Ahab humbled himself before God, and the punishment was deferred until his grandson's days. When Jehu slew Jehoram, he cast his body into Naboth's vineyard. (*I Kings 21:2 Kings 9:21–26*)

Above: Naboth turns down King Ahaz's offer to purshase his vineyard.

NADAB Eldest son of Aaron. He was appointed to the priesthood but offended God with incorrect ritual and was punished: 'And Nadab and Abihu died before the Lord, when they offered strange fire before the Lord, in the wilderness of Sinai.' (*Numbers 3:4*)

NADAB Second King of Israel and son of Jeroboam I. He reigned for only two years before being treacherously slain by one of his officers, Baasha, while besieging the Philistine city of Gibbethon. Baasha then slaughtered all Nadab's family, fulfilling the prophecy of Ahijah. (*I Kings 15:25–30*)

NAHUM One of the minor prophets, an Elkoshite, the location of which is now unknown. His book is a sequence of auguries focused on Nineveh, capital of the Assyrian Empire,

Above: Naaman visits Elisha.

predicting its downfall and blaming this upon the wickedness therein. Unlike other Hebrew prophets, he presents no message concerning Israel or Judah. *The Book of Nahum* is thought to have been written shortly before the destruction of that city and the fall of the Empire.

NAOMI Mother-in-law of Ruth, wife of Elimelech; she bore him two sons, Maklon and Chilion. During a time of famine, the family moved temporarily to Moab. There the sons married local girls, Orpah and Ruth respectively. Elimelech died; and ten years later both the sons died. Facing destitution, the three women moved back to Naomi's native Bethlehem to be near Naomi's family, but

Above: The prophet Nahum.

Right: Ruth refuses to leave Naomi.

Orpah was persuaded to return to her family in Moab. Ruth loyally remained with Naomi, knowing that she would not be able to marry again and faced hardship. When Ruth began gleaning in the fields of Naomi's rich kinsman Boaz, Naomi encouraged her daughter-in-law towards Boaz, and the two eventually married. Naomi later nursed her daughter-in-law's child, Obed, who would be an ancestor of David and Jesus. (*The Book of Ruth*)

NATHAN Prophet during the reign of King David, and advisor to the King. When David resolved to build a permanent Temple for the Ark of the Covenant to replace the tabernacle that had been brought from the wilderness, God told Nathan that this would be a task for his son, and Nathan reported this to David. (*II Samuel 7:1*) Nathan was later sent by the Lord to David to explain God's judgement on the King's conduct concerning Uriah, whose death he had contrived in order to take his wife, Bathsheba. He told him a parable about a poor man whose pet lamb was taken by a rich man to feed a visitor, which enraged David, saying that the rich man should be punished. But, said

Above: Nathan tells David the uncomfortable truth about the King's dealings with Uriah and Bathsheba.

Nathan, 'Thou art the man. Thus saith the Lord God of Israel, I anointed thee king over Israel … Wherefore hast thou despised the commandment of the Lord, to do evil in his sight? thou hast killed Uriah the Hittite with the sword, and hast taken his wife to be thy wife, and hast slain him with the sword of the children of Ammon. Now therefore the sword shall never depart from thine house; because thou hast despised me, and hast taken the wife of Uriah the Hittite to be thy wife.' (*II Samuel 12:7–10*) In consequence, David was punished by the death of the first child born to him by Bathsheba.

Nathan was still a close advisor to David many years later, when he was much advanced in age, and he was one of the first to hear that David's eldest son Adonijah (by Haggith) was preparing to usurp the throne; he hastened to tell Bathsheba, and together they told David and warned him. David then sent Nathan with Zadok and Benaiah to anoint Solomon as his heir at Gihon. (*I Kings 1*) Nathan's sons Azariah and Zabud held high office during the reign of Solomon. (*I Kings 4:5*)

NATHAN A son of David by Bathsheba (*I Chronicles 3:5*), and an ancestor of Christ. (*Luke 3:31*)

NEBUCHADNEZZAR King of Babylon who conquered the Kingdom of Judah, destroyed Jerusalem and took the people captive. With the demise of the Assyrian Empire and the fall of its capital, Nineveh, the foremost power in the Middle East became Babylon. Its principal rival was Egypt, which during the reigns of Jehoahaz and Jehoiakim attained control of Judah. At the Battle of Carchemish, the forces of Egypt and the remnant of Assyria's army were defeated by the Babylonians led by Nebuchadnezzar, then crown prince, leaving Judah within the power of Babylon. Shortly after this, the King of Babylon died and Nebuchadnezzar ascended the throne as Nebuchadnezzar II. For three years King Jehoiakim in Jerusalem paid tribute to him, but then he rebelled, only to be overwhelmed by Nebuchadnezzar's troops and carried off to

The conqueror of Jerusalem. Nebuchadnezzar receives the humble submission of King Jehoiachin.

Above left: The idol that Daniel's companions refused to worship. Above right: The dream of Nebuchadnezzar that led to his madness. Below: The King of Babylon reduced to the state of a wild animal.

Babylon, while bands of various tribes ravaged Judah. In this state of near-anarchy, Jehoiachin, Jehoiakim's successor, lasted just three months and ten days, his defiance being met by another Babylonian army occupying Jerusalem, and Jehoiakim being taken off to Babylon. His successor, the last King of Judah, was Zedekiah, who broke his oath of loyalty to Nebuchadnezzar and paid the penalty. Nebuchadnezzar besieged Jerusalem for two years then destroyed the city, including the palace and Temple. The Judaean capital was thoroughly looted, all the ornaments and utensils of precious metal surviving in the Temple being carried off. (*II Chronicles 36, II Kings 24–5*)

So too were the people, among whom was the prophet Daniel. It was Nebuchadnezzar who decreed the education and special treatment of a number of the Jewish

deportees, seeing them as useful future officers in his administration. Daniel was one of these, and interpreted three dramatic dreams that had been experienced by the King. After the last of these, Nebuchadnezzar appears to have descended into a bout of madness (generally thought to have been the rare delusional syndrome of lycanthropy, the belief that one is an animal), from which he eventually recovered. His attempts to make the Jews worship Babylonian gods met with little success: when he cast three of Daniel's companions into a fiery furnace for not complying with his edict, they escaped unharmed, and Nebuchadnezzar decreed freedom of worship for the Jews in exile. (*Daniel 1–4*) He is generally credited, during his long reign, of constructing the hanging gardens of Babylon, deemed one of the seven Wonders of the World.

NECHO Pharaoh of Egypt who defeated and killed King Josiah of Judah but lost the Battle of Carchemish to Nebuchadnezzar. When

Josaiah's son Jehoahaz became king, Necho took him captive to Egypt after a three-month reign, exacting tribute from Judah and replacing him with Jehoiakim. (*II Kings 23:38–35, II Chronicles 35:20, 36:4*)

NEHEMIAH Cupbearer to King Artaxerxes of Persia who, with Ezra, revived Jerusalem after the exile. A high-born member of the Jewish community in exile after the fall of Jerusalem, Nehemiah rose to a position of prominence in the royal court at Shushan (Susa). When one of his kinsmen, Hanani, came back from Jerusalem with news of the poor state of affairs there, Nehemiah asked the King for leave of absence to go to Jerusalem and attempt to put matters right. The King readily agreed, giving Nehemiah letters of authority, and he set out on the thousand-mile journey in company with a large party. Among these was Ezra, who would be his partner in re-establishing the native Hebrew religion in Jerusalem. When he arrived at the city he spent three days unobtrusively observing how bad the situation

Right: Nehemiah asks permission of King Artaxerxes to become governor of Jerusalem.

Above: By night, Nehemiah covertly observes the poor state of affairs in Jerusalem before beginning his work.

was. Then he sought out the leading men of the city and spoke to them: 'Ye see the distress that we are in, how Jerusalem lieth waste, and the gates thereof are burned with fire: come, and let us build up the wall of Jerusalem, that we be no more a reproach. Then I told them of the hand of my God which was good upon me; as also the king's words that he had spoken unto me. And they said, Let us rise up and build. So they strengthened their hands for this good work.' (*Nehemiah 2:17–18*) Re-energized by Nehemiah's enthusiasm and organizational ability, they rapidly repaired the walls of Jerusalem, and Nehemiah invited people from outlying communities to resettle within the city's boundaries. His work provoked considerable hostility, however, especially from Sanballat, a local official – was Nehemiah about to set up in rebellion against the King? The objectors attempted to impede the reconstruction at every turn, and Nehemiah was forced to set armed guards about the works, even arming the laborers. With Ezra, he also attempted to restore the religion of the Jews, to clean up Jerusalem's religious practices, reintroducing celebration of the age-old holy days and festivals and renewing the Covenant. Then, at a great assembly of the people, Ezra read the book of the law.

After twelve years, Nehemiah returned to Susa, but he later came back to Jerusalem and

Nehemiah sets the people to work rebuilding the city walls of Jerusalem. But (above right) there was violent opposition to his work in certain quarters, so he shut the city gates and put sentries on the walls as work carried on.

found that his religious reforms had already become eroded, including the flagrant desecration of the sabbath and the occupation of a room in the Temple by Tobiah, one of the leading objectors to his reconstruction work. Again, and for the last time in the narrative of the Old Testament, an attempt was made to draw back the Jews to their God. (*The Book of Nehemiah*)

NIMROD Son of Cush, grandson of Ham and great-grandson of Noah: 'And Cush begat Nimrod: he began to be a mighty one in the earth. He was a mighty hunter before the Lord: wherefore it is said, Even as Nimrod the mighty hunter before the Lord.' (*Genesis 10:8–9*) Central Mesopotamia is referred to as 'the land of Nimrod' in *Micah 5:6*, and in legend he was the founder of the Assyrian Empire.

NOAH God's chosen survivor at His purging of the Earth. 'And God saw that the wickedness of man was great in the earth ... And the Lord said, I will destroy man whom I have created from the face of the earth ... But Noah found grace in the eyes of the Lord.'

(*Genesis 5:5–8*) God commanded Noah to build an ark to very strict specifications, and then to fill it: 'Of every clean beast thou shalt take to thee by sevens, the male and his female: and of beasts that are not clean by two, the male and his female. Of fowls also of the air by sevens, the male and the female; to keep seed alive upon the face of all the earth.' (*Genesis 7:2–3*) When the ark had been constructed, the rain began, covering the surface of the whole world and lifting the ark from the ground, until even the highest mountains were covered, 'and Noah only remained alive, and they that were with him in the ark'. (*Genesis 7:23*) For 150 days the ark drifted upon the ocean before the rain stopped and the waters gradually abated; then Noah set out a raven and then a dove so see whether they would find dry land. Seven days later he sent forth the dove a second time, and it returned with an olive leaf in its beak; after a further seven days he sent the dove again, and this time it did not return, implying the existence of dry land. Gradually the earth dried out and the ark came to rest upon dry ground once more. Noah and his family emerged from the ship and set loose the

Right: Building the ark that would preserve Noah, his family and the animals stipulated by God. The precise specifications of the ark were given by God, together with instructions on the materials to use in its construction.

Top left: The animals embark. Top right: Noah sends out the dove to find dry land. Above left: The ark comes to rest as the waters subside. Above right: Noah gives sacrifice to the Lord, who signifies his Covenant with a rainbow.

animals that were on board to repopulate the Earth. Then Noah built an altar and made burnt sacrifice, and 'God blessed Noah and his sons, and said unto them, Be fruitful, and multiply, and replenish the earth'. (*Genesis 9:1*) He set out his Covenant, promising never to destroy all flesh again, in token of which Noah would see a rainbow – his 'bow in the cloud'. (This was the Covenant that would in time be renewed with Abraham and the people of Israel through Moses and David.) Noah had three sons, Ham, Shem and Japheth, 'and of them was the whole earth overspread'. (*Genesis 9:19*) He planted a vineyard but drank too much, lay down naked in a stupor to be discovered and shamed by his sons. (*Genesis 6–9*)

NUN The father of Joshua, conqueror of the Promised Land (*Numbers 13:8, 16; I Chronicles 7:26, 27*); he is called Non in *Chronicles*.

OBADIAH The governor of Ahab's palace and a prominent man during the period of Elijah's prophecies. (*I Kings 18:3*)

OBADIAH An overseer of the Temple in Josiah's reign. (*II Chronicles 24:12*)

OBADIAH One of the Minor Prophets. *The Book of Obadiah* is the shortest of the Old Testament and consists of an attack on Edom, the ages-old enemy of the Israelites. It condemns them for taking advantage of the fall of Jerusalem to the Babylonians to loot both the city and the surrounding lands, and predicts the inevitable destruction of Edom.

OBADIAH A priest with Nehemiah. (*Nehemiah 10:5*)

ODED Prophet of Israel during the reign of King Pekah. When that king's victorious army returned from Jerusalem to Samaria with much loot and captives, Oded saved the prisoners from slavery: 'and he went out before the host that came to Samaria, and said unto them, Behold, because the Lord God of your fathers was wroth with Judah, he hath delivered them into your hand, and ye have slain them in a rage that reacheth up unto heaven. And now ye purpose to keep under the children of Judah and Jerusalem for bondmen and bondwomen unto you: but are there not with you, even with you, sins against the Lord your God? Now hear me therefore, and deliver the captives again, which ye have taken captive of your brethren: for the fierce wrath of the Lord is upon you.' (*II Chronicles 28:9–11*)

OG King of Bashan, east of the Sea of Galilee and part of the Amorite kingdom. He was defeated by the Hebrews at Edrei, and all his land conquered. (*Numbers 21:33–5, 32:33, Deuter–*

Above: The prophet Obadiah.

Above: King Og of Bashan.

onomy 1:4, 3:1–13, 4:47, 29:7, 31:4, Joshua 2:10, 9:10, 12:4, 13:12,30,31, I Kings 4:19, Nehemiah 9:22) *Deuteronomy* has him as a giant: 'For only Og king of Bashan remained of the remnant of giants; behold, his bedstead was a bedstead of iron; is it not in Rabbath of the children of Ammon? nine cubits was the length thereof, and four cubits the breadth of it, after the cubit of a man.' (*Deuteronomy 3:11*)

OMRI Grandson of Benjamin. (*I Chronicles 7:8*)

OMRI A son of Imri. (*I Chronicles 9:4*)

OMRI A son of Michael in David's reign, (*I Chronicles 27:18*)

OMRI Sixth king of Israel after the division of the kingdom, usurper. He was proclaimed king by the army, while it was besieging the

Above: King Omri of Israel, an idol-worshipper.

Philistine city of Gibbethon, after news reached them of Zimri's successful revolt in the capital, Tizrah. The army overthrew Zimri after just seven days, and a period of strife ensued between the supporters of Omri and a rival, Tibni, son of Ginath. Omri reigned for twelve years, a period of relative peace and of a slackening in hostilities with Judah. He built a new capital for Israel, Samaria (the area in general soon taking this name, and the people becoming known as Samaritans). But the Bible records that he too led the people into idolatry; this may not be unconnected with his good relations with the Phoenician coastal cities, which led to his son and successor, Ahab, marrying Jezebel, daughter of King Ethbaal of Sidon, who worshipped Baal. (*I Kings 16–28, II Chronicles 22:2, Micah 6:16*)

ON A Reubenite who joined Korah in revolt against Moses. God caused the earth to open up and swallow his fellow conspirators – Korah, Daran and Abiram and their families – but the fate of On is not mentioned. (*Numbers 16*)

ONAN Second son of Judah, second husband of Tamar with whom he refused to lie, for which God punished him with death. (*Genesis 38:1–10*)

ORPAH Wife of Mahlon, son of Elimelech and Naomi, sister-in-law to Ruth. When all the men of the family died, the three women moved from Moab to Naomi's native Bethlehem. Then, at Naomi's suggestion, she returned to her family in Moab, leaving Ruth with her mother-in-law. (*The Book of Ruth 1:1–14*)

PASHUR Temple overseer who, angered at Jeremiah's prophesies of the destruction of Jerusalem, had him scourged and then placed in the stocks. Jeremiah's response was to reiterate his prophecy and to curse him: 'Then said Jeremiah unto him, The Lord hath not called thy name Pashur, but Magor-missabib. For thus saith the Lord, Behold, I will make thee a terror to thyself, and to all thy friends: and they shall fall by the sword of their enemies, and thine eyes shall behold it: and I will give all Judah into the hand of the king of Babylon, and he shall carry them captive into Babylon, and shall slay them with the sword. Moreover I will deliver all the strength of this city, and all the labours thereof, and all the precious things thereof, and all the treasures of the kings of Judah will I give into the hand of their enemies, which shall spoil them, and take them, and carry them to Babylon. And thou, Pashur, and all that dwell in thine house shall go into captivity: and thou shalt come to Babylon, and there thou shalt die, and shalt be buried there, thou, and all thy friends, to whom thou hast prophesied lies.' (*Jeremiah 20:1–6*)

PEKAH Eighteenth king of Israel after the division of the kingdom. During his reign, the Assyrian King Tiglath-Pileser III took possession of Gilead, Galilee and Naphtali and deported the inhabitants. However, God had decided to punish Judah for the sins of its king, Ahaz (who, the Bible tells us, even sacrificed his own sons to idols). Pekah attacked Judah and inflicted a heavy defeat, returning to Samaria with large numbers of Judaean prisoners. But, as they approached the capital of Israel, the prophet Oded stood forth and told the victorious Israelites that what they did was wrong, for their prisoners were their own kin. Four prominent and influential citizens of Israel supported him, and the prisoners were sent back to Judah.

After a twenty-year reign, Pekah was assassinated by Hoshea. (*II Kings 15:25–31, II Chronicles 28:5–15*)

PEKAHIAH Seventeenth king of Israel after the division of the kingdom. He inherited the kingdom from his father, Menahem, who had usurped the throne, and ruled for two years before being assassinated by Pekah, one of his officers. (*II Kings 15:23–6*)

PENINNAH Wife of Elkanah, a Levite of Ephraim, who taunted his other wife, Hannah, for her barrenness before the birth of the prophet Samuel. (*I Samuel 1:2, 4*)

PHARAOH Kings of Ancient Egypt. Those who feature largely in the stories of Abraham, Joseph and Moses in Genesis and Exodus are not named in the Bible. The first of these pharaohs is mentioned during the episode when Abram (Abraham) and Sarai (Sarah) spent time in Egypt (*Genesis 12:14–20*); the second in the story of Joseph, his service in Egypt and imprisonment, (*Genesis 37:36, 39:1*); his interpretation of Pharaoh's dreams and ensuing service as his minister (*Genesis 40–1*); and Joseph's dealings with his brothers and father. (*Genesis 42:15, 45, 46:33, 47, 50:4–6*)

Above: Pharaoh confronted by Moses and Aaron, demanding that the Hebrews be set free to leave Egypt.

Above: The Hebrews reduced to bondage in Egypt.

A much later Pharaoh features in the story of Moses's calling, the subsequent harsh treatment of the Hebrews in Egypt ('a new king over Egypt, which knew not Joseph') who issued the order to kill new-born Hebrew boys ('Every son that is born ye shall cast into the river, and every daughter ye shall save alive'). (*Exodus 1:8–22*) This Pharaoh died during the time that Moses was in Midian (*Exodus 2:23*), and it was his successor whom God told Moses to demand that the Hebrews be freed, upon whom the ten plagues were inflicted (*Exodus 3:10–19, 5–12*) and whose army pursued the Hebrews but was swallowed up by the closing waters of the Red Sea. (*Exodus 14:3–28*)

Later, during the reign of David in Israel, a pharaoh is mentioned in the story of Hadad, a prince of Edom who found refuge in Egypt. (*I Kings 11:14–22*) Solomon, third king of Israel, married the daughter of a pharaoh and built her a house (*I Kings 3:1, 7:8, 11:1*); that pharaoh later captured Gezer in Philistia and gave it to his daughter as a present. (*I Kings 9:16, 24*)

During the period of the two kingdoms, Egypt became a more malevolent force, the area becoming a battleground between Egypt

Above: Pharaoh Rameses II, the Great, may have been the king 'which knew not Joseph'.

and Assyria, then Babylon, then Persia. It was from the court of Pharaoh Shishak I that Jeroboam I returned to Israel after the death of Solomon and became king: he had fled there after a failed attempt to seize power during Solomon's reign. (*I Kings 11:28–40*) During the fifth year of the reign of King Rehoboam of Judah, Shishak invaded Judah with 'twelve hundred chariots, and threescore thousand horsemen: and the people were without number that came with him out of Egypt; the Lubims, the Sukkiims, and the Ethiopians. And he took the fenced cities which pertained to Judah, and came to Jerusalem.' (*I Kings 14:25–6, II Chronicles 12:3–9*) He returned to Egypt with gold and treasure from the Temple, including the shields of gold that Solomon had made.

Pharaoh Necho subsequently invaded the area, this time to counter the increasing influence of Babylon in the area, and he defeated and killed King Josiah at the Battle of Meggido. Three months into the reign of Jehoahaz, Necho returned and carried him off to Egypt, placing his brother Eliakim (Jehoiakim) on the throne. (*II Chronicles 35:20–22, 36: 3–4, II Kings 23:29–35*) Necho was later defeated by the Babylonian Nebuchadnezzar at Carchemish.

Jeremiah 37:5–11 records that the Babylonian army besieging Jerusalem was temporarily distracted by an incursion of Pharaoh Hophra's army; but later that God foretold the defeat of Hophra by Babylon. (*Jeremiah 44:30*)

POTIPHAR Captain of Pharaoh's guard who bought Joseph as a slave from the Midianites, to whom Joesph's brothers had sold him. Potiphar found merit in the young man and eventually promoted him to oversee his entire household. However, Potiphar's wife attempted to seduce Joseph, who rebuffed her advances. In revenge she alleged that he had insulted her, and Joseph was thrown into prison. (*Genesis 37:36, 39*)

Right: Pharaoh's army engulfed by the Red Sea, which had parted to allow the passage of the Hebrews but closed over again as the Egyptian pursuing force attempted to follow them.

R

RABSHAKEH Sennacherib's chief captain who came to demand the surrender of Hezekiah as the Assyrians besieged Jerusalem. (*Isaiah 36:2ff*)

RACHEL Wife of Jacob, mother of Joseph and Benjamin. She was the younger daughter of Laban, brother-in-law of Isaac, and a great beauty. When Jacob came to live with Laban, he encountered Rachel at a well; it was love at first sight, and Jacob lost no time in asking Laban for her hand. This was granted but delayed seven years. However, Jacob was cruelly deceived, for Laban substituted her sister Leah. Laban was merely following the custom of the land that daughters be married in order of their age; and polygamy was normal in these ancient times. So Laban allowed Rachel to wed Jacob a week later. When Jacob left

Above: Rabshakeh demands the surrender of Jerusalem.

Left: Rachel encounters Jacob at the well.

Laban to return to his homeland, taking his family and flocks, Rachel stole Laban's effigies of the household gods, and Laban pursued Jacob's caravan. But though he searched the tents, he could not find the images. (*Genesis 31*)

While Leah bore Jacob children, Rachel remained childless and grew restive. But since God had evidently judged her, she gave her handmaiden Bilhah to Jacob as a concubine, and she bore him children in Rachel's stead. (*Genesis 29:29, 30:3–7*)

In time, God remembered Rachel, and she bore Jacob two sons, Joseph and Benjamin, but died during the birth of the latter. (*Genesis 35:16–20*)

Right: Rahab helps the Hebrew spies escape from Jericho prior to its conquest and destruction by Joshua.

RAHAB Harlot of Jericho who helped Joshua's spies and enabled their return to the Hebrew camp by letting them down by a rope. At the destruction of the city, her life and those of her family were spared and they joined the Hebrews. (*Joshua 6:17, 22–5*)

REBEKAH Wife of Isaac, daughter of Bethuel, mother of Jacob and Esau. It was she who instigated the deception of her husband and ensured his birthright passed to Jacob. Not wishing his forty-year-old son Isaac to marry a local Canaanite, Abraham sent his servant to Nahor, where dwelt his kinsman Bethuel. When he was near to the town, the servant

stopped and asked God for a sign: that whichever young woman responded to his request for water from the well would be Isaac's wife. Rebekah approached the well, gave the servant and his camels water and invited him to stay with her family. The servant explained to Bethuel and to Laban, Rebekah's brother, who he was and what had happened, and they readily agreed to the match. The servant returned to Abraham with Rebekah; Isaac met them on the way, and they became man and wife. (*Genesis 24:15–67*) Rebekah became the object of Abimelech of Gerar's interest until he discovered she was married to Isaac. (*Genesis 26: 1–30*). She bore Isaac two sons, Esau and Jacob. (*Genesis 25:20–4*) Rebekah and Isaac disapproved of Esau marrying two Hittite women (*Genesis 26:35*);

Above: Rebekah responds to the request by Abraham's servant for a drink. By this sign, he knows that she will be the woman to wed Isaac.

Above: Rehoboam and the division of the Jewish kingdom.

indeed, Jacob was her favorite, and she incited him to deceive Isaac into giving Jacob his blessing instead of Esau, providing the clothes and kid skin for the deception, since Esau was hairy while Jacob was not. (*27:1–17*) To avoid the wrath of Esau, she warned Jacob to flee. (*Genesis 27:42–6*) When she died, she was buried with Isaac at Machpelah.

REHOBOAM First King of Judah after the division of the Kingdom of David and Solomon. Upon the death of his father, Rehoboam was faced with a mighty crisis. At Shechem, representatives of the ten northern tribes confronted him and demanded reforms to the harsh regime and high taxes that Solomon had imposed. Ignoring the advice of his counsellors, the new king replied intemperately, so angering the northerners that he was forced to flee and his labor minister, Adoniram, was stoned to death. Thus Rehoboam's kingdom consisted only of the lands of Judah and Benjamin. He was warned by the prophet Shemaiah against plans he had to attempt to reunite the country by force, for this would mean attacking their kinsmen. (*I Kings 12:24*) Instead, Rehoboam set about strengthening the defenses of Judah by fortifying cities – but this proved of no avail when, in the fifth year of his reign, the kingdom was invaded by Pharaoh Shishak. The Egyptians withdrew only after the Temple had been ransacked and its treasures taken. Shemaiah explained why God had not come to his aid: they had abandoned God, so God had abandoned them. Pagan cults and idols had been imported along with foreign wives, negating the beneficial effects Judah experienced when the priests and Levites of Israel, banned from office there, came to Jerusalem. (*I Kings 14, II Chronicles 10–12*)

REUBEN Eldest son of Jacob and Leah. (*Genesis 29:32*) It was Reuben who found mandrakes in the field for his mother, which ended her period of barrenness so that she bore Jacob a fifth son, Isschar. (*Genesis 30:14–18*) He sinned in sleeping with his father's concubine (*Genesis 35:22*), for which he paid later when Jacob was making his last blessings to his sons: 'Reuben, thou art my firstborn, my might, and the beginning of my strength, the excellency of dignity, and the excellency of power: Unstable as water, thou shalt not excel; because thou wentest up to thy father's bed; then defiledst thou it: he went up to my couch.' (*Genesis 49:3–4*)

When the brothers decided to rid themselves of their step-brother Joseph, Reuben prevented them from killing him outright and persuaded them to throw him into a well, thinking to rescue him after the others had departed for home. But Reuben was not there when a company of Midianites passed by and Judah led the brothers into selling Joseph to

them as a slave; so when Reuben returned later and found the pit empty, he was greatly dismayed. (*Genesis 37:21–9*)

During the famine and the visits of the brothers to Egypt to buy corn, Joseph demanded their youngest brother, Benjamin as hostage, which made the brothers talk among themselves guiltily, Reuben declaring that that should not have treated Joseph as they did. (*Genesis 42:22*) It was Reuben who guaranteed to his father that Benjamin would be safe. (*Genesis 42:17*)

REZIN King of Aram in Syria who allied with King Pekah of Israel to attack Judah. King Ahaz of Judah appealed to Assyria for help, and Tiglath-Pileser III captured Damascus, killing Rezin. (*II Kings 15:37, 16:5–9, Isaiah 7:1,4,8, 8:6*)

RIZPAH Concubine of Saul and heroine of David's Gibeonite famine crisis. She bore Saul two sons, and after his death may have had a relationship with Abner, the power behind the throne of the northern kingdom, now ruled by

Above: Rizpah protects the bodies of her sons from the carrion crows.

Ishbosheth. When the general and the king quarreled over her, Abner deserted to Hebron, where David ruled the rival kingdom of Judah.

Later in David's reign, a famine took hold on the land for three years, and God revealed to him that this was caused by Saul's slaughter of the Gibeonites (remnant of the Amorites) years before. David spoke to them and asked what atonement he could make: they replied that they wanted seven of Saul's surviving sons handed to them to be executed. This was done and their bodies left hanging on a hillside. Rizpah, mother of two of the victims, stayed faithfully by the bodies, keeping the birds and beasts from feasting on them. When David heard this, he was moved and gathered together both the bones of these seven and those of Saul and his other sons who had fallen at the Battle of Mount Giilboa, and gave them proper burial in the tomb of Saul's father. (*II Samuel 3:7, 21:1–14*)

RUTH Wife of Chilion, then of Boaz, daughter-in-law of Naomi. *The Book of Ruth* is the story of one of David's – and thus Christ's – ancestors. Set during the time of the Judges of Israel, it tells of the family of Elimelech and Naomi, who lived in Bethlehem. In time of famine they moved, with their two sons Mahlon and Chilion, to Moab, and there the two sons married Moab girls, Orpah and Ruth. Elimelech died while they were there; and ten years after this both Mahlon and Chilion died, leaving three widows. For Naomi, destitution loomed; they moved to her native Bethlehem, but Orpah then returned to her family in Moab. Ruth loyally remained with her mother-in-law, who was now too old to marry again, and for whom, even with local kinsmen, life would be hard. Ruth went to glean in the fields of Boaz, a kinsman of Naomi's late husband, gathering wheat and barley left by the reapers in order to earn a precarious living. Touched

Above: Ruth gleaning in the fields of her distant kinsman, Boaz.

by the beauty of Ruth and her selfless loyalty to Naomi, Boaz showed her kindness, and Naomi saw Ruth's opportunity. She told Ruth to wait until Boaz and his company had finished harvesting for the day, had eaten and laid down in the fields to sleep; she was then to lie down at Boaz's feet. When Boaz awoke to find here there, she told him that she was a near kinsman. Boaz arranged for her to take six measures of barley back to Naomi, then approached his kinsmen: it was customary for the brother of a dead man to raise an heir to the deceased by the widow. Boaz was more distantly related but made an arrangement whereby he bought Elimelech's land and took Ruth to wife. She bore him a son, Obed, who would be father to Jesse, and he to David. (*The Book of Ruth*)

SAMSON Twelfth judge of Israel, son of Manoah, a Danite, and a man of legendary strength. An angel appeared to his mother promising her that if she drank no wine or strong drink she would bear 'a Nazarite* unto God from the womb: and he shall begin to deliver Israel out of the hand of the Philistines'. (*Judges 13:1–5*)

When he had grown into a man, he took a Philistine woman of Timnath to wife, much to the chagrin of his father and mother. At his wedding feast, he gave the guests a riddle concerning the honey that he had eaten from a bees' nest, which had grown in the carcass of a lion he had killed: 'Out of the eater came forth meat, and out of the strong came forth sweetness.' (*Judges 14:14*) But his wife spoilt the riddle by telling the Philistine guests the answer. Angry, Samson killed thirty Philistines at Ashkelon, but when he later returned to get his wife he found her father had given her to another. So Samson caught three hundred foxes and burned down the standing corn, vines and olive trees of the Philistines by releasing them with fiery brands attached to their tails. In reprisal, the Philistines burnt Samson's wife and father-in-law to death; for which Samson exacted revenge by more killing; and in turn the Philistines set out in force to capture him. They were pre-empted by the men of Judah, who did not want this escalating conflict, and he allowed them to tie him and deliver him to the Philistines. But when they did so, he burst the cords that bound him, took up the jawbone of an ass and slaughtered the Philistines (which, *Judges 15:15* relates, numbered one thousand).

And so the legend of Samson's superhuman strength spread, enhanced by a nocturnal visit to a harlot in Gaza. The inhabitants, realizing that he was there, locked the city gates and thought they had him trapped; but Samson simply lifted up the gate and its pillars and carried it off.

Samson's downfall was due to another woman: Delilah. When the Philistine leaders heard of this dalliance, they visited her clandestinely at her home in the valley of Sorek and offered her money to root out the

Left: Samson wrestles a lion to death. In the carcass grew a hive of bees.

* Nazarites made a special lifelong vow to dedicate their lives to the Lord; additionally they would not cut their hair; would abstain from the fruit of the vine; would avoid contact with the dead; and would eat no unclean food.

secret of Samson's phenomenal strength. Three times she asked, and he gave her fanciful answers, but she relentlessly pursued the matter, nagging and questioning until Samson could stand it no more. 'And she said unto him, How canst thou say, I love thee, when thine heart is not with me? thou hast mocked me these three times, and hast not told me wherein thy great strength lieth ...' and in the end 'he told her all his heart, and said unto her. There hath not come a razor upon mine head; for I have been a Nazarite unto God from my mother's womb: if I be shaven, then my strength will go from me, and

Above: Samson slays Philistines with the jawbone of an ass.

Right: Samson breaks loose from his bonds.

Below: Samson's captors put him to work in a mill, blinded, his hair shorn and his strength lost.

I shall become weak, and be like any other man.' (*Judges 16:15–17*)

When he was asleep, Delilah cut off his hair, the Philistines seized him, blinded him and took him prisoner. In the prison at Gaza they set him to work in the mill, but after a time his hair began to grow, and with it returned his strength. Not perceiving this, the Philistines decided to show him off in the temple of their god, Dagon, chaining him between two of the main pillars of the building. 'And Samson said, Let me die with the Philistines. And he bowed himself with all his might; and the house fell upon the lords, and upon all the people that were therein. So the dead which he slew at his death were more than they which he slew in his life.' (*Judges 13–16*)

Above: In accordance with her vow, Hannah entrusts her son Samuel to the priest, Eli.

Above: Samson brings the Philistine temple to Dagon crashing down.

SAMUEL Prophet and last Judge of Israel. He was born into the service of God, for his mother, hitherto barren, had promised that if he gave her a son she would dedicate his life to the service of the Lord as a Nazirite (see page 142). (*I Samuel 1:1–18*). After he had been weaned, she took him to the High Priest, Eli, at Shiloh, and when he was still a child, God used Samuel to tell Eli that his two sons, who were corrupt, would be punished for their sins. (*I Samuel 1:9, 2, 3, 4:12–18*)

Samuel became recognized as a prophet; but following the death of Eli, after the capture of the Ark of the Covenant by the Philistines and the death of his two sons, we hear nothing more of him for twenty years. He then gathered the Israelites together at Mixpeh, and they fasted and prayed, and God gave them deliverance from an attack by the Philistines. (*I Samuel 7:2–15*).

Samuel's home was in Ramah, where he established a school of prophets; but he went every year to Bethel, Gilgal and Mixpeh to judge Israel. (*I Samuel 15–17*) When he was old he appointed his sons to act as judges, but they were corrupt and took bribes, so the people complained to Samuel and clamored for a king. Samuel consulted the Lord, who instructed him to tell the people the implications of such a thing: and he explained to them how a ruler would command them, oppress them and tax them – yet still they demanded a king. (*I Samuel 8*) So God directed

Above: The child Samuel, hearing the voice of God one night, mistakenly thinks he has been called by Eli.

Above: Samuel anoints David king of Israel amidst his brethren.

Samuel's footsteps to the family of Kish, a Benjamite (*I Samuel 9*) and he anointed Kish's son Saul as king. (*I Samuel 10*)

But Saul soon disappointed both Samuel and the Lord. Needing to fight a battle against the Philistines, Saul concentrated his army at Gilgal and awaited Samuel's coming to make the customary sacrifice before battle. He waited seven days; then Saul's patience was exhausted, and he made the burnt offering himself. As soon as he had done this, Samuel appeared and rebuked him angrily, beginning the dispute between God, prophet and king. (*I Samuel 13:1–16*)

There was soon another source of friction: for a campaign against Agag, the king of the the Amalekites, the Lord decreed wholesale slaughter of the enemy and their animals. 'But Saul and the people spared Agag, and the best of the sheep, and of the oxen, and of the fatlings, and the lambs, and all that was good, and would not utterly destroy them.' (*I Samuel 15:9*) God spoke to Samuel, telling how he now regretted making Saul king. Samuel confronted

Saul, condemned him for not obeying the letter of God's command and slew the unfortunate Agag himself. (*I Samuel 15*)

Saul's monarchy was doomed. Samuel was directed again to anoint a king, this time to the family of Jesse in Bethlehem, where he ordained the young David. (*I Samuel 16:1–13*) After the combat with Goliath, David became famous and lived at Saul's palace, but in time the increasingly depressed King grew jealous and eventually David had to flee for his life, taking refuge with the now aged Samuel in Ramah. Saul's men attempted to seize David there, but three times the prophet outfaced them. (*I Samuel 19*)

After Samuel died and was buried at Ramah, God abandoned Saul entirely, and this eventually drove the King to go in disguise and consult a necromancer at Endor, who conjured up the spirit of the dead prophet. The spirit testily complained at being disturbed and then told Saul that the Lord had taken the kingdom from him, and that he was doomed to die in the battle to come. (*I Samuel 28*)

The Book of Samuel is divided into two parts and is entirely narrative in structure; only the first part tells the story of Samuel; the second relates the story of King David.

SANBALLAT A Horonite and one of the leading opponents of Nehemiah's reconstruction work in Jerusalem. He threatened to send a letter to the Persian king accusing Nehemiah of planning to set himself up in rebellion; and with Tobiah and others he conspired to make an attempt on Nehemiah's life. (*Nehemiah 2:10, 4:1–7, 6:1–14, 13:28*)

SARAH (Sarai) Wife and half-sister of Abraham (Abram) and father of Isaac. Her name was changed by God to Sarah at the same time as Abram became Abraham. Despite assurances from God that she would bear Abraham a child, she remained barren, and in despair she gave her maid, Hagar, to Abraham as a concubine: she bore him a son, Ishmael. This engendered much jealousy and friction, however.

Above: When God appeared to Abraham in the form of three travelers, Sarah overheard Him repeat the promise of the Covenant and that she would bear Abraham a child.

Then, in old age, she was miraculously delivered of a boy child at last – Isaac. However, the friction with Hagar continued, stimulated in part at least by fears for Isaac's inheritance, and in the end Abraham was persuaded to send Hagar and Ishmael away. Abraham buried Sarah at Machpelah in Hebron, which was also to be the final resting place for Abraham himself, Isaac, Rebekah, Leah and Jacob. (*Genesis 1–18 passim*)

SARGON II King of Assyria who captured Samaria after a two-year siege begun by his predecessor, Shalmaneser V, and thereby ended the Kingdom of Israel. He subsequently took Ashdod after a revolt there. (*II Kings 18:10–11, Isaiah 20:1*)

SAUL First king of Israel, son of Kish, a Benjamite. By popular demand for a king, God sent the prophet Samuel to find Saul and anoint him. It was an unfortunate monarchy, ending with God's abandonment of Saul, the King's descent into depression and his eventual defeat and death on Mount Gilboa; but he did pave the way for David, playing a significant role in unifying the tribes into a cohesive kingdom, which only broke apart on the death of Solomon.

God sent Samuel to find Saul and anoint him king, after which he was presented to the people, who acclaimed him: 'And they ran and fetched him thence: and when he stood among the people, he was higher than any of the people from his shoulders and upward. And Samuel said to all the people, See ye him whom the Lord hath chosen, that there is none like him among all the people? And all the people shouted, and said, God save the king. (*I Samuel 10:23–4*) However, in truth there were now two rulers in Israel: Saul and Samuel, for the prophet spoke the word of God.

Within two years of his accession, Saul was involved in campaigns against the Philistines, Ammonites and Zobamites, during which his eldest son, Jonathan, played a heroic part. (*I Samuel 13–14*) He was successful, but the first sign of friction between Saul and Samuel came during a Philistine incursion, when Saul concentrated his forces at Gilgal. The King awaited Samuel's customary burnt offering before battle, but he had to wait for seven long days before the prophet arrived. Just before he did so, Saul realized he could wait no longer

Above: Saul is anointed King of Israel by Samuel.

Above: Samuel's garment rent by Saul.

and made the sacrifice himself. Then Samuel arrived and told him he had acted foolishly and that his kingship would be compromised as a result. (*I Samuel 13:1–14*)

In a subsequent campaign, Saul defeated and captured Agag, King of the Amalekites, but he disobeyed God's command for whole-sale destruction and slaughter, taking the enemy's animals and sparing the King. When Samuel discovered this he was enraged and passed judgement: 'For rebellion is as the sin of witchcraft, and stubbornness is as iniquity and idolatry. Because thou hast rejected the word of the Lord, he hath also rejected thee from being king.' (*I Samuel 15:23*) As Samuel turned to leave, Saul reached out to stop him and Samuel's mantle was torn, 'and Samuel said unto him, The Lord hath rent the king-dom of Israel from thee this day, and hath given it to a neighbour of thine, that is better than thou.' (*I Samuel 15:28*) Samuel anointed David, and Saul's reign was doomed.

David's triumph over Goliath and his other exploits made him so popular – 'Saul hath slain his thousands, and David his ten thousands', sang the people (*I Samuel 18:7*) – that Saul became increasingly depressed. Eventually

Above: Saul is soothed by the music of David's harp.

Below: Saul at the mercy of David.

even David's harp could no longer sooth him (*I Samuel 16–17*) and Saul actively sought David's death. (*I Samuel 18–19*) David fled the court, and Saul's attempts to find him proved futile. And so 'the evil spirit from God came upon Saul'. (*I Samuel 18:10*) He became disturbed in his mind, ordering the massacre of the priests at Nob who had given David refuge (*I Samuel 22:17–19*) and felt isolated and friendless.

Samuel died, and when Saul asked the Lord for help against a Philistine invasion, he even

Left: The death of Saul. 'Then said Saul to his armourbearer, Draw thy sword, and thrust me through therewith; lest these uncircumcised come and abuse me. But his armourbearer would not; for he was sore afraid. So Saul took a sword, and fell upon it.' (I Chronicles 10:4)

Right: Sennacherib before the walls of Jerusalem.

resorted to witchcraft, but the spirit of Samuel, whom the necromancer he consulted at Endor invoked, merely confirmed Saul's doom. (*I Samuel 28*) At the Battle of Gilboa, facing defeat, Saul was badly wounded by an arrow and fell upon his own sword. Three of his sons, Jonathan, Abinadab and Malchishua, died with him. (*I Samuel 31, I Chronicles 10*)

SENNACHERIB King of Assyria, son and successor of Sargon II. He invaded Judaea and besieged Jerusalem, but his army was destroyed in answer to the prayer of Hezekiah (*II Kings 18:13–16; 2 Chronicles 32:1–22*). 'Then the angel of the Lord went forth, and smote in the camp of the Assyrians a hundred and fourscore and five thousand: and when they arose early in the morning, behold, they were all dead corpses. So Sennacherib king of Assyria departed, and went and returned, and dwelt at Nineveh. And it came to pass, as he was worshipping in the house of Nisroch his god, that Adrammelech and Sharezer his sons

smote him with the sword; and they escaped into the land of Armenia: and Esar-haddon his son reigned in his stead. (*Isaiah 37:36–8*)

SETH Third son of Adam and Eve, after the murder of Able by Cain, through whom the chosen line continued. (*Genesis 4:25; 5:3*)

SHADRACK (Jewish name Hananiah) One of Daniel's three companions during the early years of the exile, Jewish nobles educated by the Babylonians and promoted to high office. When they refused to worship Nebuchadnezzar's giant golden idol, they were thrust into a fiery furnace but came out unscathed. So impressed was Nebuchadnezzar that he promoted them. (*Daniel 1:6–7,11–21, 3*)

SHALLUM Fifteenth king of Israel after the division of the kingdom. He assassinated his predecessor, Zechariah, but was himself murdered within a month by Menahem. (*II Kings 15:13–15*)

SHALMANESER V King of Assyria, successor to Tiglath-Pileser. When Hoshea, King of Israel, rebelled against Assyrian overlordship, Shalmaneser besieged Samaria but died before the city fell. (*II Kings 17:3–6, 18:9–11*)

SHAPHAN Secretary to King Josiah of Judah. He received the rediscovered Book of the Law from the High Priest, Hilkiah, and brought it to the King's attention. (*II Kings 22:3, II Chronicles 34:8, Jeremiah 26:24, 36:10-12*)

SHEBA, QUEEN OF Ruler of an unidentified region on the southern shores of the Red Sea who famously visited Solomon. 'And when the queen of Sheba heard of the fame of Solomon concerning the name of the Lord, she came to prove him with hard questions. And she came to Jerusalem with a very great train, with camels that bare spices, and very much gold,

Right: Solomon and the Queen of Sheba.

and precious stones: and when she was come to Solomon, she communed with him of all that was in her heart ... And she gave the king an hundred and twenty talents of gold, and of spices very great store, and precious stones ... And king Solomon gave unto the queen of Sheba all her desire, whatsoever she asked, beside that which Solomon gave her of his royal bounty. So she turned and went to her own country, she and her servants.' (*I Kings 10:1–13*) In the New Testament, Luke also mentions this visit: 'The queen of the south ... came from the utmost parts of the earth to hear the wisdom of Solomon ...' (*Luke 11:31*)

SHELAH Third son of Hudah, who failed to be married to Tamar. (*Genesis 38:5–26*)

SHEM One of the sons of Noah, therefore one of the three ancestors of the peoples of the world, having survived the Flood on board the ark. He had five sons, Elam, Asshur, Arphaxad, Lud and Aram, from whom, according to *Genesis*, descend the Elamites (Persians), Assyrians, Chaldeans, Libyans, Syrians and Armenians. With his brother Japheth, he tactfully covered Noah when Ham found their father asleep and intoxicated. It is through Shem that the lineage of David and of Jesus runs from Adam via Noah. (*Genesis 5:32, 6:10. 7:13, 9, 10*)

SHEMAIAH Prophet who warned King Rehoboam not to attack Israel when the ten northern tribes seceded; he also explained the absence of God's help when the kingdom was overrun by Pharaoh Shishak's Egyptian army five years later. (*I Kings 12:21–4, II Chronicles 11:1–4, 12:7–12*)

SHESHBAZZAR A prince of Judah by whom Cyrus restored the Temple vessels carried off to Babylon by Nebuchadnezzar. (*Ezra 1:8*).

SHIMEI An opponent of David, a member of the house of Saul. When Absalom seized power in Jerusalem, Shimei cast stones at the King and his retinue as they left the city and cursed him,

calling him a 'bloody man'. When David returned in triumph, Shimei begged forgiveness, and David spared his life on the understanding that he should not leave the city. When, some years later, he broke this undertaking in pursuit of a runaway slave, Solomon sent Benaiah to execute him. (*II Samuel 16:5, 19:16–23, I Kings 2:8, 9, 26–46*)

SHISHAK Pharaoh who gave sanctuary to Jeroboam, who later became King of Israel at the division of the kingdom, when he failed in his attempt to assassinate King Solomon. He invaded Israel and Judah in the fifth year of the reign of King Rehoboam of Judah and took away the Temple treasures as tribute. (*I Kings 11:40, 14:25–6, II Chronicles 12:2–9*)

SIMEON Second son of Jacob by Leah (*Genesis 29:33*). After their sister Dinah was seduced or raped, he and Levi took matters into their own hands and meted out brutal justice to the men of Sechem who had perpetrated the deed. (*Genesis 24*) When the brothers went to Egypt to buy corn and, unknown to them, encountered their brother Joseph, Simeon was left as a hostage when the brothers returned to Jacob. (*42:24*)

Above: Sheshbazzar and the restoration of the Temple vessels.

SISERA General of King Jabin of Hazor, defeated in battle by the judge Deborah and her general Barak. He fled the battlefield alone, his army having been slaughtered to a man, and found sanctuary at the tent of Heber, a Kenite. As he was sleeping, Heber's wife, Jael, treacherously despatched him with a tent peg through the temples. (*Judges 4, 5*)

SOLOMON Third king of Israel, son of David and Bathsheba. Solomon's accession to the throne was threatened before the death of his father by one of his older step-brothers, Adonijah, but the prompt action of David's counsellor, Nathan, pre-empted Adonijah's coup: then, following David's advice, the new king ensured his tenure on power by banishing or executing potential opponents, including Adonijah, Abiathar, Joab and Shimei. (*I Kings 2*) Securely enthroned, Solomon prayed to God for wisdom, and he became renowned for this attribute as well as his wealth. He most famously displayed his judgement in a case where two women claimed the same child, and Solomon was able to uncover the real mother. (*I Kings 3:16–28*)

Above: Sisera finds refuge at the tent of Heber and Jael.

Right: The judgement of Solomon.

153

The Kingdom of Israel reached its zenith during Solomon's reign. The wealth of both king and kingdom became legendary (*I Kings 3:20–34, 10:14-29, I Chronicles 13–17, 9:13–28*), and he mounted maritime expeditions to add to the prosperity of Israel. (*I Kings 9:26–7, I Chronicles 8:17–18*) As the reputation of Solomon's kingdom spread, Solomon's trading ships attracted the attention of more distant kingdoms and occasioned the visit of the Queen of Sheba, who was received in unsurpassed pomp and splendor. (*I Kings 10, I Chronicles 9:1–12*)

Above: The wealth of Solomon's kingdom.

His father had planned the construction of a permanent site to house the Ark of the Covenant, but God had told him this would be his son's task. Putting the considerable resources of Israel to work, Solomon also brought in Hiram of Lebanon's skilled artisans as well as Israelite forced labor to construct the first Temple in Jerusalem (*I Kings 5–6, I Chronicles 2–4*), installing the Covenant box and dedicating the building in a grand ceremony. (*I Kings 8, I Chronicles 5–7*) He also built an imposing, and similarly lavishly decorated, royal palace and rebuilt many cities in the land. (*I Kings 7, 9: 15–24, I Chronicles 8*)

However, 'king Solomon loved many strange women, together with the daughter of Pharaoh (*I Kings 3:1, 7:8, 11:1*), women of the Moabites, Ammonites, Edomites, Zidonians, and Hittites … And he had seven hundred wives, princesses, and three hundred concubines: and his wives turned away his heart. For it came to pass, when Solomon was old, that his wives turned

away his heart after other gods: and his heart was not perfect with the Lord his God, as was the heart of David his father. For Solomon went after Ashtoreth the goddess of the Zidonians, and after Milcom the abomination of the Ammonites. And Solomon did evil in the sight of the Lord, and went not fully after the Lord, as did David his father. Then did Solomon build an high place for Chemosh, the abomination of Moab, in the hill that is before Jerusalem, and for Molech, the abomination of the children of Ammon. And likewise did he for all his strange wives, which burnt

Above: The dedication of the Temple, exactly 3,000 years after completion of the Creation and 1,000 years before the birth of Jesus Christ.

incense and sacrificed unto their gods.' (*I Kings 11:1–8*) God had warned him against this – that punishment would follow his failure to be faithful to Him and abide by His laws. Through the prophet Ahijah, God told Jeroboam, the would-be usurper, that he would rend the kingdom in two after Solomon's death (*I Kings 41–3*), and his successor, Rehoboam, faced revolt by the ten northern tribes, who made Jeroboam their king.

T

TAMAR Canaanite wife to Er, then Onan, sons of Judah. When Er, being of a wicked disposition, was struck down by the Lord, Jacob married her to his second son, Onan, in order to carry on his line. But Onan would not cooperate, and he too died.

When Jacob's wife, Shuah, died, Tamar put aside her widow's dress and, disguised as a harlot, seduced Judah. When Judah discovered the deception, he realized that he should have given Tamar to his third son, Shelah. Tamar bore Judah twin sons, Zarah and Pharez. (*Genesis 38*)

TAMAR Daughter of David and Maacah, sister of Absalom. She was violated by her half-brother Amnon. Absalon had Amnon murdered in revenge. (*I Chronicles 3:9*)

TERAH Father of Abraham (Abram). The son of Nahor, he had two other sons, Haran and Nahor, and accompanied Abram and Lot when they migrated from Ur of the Chaldees to Haran. (*Genesis 11:24–32, Joshua 24:2, I Chronicles 1:26*)

TIBNI Rival to Omri for the throne of Israel after the crisis brought about by the murder of Elah by Zimri. Omri became king and Tibni died. (*I Kings 16:21–3*)

TIGLATH-PILESER III (also called Pul) King of Assyria, whose armies conquered much of the Holy Land during the reigns of Kings Menahem, Pekahiah and Pekah of Israel and Ahaz of Judah. As the Assyrian advance began, Menahem paid tribute to Tiglath-Pileser 'that his hand might be with him to

Above: The rape of Tamar.

Left: Terah, father of Abraham.

155

confirm the kingdom in his hand'. During the reign of Pekah, Assyria's conquests included Hazor, Gilead, Galilee and Naphtali, whose inhabitants were carried off; and it was to Tiglath-Pileser that Ahaz applied for help against attacks by Pekah and King Rezin of Damascus; the Assyrians captured the Syrian capital and it was in Damascus that Ahaz saw the Assyrian altar to Baal that he copied in Jerusalem. (*II Kings 15:19,29, 16:7, II Chronicles 28:20–1*)

TOBIAH One of the leading men of Jerusalem opposed to Nehemiah's reconstruction of Jerusalem's walls and Temple. With Sanballat and others he did all in his power to ridicule and hinder the works, even conspiring to have Nehemiah assassinated. On his second visit to Jerusalem, Nehemiah found Tobiah, in league with the priest Eliashib, installed within the grounds of the Temple and had him thrown out. (*Nehemiah 2:3,19, 4:3,7, 6:1,12,14,17–19, 7:72, 13:4–8*)

TUBAL-CAIN Son of Lamech and Zillah. He was a worker in metals: 'And Zillah, she also bare Tubal-cain, an instructer of every artificer in brass and iron: and the sister of Tubal-cain was Naamah.' (*Genesis 4:22*)

Above: Tubal-Cain.

U

UZZIAH (Azariah in Kings) Ninth king of Judah, son of Amaziah. Succeeding to the throne at the age of sixteen, Uzziah led a life faithful to the Lord but in time grew arrogant, which led to his downfall.

Judah's military fortunes rose dramatically after the humiliation of his father's reign, when much of Jerusalem's walls were pulled down by the victorious King Jehoash of Israel. Uzziah rebuilt and strengthened the defenses with new towers, equipping them with the latest artillery (catapults and early forms of ballista). With a large and newly equipped army, he made war on Philistia, taking Gath, Jabneh, Ashdod and built forts there; he also fought successful campaigns against the Arabs at Gur-baal, the Mehunims, and forced the Ammonites to pay tribute.

He took considerable interest in agriculture and encouraged the planting of vines; he also built Elath, on the eastern arm of the Red Sea.

But in time, the prosperity of the kingdom and his burgeoning international reputation turned his head, and he grew proud. His religious adviser, Zechariah, was no longer there to prevent a terrible error – in the Temple he dared to burn incense. The priests recoiled in horror, telling him that only those descended from Aaron (the first High Priest, of Moses' time) were permitted to do this; and at that very moment he was struck with leprosy. He reigned for 52 years, but for the latter part of his reign he kept from public view, never again entering the Temple, while affairs of state were placed in the hands of his son, Jotham, as Regent. (*II Kings 15:1–7, II Chronicles 26*)

Right: Machines of war strengthen the walls of Jerusalem.

V-W

VASHTI Queen of King Ahasueras who refused to obey him and was put aside. The King also issued an edict 'that all the wives shall give to their husbands honour, both to great and small ...' and 'that every man should bear rule in his own house'. The King then sought another wife, and Esther was chosen. (*Esther 1*)

Above: Queen Vashti's downfall.

X·Y·Z

ZABUD Son of Nathan, brother of Azariah and one of King Solomon's ministers. (*I Kings 4:5*)

ZADOK One of the two High Priests during the reign of King David. Eleazar, son of Aaron, was his ancestor, and the priesthood stayed in his line until the time of the Maccabees. During Absalom' usurpation attempt, Zadok and Abiathar, the other High Priest, took the Ark of the Covenant from Jerusalem for safety but were told by David to go back and remain in Jerusalem. There they stayed, relaying intelligence couriered by their sons to the King. Later, in David's old age, Zadok went with Nathan to anoint Solomon king at Gihon when Adonijah's plans to usurp the throne became known. (*I Kings 1*)

ZEBULUN Tenth son of Jacob, sixth by Leah, and the founder of the tribe that bore his name. When Jacob gave his blessing to his sons shortly before he died, he said of Zebulun: 'Zebulun shall dwell at the haven of the sea; and he shall be for an haven of ships; and his border shall be unto Zidon.' (*Genesis 30:20, 49:13*)

ZECHARIAH Fourteenth king of Israel after the division of the kingdom, son of Jeroboam II. His reign was cut short after just six months when he was assassinated by Shallum, bringing the dynasty of Jehu to an end as God had foretold: 'And the Lord said unto Jehu, Because thou hast done well in executing that which is right in mine eyes, and hast done unto the house of Ahab according to all that was in mine heart, thy children of the fourth generation shall sit on the throne of Israel.' (*II Kings 10:30, 15:10–15*)

ZECHARIAH One of the Minor Prophets. A contemporary with Haggai and Zerubbabel, he was the son of Berechiah and grandson of Iddo, a prophet. (*Nehemiah 12:4, 16; Zechariah 1:1*) His book lays stress upon the importance of worship in the Temple and looks forward to

Above: Zebulun. Below: The prophet Zechariah.

159

the restoration of Jerusalem and the coming of the Messiah. Jesus quoted verse *13:7* of *The Book of Zechariah* according to *Mark 14:27*: 'for it is written, I will smite the shepherd, and the sheep shall be scattered.'

ZECHARIAH Son of Jehoiada, High Priest of Judah. Upon his father's death, Zechariah saw Judah turn once more to idolatry and condemned it, for which the King, Joash, had him stoned. (*II Chronicles 24:14–17*)

Above: The stoning of Zechariah.

ZEDEKIAH False prophet named together with Ahab in *Jeremiah 29:21* – 'Thus saith the Lord of hosts, the God of Israel, of Ahab the son of Kolaiah, and of Zedekiah the son of Maaseiah, which prophesy a lie unto you in my name; Behold, I will deliver them into the hand of Nebuchadnezzar king of Babylon; and he shall slay them before your eyes.'

ZEDEKIAH (Mattaniah) Nineteenth and last king of Judah. Uncle of Jehoiachin, his original name was Mattaniah, and he ruled Judah – which by now consisted of little but Jerusalem – for its final eleven years. The kingdom had now come under the thumb of the Babylonians, and when Zedekiah broke his oath to King Nebuchadnezzar and rebelled, the Babylonian king responded with massive force. Even then, it took a two-year siege before the Babylonians could break into the city, where they found the population starving. Zedekiah and the remnant of his army managed to escape, but the Babylonians soon caught up with them. The men of Judah scattered, while the King was captured and taken to face the wrath of Nebuchadnezzar at Riblah. He was shown no mercy: his sons were killed before his eyes and then he was blinded and carried off in chains to Babylon. Since Jerusalem had not surrendered but had to be taken by force, Nebuchadnezzar decreed the destruction of the Temple, the palace, the grand houses of the city, and the city walls were demolished, leaving Jerusalem an empty shell. Everything of value was looted, even the large, bronze objects installed in the Temple by Solomon. The kingdom of Judah was no more. *(II Kings 24:17–25:7, II Chronicles 36:11–21)*

ZEPHANIAH Prophet during the reign of King Josiah of Judah and a contemporary of Jeremiah. He echoed Jeremiah's message – the people had transgressed God's laws to such an extent, with idolatry, fraud, violence and wanton behaviour, that there was now no other way but the destruction of Jerusalem and a new beginning: 'The great day of the Lord is near, it is near, and hasteth greatly, even the voice of the day of the Lord: the mighty man shall cry there bitterly. That day is a day of wrath, a day of trouble and distress, a day of wasteness and desolation, a day of darkness and gloominess, a day of clouds and thick darkness ... And I will bring distress upon men, that they shall walk like blind men, because they have sinned against the Lord: and their blood shall be poured out as dust ... Neither their silver nor their gold shall be able to deliver them in the day of the Lord's wrath; but the whole land shall be devoured by the fire of his jealousy: for he shall make even a speedy riddance of all them that dwell in the land.' However, there was hope after the despair: 'I will also leave in the midst of thee an afflicted and poor people, and they shall trust in the name of the Lord. The remnant of Israel shall not do iniquity, nor speak lies; neither shall a deceitful tongue be found in their mouth: for they shall feed and lie down, and none shall make them afraid. Sing, O daughter of Zion; shout, O Israel; be glad and rejoice with all the heart, O daughter of Jerusalem.' (*The Book of Zephaniah*)

Above: The cruel fate of Zedekiah, last King of Judah.

ZERAH Cushite King of Ethiopia who invaded Judah during the reign of King Asa, who repulsed his incursion. (*II Chronicles 14:9*)

ZERUBBABEL Jewish prince who led the initial return of the Jews from captivity in Persia to Jerusalem. After the Persian conquest of the Babylonian Empire, Cyrus gave permission for the Jews to go back to their homeland and returned to them more than 4,500 gold and silver objects that had been taken from the Temple by Nebuchadnezzar. The King also encouraged the Jews to begin reconstruction. Local opposition was vociferous, however, led by local Jews who had intermarried with Samaritans and who distrusted those returning. After the foundations of the Temple had been laid and the Passover celebrated, the opposition wrote to the Persian court demanding that work be stopped. During the reign of Cyrus's successor, Artaxerxes, work was indeed halted, but a fresh appeal during the reign of Darius succeeded in allowing the reconstruction work to begin again. (*The Book of Ezra*)

ZIBA A servant of Saul, to whom David inquired whether there were any members of the house of Saul still alive. Ziba told him of Meshibosheth, son of Jonathan, and David brought him to court, charging Ziba with the management of Meshibosheth's estate. *(II Samuel 9)* When Absalom temporarily usurped David's throne, Ziba remained loyal to David and sent him supplies. *(II Samuel 16:1–4)* But he lied about Meshibosheth's loyalty, telling him that Meshibosheth had remained in Jerusalem with the usurper, and David made Meshibosheth's land over to Ziba. When the truth came out, David divided the land between the two. (*II Samuel 19:24–30*)

ZILPAH Concubine of Jacob, formerly maid to Leah, who bore Jacob two sons, Gad and Asher. (*Genesis 30:9–13*)

ZIMRI Fifth king of Israel after the division of the kingdom, usurper. While the Israelite army was away in Philistia besieging the city of Gibbethon, he took advantage of King Elah's drunken state to assassinate him and stage a palace revolt. On hearing of this, the army at once elected its commander, Omri, as king and marched back to besiege Zimri in the Israeli capital, Tirzah. Zimri perished as the citadel was set on fire, after a reign of just seven days. (*I Kings 16:9–20*)

ZIPPORAH Wife of Moses, daughter of Jethro. In Midian she bore Moses two sons, Gershom and Eliezer. When Moses went with Aaron to confront Pharaoh, Zipporah stayed in Midian with Jethro, only joining Moses in the wilderness when Jethro visited him. (*Exodus 2:21-2, 18:1–7*)

ZURISHADDAI A Simeonite and father of Shelumiel, who represented the tribe at the census in the wilderness. (*Numbers 1:6; 2:12, 7:36,41,10:19*)

The
New Testament

ABADDON The angel of the bottomles pit in *Revelation 9:11*.

AENEAS An inhabitant of Lydda, bedridden for eight years with paralysis until healed by Peter. (*Acts 9:33–5*)

AGABUS Prophet at the time of Paul. He foretold a great famine, causing the Christians of Antioch to send aid to Judaea (*Acts 11:28–30*), and subsequently correctly warned Paul, then at Caesarea, that he would be imprisoned if he went to Jerusalem. (*Acts 21:10*)

AGRIPPA See Herod Agrippa.

Above: Aeneas.

Left: Agabus predicts Paul's incarceration upon his return to Jerusalem, demonstrating this symbolically with Paul's belt.

Right: The gift of Ananias.

Far right: Jesus calls Andrew and Peter to be his disciples.

ALEXANDER A relative of the High Priest Ananias (Annas), and who was present when Peter and John were examined. (*Acts 4:6*)

ALEXANDER The son of Simon the Cyrenian, who bore the cross for Christ. (*Mark 15:21*)

ALEXANDER A Jew who took part in the uproar raised at Ephesus by the preaching of Paul. (*Acts 19:33*)

ALEXANDER The coppersmith who taught certain heresies concerning the Resurrection and who was excommunicated by Paul. (*I Timothy 1:19; II Timothy 4:14*)

ALPHAEUS Father of James the Younger, or Lesser. (*Matthew 9:9, Mark 2:14, 3:18, Luke 5:27*)

ALPHAEUS Father of Matthew (Levi) the apostle who was previously a tax-collector. (*Mark 2:14*)

ANANIAS Supporter of the early Christians who, with his wife Sapphira, sold property to donate to the early Christians but kept part of it back; for which he was reproved by Peter and was struck dead on the spot. (*Acts 3:1–11*)

ANANIAS Restorer of Paul's sight at Damascus. (*Acts 9:10–19*)

ANANIAS (Annas) High Priest in Jerusalem before whom Paul appeared; he ordered Paul to be struck, and Paul called him a 'whited wall'. (*Acts 23:2*)

ANDREW Apostle and brother of Simon Peter (*Matthew 10:2*), with whom he lived in the family home at Bethsaida in Galilee. Working with his brother, he was a fisherman before being recruited by Jesus.

Initially he was a disciple of John the Baptist, who trhen directed his followers toward Jesus. When John pointed Jesus out, Andrew was the first to recognize him and next day told Simon Peter that they had found the Messiah. (*John 1:40–4*)

Although he was one of the inner circle of disciples (*Mark 13:3*), mentions of him in the Gospels are few: he was present on the Mount of Olives when Jesus predicted the destruction of the Temple; was on the mountainside with the other disciples when Jesus delivered the

Above: The feeding of the five thousand. Andrew discovers a lad who has five loaves and two fishes, with which Jesus then miraculously feeds the crowd.

Beatitudes (*Luke 6:14*); and it was Andrew, before the feeding of the 5,000, who discovered the boy with the five loaves and two fishes. (*John 6:8*)

After the Ascension he preached in Jerusalem, subsequently, according to tradition, working as a missionary to the Scythians. A later tradition has his martyrdom at Patrae in Achaia on an x-shaped cross; and that his remains were taken to Scotland, of which he became patron saint. (*John 1:44*)

ANDRONICUS A believing Jew, a kinsman and fellow-prisoner of Paul. (*Romans 16:7*)

ANNA The 84-year-old prophetess who, with Simeon, recognised Jesus when Joseph and Mary brought the child into the Temple. (*Luke 2:36–8*)

ANNAS Father-in-law to Caiaphas and a High Priest of the Jews at the time of the tax census that caused Joseph and Mary to journey to Bethlehem. Upon his arrest at Gethsemane, it was to Annas's house that Jesus was taken. (*Luke 3:2, John 18:13–24, Acts 4:5–6*)

APOLLOS A Jewish convert 'born at Alexandria'. He was well read in the Scriptures (*Acts 18:24*) and spoke 'boldly' in the synagogue at Ephesus (*18:26*), although he was ignorant that Jesus was the Messiah. Aquila and Priscilla made 'the way of God' more clear to him, after which he went to Corinth, where Paul was. (*Acts 18:27, 19:1*) He there undertook to 'water the seed' sown by Paul (*I Corinthians 2:9*) and endeared his disciples to him. (*I Corinthians 3:4–7, 22*) When Paul wrote the First Epistle to the Corinthians from Ephesus Apollos was with him, and kindly reference to him occurs in the letter to Titus. (*Titus 3:13*)

APOSTLES These are listed in *Matthew 10:3, Mark 3:18, Luke 6:14* and *Acts 1:13*.

APPHIA A Christian woman at Colosse. (*Philemon 2*)

AQUILA A tent-maker, whom Paul met when he first visited Corinth. (*Acts 18:2*) He and his wife Priscilla had fled from Rome in obedience to the decree of Claudius commanding all Jews to leave the city. At Corinth he and Paul worked together, making hair-cloth for tents. Paul left Corinth for Ephesus eighteen months later, and Aquila and his wife went with him. They remained at Ephesus, but he went into

Above: Annas. Right: Aquila, the tent-maker.

Syria. (*Acts 18:25, 26*) In Ephesus they became Paul's helpers. Afterwards Aquila was at Rome (*Romans 16:3*), and some years later both he and his wife were at Ephesus. (*II Timothy 4:19*)

ARCHELAUS See Herod Archelaus.

ARCHIPPUS A 'fellow-soldier' of Paul (*Philemon 2*), whom he exhorts to renewed activity. (*Colossians. 4:17*) He belonged to Philemon's family.

ARISTARCHUS A native of Thessalonica (*Acts 20:4*) and companion of Paul in his third missionary journey. (*Acts 19:29, 27:2*) He was also Paul's 'fellow prisoner' and 'fellow labourer'.

(*Colossians 4:10 Philemon 24*)

ARISTOBULUS A Roman whose household Paul salutes in *Romans 16:10*.

ARTEMAS A companion of Paul. (*Titus 3:12*)

AUGUSTUS (C. Julius Caesar Octavius) First emperor of Rome, victor in civil wars with the assassins of his great uncle, Julius Caesar, and later with Mark Antony and Cleopatra. It was his decree for a tax census that brought the Holy Family to Bethlehem shortly before Jesus' birth (*Luke 2:1*), and Luke also records (*3:1*) that it was in the fifteenth year of his reign that John the Baptist began to preach.

Right: The famous Prima Porta statue of the Roman Emperor Augustus, in whose reign Jesus was born.

BAR-JESUS (also known as Elmyas) A Jewish magician and false prophet in the pay of the Roman proconsul of Cyprus, Sergius Paulus. When Paul began speaking of the Word of God to the Roman governor, Bar-Jesus attempted to stop him; upon which Paul placed a curse on him and temporarily blinded him. (*Acts 13:6*)

BARABBAS A condemned criminal and murderer sentenced to death in Jerusalem at the

Above: The false prophet, Bar-Jesus, blinded by Paul.

Above: Pilate, unconvinced by the priests' demands for the crucifixion of Jesus, attempts to free him. It was customary at the time of the Passover for the Romans to release a prisoner, chosen by the people. Pilate offered them Jesus, but they insisted upon Barabbas.

He was sent to Antioch to oversee the infant church there, before collecting Paul from Tarsus and taking him on their first missionary journey to Cyprus, Pisidia, Lycaonia and Lystria. On their return to Jerusalem he took part in the fierce debate with the apostles about whether Gentiles could be converted to Christianity.

He then quarrelled with Paul about whether to take his nephew, John Mark, on the next mission, with the result that he and his nephew went to Cyprus while Paul went to Galatia. Their disagreement was not long-lasting. (*Acts 15:36–9*) His Jewish name was Joseph. (*Acts 4:36, 11:22–5, 30, 12:35, 13:1–50, 14:12–20, 15:7–37, I Corinthians 9:6; Galatians 2:1, 9, 13, Colossians 4:10*)

BARSABAS Surname of Joseph called Justus. (*Acts 1:23*)

BARTHOLOMEW One of the twelve apostles, introduced to Jesus by Philip (*John 1:45–51*), where he is referred to as Nathanael. He was

same time as Christ. He was possibly a Zealot, a guerrilla fighter dedicated to overthrowing the Roman occupation. When Pilate offered to release Jesus in the customary Passover amnesty, the mob (incited by the priests) called for Barabbas to be released instead. (*Matthew 27, Mark 15, Luke 23, John 18*)

BARNABAS A Levite from the island of Cyprus and one of the key missionaries spreading the Gospel to the Gentiles in the early years of the Christian church. He is portrayed in the Bible as a good and kindly man, with an impressive, commanding personality – the Lycaonians were so impressed that they called him 'Jupiter' (while calling Paul 'Mercury'). His generosity was demonstrated early on when he sold his plot of land in Jerusalem and donated the proceeds to the apostles. (*Acts 4:32–7*) When Paul was converted, it was Barnabas who introduced him to the Christian leaders in Antioch and to the apostles in Jerusalem. (*Acts 9:27*)

Above: Barnabas with Paul preaching in a synagogue.

Above: Barnabas with the apostles in Jerusalem; and , right, farther afield as they spread the Gospel to the Gentiles of Asia Minor.

Left: Philip calls Bartholomew to Jesus.

possibly from Cana in Galilee, and was with the disciples when Christ appeared to them after his Resurrection by the Sea of Galilee. (*John 21:2*) According to tradition, he met his martyrdom by being flayed alive in Armenia.

BARTIMAEUS A blind beggar of Jericho whose sight was restored by Jesus. Squatting by the roadside, Bartimaeus heard that Jesus of Nazareth approached and called out, 'Jesus, thou son of David, have mercy on me', thus recognizing Jesus as the Messiah. Jesus called him forward through the throng and cured him, saying, 'Thy faith hath made thee whole.' (*Mark 10:46–52, Luke 18:35*)

BEELZEBUB See Satan, page 7.

BERNICE Eldest daughter of Herod Agrippa I and sister of Herod Agrippa II, with whom it was rumored that she had an incestuous relationship after the death of her first husband (she married King Polemon of Olba in Cicilia to avert such suspicions). She was present at the Roman procurator Festus's investigation of Paul preparatory to his being sent to Rome. Non-Biblical sources suggest she married her uncle; was involved in preventing the massacre of Jews by Gessius Florius; and was at one time the mistress of the Emperors Vespasian and Titus. (*Acts 25: 14, 23, 26:30*)

BOANERGES A surname given by Christ to James and John (*Mark 3:17*) on account of their temperaments. (*Luke 9:54*)

Left: Blind Bartimaeus cries out and comes to Jesus to be healed.

C

CAESAR The title assumed by all the Roman emperors. In the New Testament it is the general title given to the Roman rulers of Judea *(John 19:15, Acts 17:7)*: tribute was paid to Caesar *(Matthew 22:17)*, and all Roman citizens could appeal to Caesar *(Acts 25:11)*. Several Caesars are referred to in the New Testament: Augustus *(Luke 2:1)*, Tiberius *(3:1, 20:22)*, Claudius *(Acts 40:28)* and Nero *(Acts 25:8, Philippians 4:22)*.

CAIAPHAS The son-in-law of Annas and his successor as High Priest in Jerusalem. He was the foremost enemy and persecutor of Jesus and his followers. Identifying Jesus and his message as a threat to his authority and to other vested interests, he determined to destroy him. During Passion Week he was the prime mover in the arrest, conviction and execution of Jesus, and he convened the Sanhedrin after initial investigations at the

Caiaphas presides over the trial of Jesus

The walk to Emmaus, after the Resurrection of Christ, where Jesus met two of his disciples, one of whom was Cleopas. At first they did not recognize him.

house of his father-in-law. He presided over the trial and asked the key question: 'I adjure thee by the living God, that thou tell us whether thou be the Christ, the Son of God.' (*Matthew 27:63*) He took Jesus' answer as blasphemy, and conviction followed. After the Crucifixion and Ascension, Caiaphas zealously persecuted the disciples, inconclusively bringing Peter and John to trial, presiding at the trial of Stephen and commissioning Saul to seek out and eradicate the Christians of Damascus. (*Matthew 26:3, 26:57–68, Mark 14:63, Luke 3:2, John 11:49,51–2, 18:13, 14, 24, 28; Acts 4:6,21, 6:12–13*)

CANDACE The Queen of Ethiopia, in whose service the eunuch converted by Philip was traveling. (*Acts 8:27*)

CHUZA Steward of Herod Antipas. His wife, Joanna, was one of the women who ministered to the needs of the disciples. (*Luke 8:3*)

CLAUDIA A female Christian mentioned in *II Timothy 4:21*. She is supposed by some to have been a British woman.

CLAUDIUS The fourth Roman emperor. He succeeded Caligula and banished the Jews from Rome. (*Acts 18:2*) During his reign several persecutions of the Christians took place under Herod Agrippa (*12:2*).

CLAUDIUS LYSIAS Commander of the Roman garrison who took Paul into custody and prevented his being lynched by the mob. He did not carry out the flogging that had been ordered when he understood that Paul was a Roman citizen. It was next day that Paul demanded that he be judged in Rome. That night word reached Claudius of a plot to kill Paul, so he assembled a strong escort and sent his prisoner with a letter to Felix in Caesarea. (*Acts 21:31–40, 22–28, 23–26*)

CLEOPAS One of the two disciples to whom Jesus talked on the way to Emmaus during the evening of the Resurrection. (*Luke 24:18*)

Cornelius, the centurion, receives Peter, who baptizes him and his family.

CORNELIUS A centurion whose history is given in Acts 10. He was a 'devout man' and feared God. In obedience to an angel he sent for Peter: he and his family were baptized and welcomed as Christians. (*Acts 10:1, 44-48*)

COSAM Son of Elmodam in the genealogy of Jesus. (*Luke 3:28*)

CRESCENS One of Paul's assistants at Rome and may have been one of the seventy disciples sent out by Jesus. (*II Timothy 4:10*).

CRISPUS Ruler of the synagogue at Corinth. (*Acts 18:8*) He was converted and baptized by Paul. (*I Corinthians 1:14*)

CYRENIUS (Publius Sulpicius Quirinus) was Governor of Syria at the time of Christ's birth. (*Luke 2:2*)

D

DAMARIS An Athenian woman converted by the preaching of Paul. (*Acts 17:34*)

DEMAS A fellow laborer of Paul at Rome (*Colossians 4:14*), he afterwards deserted the apostle (*II Timothy 4:10*), 'having loved this present world'.

DEMETRIUS A silversmith of Ephesus, who made silver shrines for Diana (*Acts 19:24*), a very profitable occupation. This traffic being endangered by the spread of Christianity, he incited a riot in the city against Paul.

DIDYMUS See Thomas.

DIONYSIUS An Areopagite who was converted at Athens by Paul. (*Acts 17:34*)

DIOTREPHES A convert at Corinth, who spoke maliciously against the apostle John. (*III John 9*)

DORCAS A Christian widow at Joppa who died but was miraculously restored to life by Peter, who was called from Lydda. (*Acts 9:36–41*). She was also called Tabitha.

Left: Demetrius causes a riot in Ephesus.

DRUSILLA Youngest daughter of Herod Agrippa I. Felix, the Roman procurator of Judea, persuaded her to abandon her husband, Azizus, King of Emesa, and marry him. She sat with Felix when he interrogated Paul but reached no conclusion except to keep him in prison, hoping Paul would pay for his release. (*Acts 24:24*) She was killed in the eruption of Mount Vesuvius that the Roman historian Pliny the Younger described.

Left: The risen Dorcas. 'And it was known throughout all Joppa; and many believed in the Lord.' (Acts 9:42)

Below: Drusilla sits beside Felix as he hears Paul 'concerning the faith in Christ. And as he reasoned of righteousness, temperance, and judgment to come Felix trembled, and answered, Go thy way for this time; when I have a convenient season, I will call for thee. (Acts 24:24–5)

E

ELISABETH Mother of John the Baptist and kinswoman of Mary, mother of Jesus. Of a priestly lineage stretching back to Aaron, she married a priest, Zechariah, and they lived in Ein Karem. At the Annunciation, the angel Gabriel shared with Mary the news that Elisabeth too was expecting a child, despite her relatively advanced age, and Mary hastened to

share her own news with her cousin, staying with her for three months. The visitation is related in *Luke 1*, which includes the hymn of praise later known as the *Magnificat*. Elisabeth gave birth to John six months before Jesus was born.

ELIUD An ancestor of Jesus Christ. (*Matthew 1:14–15*)

EMMANUEL (Immanuel) Name given to the child prophesied in *Isaiah 7:14*: 'Therefore the Lord himself shall give you a sign; Behold, a virgin shall be with child, and shall bring forth a son, and they shall call his name Emmanuel, which being interpreted is, God with us.' The birth of Jesus was deemed as fulfillment of this prophesy. (*Matthew 1:23*)

EPAPHRAS Paul's 'dear fellow-servant' and a faithful minister of Christ mentioned in *Colossians 1:7, 4:12* and also in *Philemon 23.*

EPAPHRODITAS A valued aide to Paul who fell seriously ill and, upon his recovery, was sent to the Christian community at Philippi. (*Philippians 2:25–30*)

EPENETUS A Christian at Rome. (*Romans 16:5*)

ERASTUS A companion of Paul at Ephesus. (*Acts 19:22*) Corinth was his usual place of abode. (*II Timothy 4:20*)

ESLI Father of Naum in the genealogy of Christ. (*Luke 3:25*)

EUBULUS A disciple at Rome who was converted while Paul was there. (*II Timothy 4:21*)

EUNICE The mother of Timothy, a Jewess who believed. (*Acts 16:5*) She was mentioned for her 'unfeigned faith'. (*II Timothy 1:5*)

EUTYCHUS A youth who fell from the third floor of the house where Paul was preaching at Troas, and was 'taken up dead'. Paul miraculously restored him to life. (*Acts 20:9–12*)

*Left: The visitation. Mary
tells her cousin Elisabeth
that she too is with child.*

F

FELIX (Possibly Claudius Felix) Roman prefect of Judea during the time of Paul's arrest and first trial. An imperial freedman, he married three times, one of his wives being a daughter of Antony and Cleopatra. At the time of Paul's trial, he was married to Drusilla.

After his arrest in Jerusalem, Paul was sent to Caesarea by Claudius Lycias, the commander of the Roman garrison in Jerusalem. In a letter accompanying the prisoner, Claudius Lycias explained the situation to Felix: essentially the problem of his accusations by the Jewish priests, the difficulties arising from his special status as a Roman citizen and the existence of Jewish plots against Paul's life.

Felix presided over a meeting with Ananias, the High Priest, and a lawyer named Tertullus; probably, because Drusilla was Jewish, he had some knowledge of the ideas that Paul was promoting. But to appease the Jews he kept Paul in prison (or possibly some form of 'house arrest') and talked with him a number of times; the Bible text says that he was hoping Paul would attempt to bribe his way to freedom. Paul was thus incarcerated for two years before Felix was recalled to Rome. He already had a reputation for cruelty (including a massacre in Egypt) in addition to which he was accused of mishandling the Jewish situation, which was becoming increasingly violent and would lead ultimately to the Jewish revolt. He was replaced by Porcius Festus. (*Acts 21–4*)

FESTUS See Porcius Festus.

FORTUNATAS One of Paul's first converts in Achaia, a member of the household of Stephanas at Corinth. With Stephanas and Achaicus he travelled to Ephesus, as mentioned in Paul's second letter to the *Corinthians 16:17*.

Left: Paul before Felix.

G

GABRIEL An archangel, in the New Testament a messenger from God. He appeared twice: first to Zechariah, to announce that his wife Elisabeth would bear him a son, John the Baptist; second, six months later, to the virgin Mary in Nazareth, announcing that she would give birth to Jesus (the Annunciation). See also entry for Gabriel in the Old Testament. (*Luke 1:11–20, 26–38*)

GALLIO Proconsul of Achaia when Paul visited Corinth. From Cordoba in Spain, he was the brother of the philosopher Seneca. When the Jewish backlash at Paul's success in converting people in Corinth led to Paul being brought before him, Gallio was unimpressed by the charges made by the Jews, telling them that it was no business of his. (*Acts 28:12–17*)

GAMALIEL Pharisee and teacher of the law in Jerusalem at the time of the arrest of Peter and other apostles. At the hearing in the Sanhedrin, he argued that they should be set free on the grounds that, if their message was fraudulent, the sect would simply die out. (*Acts 5:33–40*) Saul (later known as Paul) was one of his students. (*Acts 22:3*)

The Annunciation: The archangel Gabriel tells Mary her joyous news. 'And the angel came in unto her, and said, Hail, thou that art highly favoured, the Lord is with thee: blessed art thou among women. And when she saw him, she was troubled at his saying, and cast in her mind what manner of salutation this should be. And the angel said unto her, Fear not, Mary: for thou hast found favour with God. And, behold, thou shalt conceive in thy womb, and bring forth a son, and shalt call his name Jesus.' (Luke 1:28–31)

H-I

HEROD AGRIPPA I (Roman name Marcus Julius Agrippa) King of Judea responsible for the execution of James, brother of John, and the imprisonment of Peter (who was miraculously freed, for which Herod Agrippa's guards paid with their lives). He spent his childhood in Rome and became Tetrarch of Iturea, Gaulanitis, Trachonitis, Galilee and Perea on the death of his uncle, Herod Philip. He seems to have had some involvement in the succession of the Emperor Claudius and was rewarded with the additional territories of Judea and Samaria. He thus reunited the kingdom of his grandfather, Herod the Great. He died dramatically at Caesarea, following trouble with Tyre and Sidon. *Acts 12: 22–3* reports: 'And the people gave a shout, saying, "It is the voice of a god, and not of a man." And immediately the angel of the Lord smote him, because he gave not God the glory: and he was eaten of worms, and gave up the ghost.' (*Acts 12: 1–23*)

HEROD AGRIPPA II (Roman name Marcus Julius Agrippa) Ethnarch of Chalcis in Lebanon, then ruler of Galilee, Iturea, Gaulanitis and Trachonitis, before whom Paul appeared at the behest of Festus. His interview with the apostle was sympathetic, Agrippa concluding, 'Almost thou persuadest me to be a Christian'; and to Festus, 'This man might have been set at liberty, if he had not appealed to Rome.' Agrippa was the last of the Herodian dynasty, surviving the Jewish Revolt and fighting alongside Titus in its suppression. He later retired to Rome. (*Acts 25:13–27, 26:1–32*).

HEROD ANTIPAS Fifth son of Herod the Great and Tetrarch of Galilee and Peraea (a non-adjacent territory beyond the east bank of the Jordan). It was Herod Antipas before whom Jesus briefly appeared between his interviews with Pilate. (*Luke 23:7–11*) He founded the city of Tiberias and made it his capital, and it was in the lands he ruled that John the Baptist and Jesus preached. Herod Antipas married the daughter of the Arabian king of Nabataea but divorced her, provoking an invasion by his enraged father in law that was only repulsed with Roman help. He then married his niece Herodias, who by a previous marriage had born a daughter, Salome. John the Baptist condemned this immoral act, which led to the prophet's imprisonment and death. Herod Antipas applied to the Emperor in Rome (now Gaius, or Caligula) to be named 'king', as was his nephew Herod Agrippa I, but this request was refused when the latter objected, and Herod Antipas and Herodias were deposed and exiled to Gaul.

HEROD ARCHELAUS Fourth son of Herod the Great and Ethnarch of Judea, Samaria and Idumea upon his father's death. He is identified in *Matthew 2:22*; Joseph feared returning to Israel even after the death of Herod the Great, but in a dream he was directed to go to Nazareth in Galilee. Herod Archelaus made a disreputable marriage with the daughter of Archelaus of Cappadocia; she had previously been married to his own half-brother and to Juba of Mauretania. An outraged deputation of Jews journeyed to Rome and secured his deposition and exile to Gaul.

HEROD PHILIP Seventh and youngest son of Herod the Great; Tetrarch of Batanea, Trachonitis, Auranitis, Gaulanitis (the Golan) and Panias. He founded the city of Caesarea Philippi, near which Peter declared that Jesus was the Messiah. (*Matthew 16:13, Mark 8:27–30*) The Bible erroneously identifies him as the husband of Herodias, his niece, who subsequently married Herod Antipas, his brother, incurring the condemnation of John the Baptist (whereas in fact she was married to Herod Beothius, Herod the Great's sixth son). Tradition has it that he later married Salome, his niece, daughter of Herodias and Antipas.

HEROD THE GREAT King of Judea at the time of Christ's birth. An Idumean (from Edom), Herod's Jewish identity was doubtful,

Herod prepares to question Jesus. Pilate, noting that Jesus was from Galilee, which was within Herod's jurisdiction, hoped that he could pass responsibility for Jesus' fate to the King. But Herod was merely interested to see if Jesus would perform a miracle.

but he saw himself as a Jew, albeit with Hellenic sympathies. Mark Antony made him governor of Galilee, but he was forced to flee to Rome during the subsequent Parthian invasion. Three years later, Rome retook Jerusalem, Octavian confirmed him as King of Judaea, and his kingdom was expanded to the north-east. Herod enjoyed the confidence of the Emperor, visiting Rome several times, and the port of Caesarea, which Herod developed, was named in his honor. This was just one of Herod's major construction projects: he built

183

Herod the Great.

foiled when the wise men, warned in a dream, returned to their native land without telling him where to find the child. In fury, King Herod decreed the 'massacre of the innocents' – the slaughter of all children of two years or less in the Bethlehem area. A dream had also warned Joseph of this, and he took Mary and Jesus to Egypt until the death of Herod.

Herod separated the roles of king and high priest, which had been united by the Parthians' puppet king, Antigonus. When he died, his kingdom became a tetrarchy, split between three sons, Herod Antipas, Herod Archelaus and Philip. (*Matthew 2:1–23, Luke 1:5*)

HERODIAS Mother of Salome and instigator of the execution of John the Baptist. She was the granddaughter of Herod the Great and daughter of his second son, Aristobulus (who perished at the hand of Herod together with his brother Alexander and their mother, Mariamne I). She first married her uncle, Herod Beothus (Herod the Great's sixth son) and bore him a daughter, Salome, then married Philip, another more distant member of the Herod family in Rome (*Matthew* and *Mark* being in error when they state that she married her uncle Philip); her third marriage was to her uncle Herod Antipas. John the Baptist's condemnation of this flagrantly incestuous marriage brought about his death, Herodias using her daughter as the instrument of John's demise – when Salome had exacted from a reluctant Herod Antipas the head of John, she presented it to her mother. Herodias later accompanied her husband into exile in Gaul when the Emperor Caligula deposed him.

HERMAS A Christian Roman to whom Paul sends greetings in *Romans 16:14*.

HYMENAEUS A heretic excommunicated by Paul for his false doctrine. (*I Timothy 1:20; II Timothy 2:17*)

ISCARIOT See Judas Iscariot.

fortresses (including that at Masada), rebuilt Samaria (destroyed by the Hasmonaean John Hyrcanus) as Sebaste, and endowed Jerusalem with a theatre, amphitheatre, hippodrome and a lavish palace. Most significantly, however, he rebuilt the Temple on a massive scale, financing it but leaving the priests to organize its construction.

He had a large family of ten wives and fifteen children, and treated them badly. He executed his first wife and her two children; and in old age became ever more brutal and cruel – his eldest son and heir was killed just prior to Herod's death. His callous inhumanity was demonstrated in the Bible at the birth of Jesus. When the three wise men told him that they came in search of a child born to be 'King of the Jews' he planned the child's death but was

J-K

JACOB The father of Joseph, the husband of the virgin Mary. (*Matthew 1:15, 16*)

JAIRUS A synagogue official in Galilee whose daughter was raised from the dead early in Jesus' ministry. When Jesus was preaching by the shores of the lake, Jairus begged him to save his twelve-year old daughter, who, he said, was dying – and as he spoke, servants rushed up and told him that the child was dead. But Jesus went with Jairus to his home, taking Peter, James and John with him. There they found that the mourning had already begun. Jesus told them that the child was merely sleeping, took her hand and bid her arise and take food. She awoke and was restored to life. While Luke says that Jesus told Jairus to tell no one about this, Matthew and Mark report that it caused a local sensation. (*Matthew 9:18–26, Mark 5:21–43, Luke 8:40–56*)

JAMES Apostle; brother of the apostle John, son of Zebedee, and the first Christian martyr. The brothers were fisherman on the Sea of

Jesus restores Jairus's daughter to life.

Left: Jesus calls James and John to follow him.

Galilee and probably lived at Capernaum. It was while they were at work that they were called by Jesus, shortly after he recruited Simon Peter and his brother Andrew. (*Mark 1:19–20*) James, together with his brother and Simon Peter, were Jesus' 'inner circle', present at the raising of Jairus' daughter (*Mark 5:37–43*) and also the Transfiguration. (*Matthew 16:1*) It was these three whom Jesus took into the Garden of Gethsemane on the eve of His arrest and who failed to keep watch that night as Jesus prayed. (*Mark 14:32–42*)

Some clue as to the characters of the two brothers can be found in the name Jesus gave them – Boanerges, 'the sons of thunder'. (*Mark 3:17, Luke 9:43*) They were evidently zealous but sometime excessively so, as when Christ rebuked them for suggesting that (in imitation

of Isaiah) they call down fire on a village that refused them hospitality. (*Luke 9:54*) They evidently also had high opinions of their worth, Jesus having to gently reproach them for asking to sit on either side of him when he attained his glory (*Matthew 20:20, Mark 10:35–41*), which request caused some little displeasure among the other disciples.

James was probably the elder of the two brothers, but he is generally placed third in the lists of the apostles in *Matthew 10:2, Mark 3:17, Luke 6:14* and *Acts 1:13*. He was the first Christian martyr (indeed, the only apostle whose death is described in the Bible), beheaded with a sword on the orders of Herod Agrippa I. (*Acts 12:1–2*) A later tradition asserted that he visited Spain, and his shrine at Santiago de Compostela in the north-west of the peninsula became a major centre of pilgrimage during the Middle Ages.

JAMES Half-brother of Jesus (*Galatians 1:19*) and first leader of the Church in Jerusalem after the Resurrection. Little is known about this James during Jesus' lifetime. Like his brothers, Joses, Simon and Judas, he found Jesus hard to understand at first – 'For neither did his brethren believe in him.' (*John 7:6*) He may have found his faith when he saw Jesus after the Resurrection just before he appeared before the apostles. (*I Corinthians 15:7*)

Not, therefore, one of Christ's disciples but joining the ranks of the apostles, he became the first leader of the Church in Jerusalem, possibly (in the traditional way) because he was next of kin to Jesus, possibly out of respect for him as a person of integrity. He is mentioned at the important meeting of the council in Jerusalem when Peter, Paul and Barnabas argued against the insistence of some that Gentile converts needed to be circumcised. James spoke last, and most sagaciously: they should not be burdened thus, but should be encouraged to accept the Jewish laws about food, so that Jews and Gentiles could sit at the same table and be as one. (*Acts 15:13–21*)

Pentecost: the Holy Spirit descends upon the apostles.

He is thought to be the author of the eponymous Epistle, which is one of the 'general epistles', addressed not to those in Palestine but to a wider circle beyond. Non-Biblical tradition relates that he died a martyr, being thrown off the roof of the Temple and then beaten to death.

JAMES the Younger, or the Lesser. Cousin of Jesus, he was the son of Alphaeus and is mentioned in lists of the apostles. (*Matthew 10:3, Mark 3:18, Luke 6:15, Acts 1:13*) He was present in the Upper Room after the Ascension and is linked with Thaddeus. Mark (*15:40*) names him as 'James the Less' whose mother was called Mary, mother also of Joses. (*Matthew 28:56, Mark 15:40, 47*) Nothing more is known of him.

JANNA son of Joseph, an ancestor of Christ. (*Luke 3:24*)

JASOU a kinsman of Paul, who entertained him and Silas in Thessalonica. (*Acts 17:5-9, Romans 16:21*).

James, half-brother of Jesus, at one of the meetings of the early Christians in Jerusalem.

JESUS CHRIST Son of God, the Messiah and the central figure in the Gospels of the New Testament.

Jesus' earthly parents were warned of His birth by angels: to His father, 'the angel of the Lord appeared unto him in a dream, saying, Joseph, thou son of David, fear not to take unto thee Mary thy wife: for that which is conceived in her is of the Holy Ghost. And she shall bring forth a son, and thou shalt call his name Jesus: for he shall save his people from their sins. Now all this was done, that it might be fulfilled which was spoken of the Lord by the prophet, saying, Behold, a virgin shall be with child, and shall bring forth a son, and they shall call his name Emmanuel, which being interpreted is, God with us.' (*Matthew 1:20–5*) To His virgin mother, Mary, 'the angel said

unto her, Fear not, Mary: for thou hast found favour with God. And, behold, thou shalt conceive in thy womb, and bring forth a son, and shalt call his name Jesus. He shall be great, and shall be called the Son of the Highest: and the Lord God shall give unto him the throne of his father David: And he shall reign over the house of Jacob for ever; and of his kingdom there shall be no end.' (*Luke 1:30–3*)

Jesus was born in Bethlehem, where Joseph had taken his wife for the Roman tax census. In the overcrowded town they were unable to find proper lodgings and were forced to stay in a stable, where the child Jesus was placed in a manger for a crib, visited by shepherds alerted by an angel: 'And the angel said unto them, Fear not: for, behold, I bring you good tidings of great joy ... For unto you is born this day in

The shepherds, summoned by an angel, pay homage to Jesus as he lies in the manger.

Left: Joseph leads Mary with Jesus into Egypt, fleeing from the massacre of innocent infants in Behtlehem decreed by King Herod.

Below: The twelve-year-old Jesus discovered in the Temple discoursing with the priests and elders.

the city of David a Saviour, which is Christ the Lord.' (*Luke 2:10–11*)

The coming of a Messiah, or 'anointed one', had long been predicted by prophets during the period covered by the Old Testament. And when Jesus was taken to the Temple for his presentation, Simeon at once recognized him, for 'it was revealed unto him by the Holy Ghost, that he should not see death, before he had seen the Lord's Christ. And he came by the Spirit into the temple: and when the parents brought in the child Jesus, to do for him after the custom of the law, Then took he him up in his arms, and blessed God, and said, Lord, now lettest thou thy servant depart in peace, according to thy word: For mine eyes have seen thy salvation, Which thou hast prepared before the face of all people; A light to lighten the Gentiles, and the glory of thy people Israel.' (*Luke 2:26–32*) Three 'wise men from the east' also sought him: 'Where is he that is born King of the Jews? for we have seen his star in the east, and are come to worship him.' (*Matthew 2:2*) But, 'when Herod the king

had heard these things, he was troubled, and all Jerusalem with him.' (*Matthew 2:3*) An angel warned Joseph, and the family fled to Egypt while a royal search for the child proved ineffective so Herod instituted a massacre of children under the age of two. Joseph, Mary and Jesus only returned after the death of the King, and Jesus grew up in Nazareth, working

189

in Joseph's carpentry shop. Even in childhood, He demonstrated a seemingly precocious knowledge, debating religious arguments with the priests in the Temple during a family visit to Jerusalem to celebrate the Passover. 'And Jesus increased in wisdom and stature, and in favour with God and man.' (*Luke 2:52*)

To the people of Israel, Jesus' coming was heralded by His cousin born six months His

elder, John the Baptist: 'In those days came John the Baptist, preaching in the wilderness of Judaea, And saying, Repent ye: for the kingdom of heaven is at hand. For this is he that was spoken of by the prophet Esaias [Elijah], saying, The voice of one crying in the wilderness, Prepare ye the way of the Lord, make his paths straight.' (*Matthew 3:1–3*) It was John who baptized Jesus, when He was about

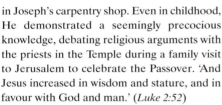

Top left: The baptism of Jesus in the waters of the Jordan.

Above: He chases the moneylenders and petty traders from the Temple.

Left: With His disciples.

thirty years of age, in the waters of the Jordan. (*Matthew 4:13–17, Luke 1:29–34*) But before His ministry could begin, He went into the wilderness, fasting, and was tempted by the devil – tempting Him to turn stone into bread, offering him power over all kingdoms of the world that could be His, 'if thou therefore wilt worship me, all shall be thine', and setting him on a high pinnacle and daring him to throw himself off. (*Matthew 4:1–11, Luke 4:1–13*)

Such was the effectiveness of John's preaching that when Jesus himself began to preach, spreading the word of God and teaching even in synagogues, people had already heard of Him and began to flock to hear him. He called forth a body of twelve disciples to help and support Him as He traveled the countryside, first about Galilee, then farther south, not only teaching but disputing the law with pharisees and sadducees, and performing miraculous healings. His message was often told in the

Above right: Jesus cures a leper: 'And it came to pass, when he was in a certain city, behold a man full of leprosy: who seeing Jesus fell on his face, and besought him, saying, Lord, if thou wilt, thou canst make me clean. And he put forth his hand, and touched him, saying, I will: be thou clean. And immediately the leprosy departed from him.' (*Luke 5:12*)

Right: The Sermon on the Mount, which includes the blessings known as the Beatitudes.

191

form of parables, using familiar themes and scenes to make it easy for the listeners to understand. At one point He ascended a mountain to pray overnight, descending to the lower slopes the next day to preach to a large crowd. In this address, which became known as the Sermon on the Mount, He set forth the Beatitudes (from the Latin meaning 'blessed' or 'happy'), elucidating His fundamental message, emphasizing the moral and spiritual aspects of the Law, the love of God, and how people should behave to one another. Great crowds gathered to hear Him speak, and twice He miraculously fed thousands with only a few fish and loaves. As His mission expanded, He sent out more of His followers to spread the word, at one point dispatching seventy. The four gospels, however, concentrate upon his personal activities – the individual conversations, the curing of lepers and blind beggars and his relationship with his disciples, some of whom were fishermen on the Sea of Galilee. Here He astounded them by calming a storm and later walking on the waters. His 'inner circle' of disciples, Peter, James and John, He took into the mountains 'and was transfigured before them: and his face did shine as the sun, and his raiment was white as the light. And, behold, there appeared unto them Moses and Elias [Elijah] talking with him … While he yet spake, behold, a bright cloud overshadowed them: and behold a voice out of the cloud, which said, This is my beloved Son, in whom I am well pleased; hear ye him.' (*Matthew 17:2–5*)

Thus His fame spread, the crowds grew large, and His followers multiplied. But those in power at the Temple, sensing that their authority, teachings and practices were threatened, became his enemies. He was perceived to be consorting with the poor and the despised, including tax men, and offended the priests by healing the sick even on the sabbath and throwing money-lenders and tradesmen from the Temple. When He raised Lazarus from the dead, they became truly concerned and began planning how to kill Him.

Such is the press of the crowd around Jesus that a sick man is let down through the roof to be healed.

Christ's joyous entry to Jerusalem the crowds laying branches in his path and crying 'Hosannah!'

192

Several times they tried to lay hands on Him or to trap Him. Their opportunity came, at last, during the week of the Passover, when Jesus and his disciples came to Jerusalem, staying just outside the city at Bethany with His friends, Mary, Martha and Lazarus. His initial entry to Jerusalem that Passover became a great celebration: 'And a very great multitude spread their garments in the way; others cut down branches from the trees, and strawed them in the way. And the multitudes that went before, and that followed, cried, saying, Hosanna to the Son of David: Blessed is he that cometh in the name of the Lord; Hosanna in the highest. And when he was come into Jerusalem, all the city was moved, saying, Who is this? And the multitude said, This is Jesus the prophet of Nazareth of Galilee.' (*Matthew 21:8–11*) Each day that week He came to the city, teaching and healing, talking to scribes, priests and ordinary people.

On the Wednesday night He did not return to Bethany but slept in the Mount of Olives; next day was the feast of the unleavened bread, and with His twelve disciples He took supper in an upper room in the city. He had already told then that He would be betrayed and crucified, and they did not want to believe Him. One of the twelve, Judas Iscariot, had

Top: The last Supper. Above: Jesus before Pilate.

been bribed for just this purpose. After eating, Jesus took his closest disciples to the garden of Gethsemane and prayed; then there came a band of armed men with torches, and Judas made the sign for which they looked: he kissed Jesus. After a scuffle, in which Peter chopped the ear off of one of the intruders, Malchus, Jesus cured the man and was taken for questioning. Before the Sanhedrin, the assembly of priests, elders and scribes presided over by Caiaphas, the High Priest, Jesus calmly parried their questions, which only enraged them, for in their hearts they had already condemned Him. But they could not punish Him. Only the Romans could do that, so He was brought before Pontius Pilate, the Roman governor, who had no interest in the case but whose great concern was the prevention of disorder. In truth, he could find no fault in Jesus; and an interview with Herod, the tetrarch, was inconclusive. Even a vicious scourging by the Roman guard, during which they mocked Him with a crown of thorns, was not enough for the mob, now incited to near-riot. To appease them, Pilate eventually consented to Jesus' crucifixion, symbolically washing his hands of the case.

The reversal of the mood in the city was reflected in the journey Jesus now made to the hill of Golgotha, called Calvary, carrying the heavy wooden cross upon which He was to meet death, through a jeering mob. When He fell, exhausted from the weight of the cross and the beating He had suffered, the Romans grabbed a man from the crowd, Simon of Cyrene, to bear the cross to its destination. There Jesus was stripped and nailed to the cross, which was hoisted into place between two criminals also being executed.

Long hours of agony ensued until 'it was

Left: The Crucifixion.

Above right: Mary Magdalene is the first to see the risen Jesus.

Above far right: The Ascension.

about the sixth hour, and there was a darkness over all the earth until the ninth hour. And the sun was darkened, and the veil of the temple was rent in the midst. And when Jesus had cried with a loud voice, he said, Father, into thy hands I commend my spirit: and having said thus, he gave up the ghost.' (*Luke 23:44–6*) Before the cross were several of his disciples, His mother and other of the women who had supported Him and the disciples during his missionary journeys. Now there came Joseph of Arimathaea, who had obtained permission to take the body, and Nicodemus, a pharisee, and they wrapped him in linen and laid Him in the tomb that Joseph had provided.

On the third day, several of the women came to the tomb to anoint the body but were amazed to find the stone door open and the tomb empty. They called Peter and John, but none of them truly understood what had happened. It was to Mary Magdalene that the risen Christ first showed himself, she mistaking him for the gardener. Three times after that He appeared to the disciples, at Emmaus, in

Jerusalem and on the shore of the Sea of Galilee, before His final appearance to them at Bethany, when He told them to continue his work, spreading the word of the Lord. Then He vanished, ascending to Heaven.

JOANNA Wife of Chuza, steward of Herod Antipas. She was among the group of women who ministered to Jesus and the disciples and was present before the cross. (*Luke 8:3; 24:10*)

JOHN Apostle, younger brother of James the Great, son of Zebedee and Salome; possibly a cousin of Jesus. (*Matthew. 4:21,25, 10:2, 27:56, Mark 1:59, 3:17, 10:35, 14:40*) The two brothers lived at Capernaum and were fishermen, working closely with Simon Peter and his brother Andrew. (*Luke 5:7–10*). John and Andrew were followers of John the Baptist until the preacher pointed out Jesus to them. After Jesus recruited Simon Peter and Andrew to be disciples, he found James and John farther along the shoreline and called them too. (*Matthew 4:21–2, Mark 1:19-20, Luke 5:10–11*)

Several times referred to in the Gospel according to John as the 'disciple whom Jesus loved' (*13:23, 19:26, 20:2, 21:7, 21:20*), John was one of the chosen 'inner circle' of disciples, with his brother and Simon Peter, who were with Jesus on three very special occasions: the raising of Jairus's daughter (*Mark 5:37–43*), the Transfiguration (*Matthew 16:1*), and in the Garden of Gethsemane on the night of Jesus' arrest (*Mark 14:32–42*). Jesus called him and James 'Boanerges, which is, The sons of thunder' because of their zeal and fiery

John with the women before the cross.

temperaments. (*Mark 3:17*) John was also the youngest of the disciples.

He sat next to Christ at the Last Supper, and upon prompting by Simon Peter asked Jesus to identify the one who would betray Him that night. (*John 13:23–5*) After the betrayal in Gethsemane he and Peter followed Christ at a distance while the others fled. (*John 18:15*) Being known to the High Priest, he was admitted to the palace but had to vouch for Peter's admittance (and it was at this point that Peter was recognized as a disciple and made the first of his three denials).

During the Crucifixion, John was with the women at the foot of the cross, and when Jesus saw them standing there he committed his mother to the care of John, 'And from that hour that disciple took her unto his own home'. (*John 19:25–7*) Later, when Mary Magdalene discovered the tomb to be open, she went at once to find Simon Peter and John, who ran back to the sepulcher, John outrunning Peter, 'And he stooping down, and looking in, saw the linen clothes lying; yet went he not in'. (*John 20:5*) After the Resurrection, he was with some of the other disciples fishing on the Sea of Galilee when Jesus appeared to them, and John was the first to recognize Him: 'Therefore that disciple whom Jesus loved saith unto Peter, It is the Lord.' (*John 21:7*)

After this, John worked with Peter in the Temple and was arrested by the authorities (*Acts 3*); he and Peter also preached among the Samaritans (*Acts 8:14*). Of his later years little is known save that he lived in Ephesus, being banished to Patmos for a time. (*Revelation 1:9*) The Gospel that bears his name is generally thought to have been written by him (possibly as long as twenty or thirty years later than the others) as are the three Epistles and *Revelation*, the full title of which is *The Revelation of St John the Divine*; the latter was written towards the end of the 1st century, when John was very old indeed. The Gospel according to John has been called the 'spiritual gospel' because it gives prominence to the teaching of Jesus and the relationship

between the Father and the Son on the one hand and that between Jesus and his disciples on the other. *Revelation*, the 66th and last book of the Bible, is the only prophetic book of the New Testament.

JOHN MARK See Mark.

JOHN THE BAPTIST Prophet, herald of the Messiah. His father, Zechariah, was a priest; his mother, Elisabeth, was also descended from Aaron and was a kinswoman of Mary, mother of Jesus. By the time of his birth his parents thought themselves too old to have children, but Zechariah was warned by the angel Gabriel that Elisabeth would bear a very special son. (*Luke 1:5–24, 57ff*) Elisabeth gave birth to John at Ein Karem six months before the birth of Jesus.

In fulfillment of Isaiah's prophesy, John became a Nazarite, with uncut hair, clad in camel's hair with leather girdle, living on locusts and wild honey in the Judaean wilderness. He began preaching, announcing the coming of the Messiah, 'And saying, Repent ye: for the kingdom of heaven is at

John the Baptist begins to preach.

Left: John the Baptist heralds the coming of Jesus.

Above: 'John seeth Jesus coming unto him, and saith, Behold the Lamb of God, which taketh away the sin of the world.' (John 1:29)

hand. For this is he that was spoken of by the prophet Esaias, [Elijah] saying, The voice of one crying in the wilderness, Prepare ye the way of the Lord, make his paths straight.' He baptized a growing number of followers in the waters of the Jordan, and when he was confronted by pharisees and sadducees he called them to repentance, naming them a 'generation of vipers'. (*Matthew 3, Mark 1:1–8, Luke 3:1–18, John 1:15ff*) He also baptized Christ (*Matthew 3:12–17*) and identified Jesus to Andrew (*John 1:40–4*), whereupon Jesus began to gather together those who would be his disciples.

As Jesus began his ministry, John continued baptizing and preaching, and word of these activities reached the palace of Herod Antipas, Tetrarch of Galilee and Peraea. When John condemned the marriage of that king to Herodias, his brother's wife, Herod imprisoned him but was afraid to execute him in view of the large numbers of followers he had built up in the countryside. In the desolation of Herod's prison, John had heard of Jesus's activities and sent word to be certain that he

was really the Messiah; Jesus sent back witnesses to his miracles. (*Matthew 11:1–6, Luke 7:18–23*)

Herod's incestuous wife finally seized the opportunity to have John executed when her daughter Salome danced before the King and was asked what reward she wanted for her performance. John was beheaded and his head presented to Herodias on a platter. (*Matthew 14:6–11, Mark 6:21–8*)

The activities of Jesus and John caused some confusion, since their identities as prophet and Messiah were not always clearly perceived. Herod too was mystified: 'And Herod said, John have I beheaded: but who is this, of whom I hear such things?' (*Luke 9:9*)

JOSEPH Father of Jesus. A descendant of David, Joseph was pledged in marriage to Mary, but before their wedding Mary conceived. An angel appeared in a dream to Joseph to reassure him and explain that the child she would bear had been conceived by the Holy Spirit and was to be called Jesus. So he married Mary, and when it was approaching the time for the child to be born they journeyed to Bethlehem in Galilee, his native

No room at the inn – Joseph finds no lodging in Bethlehem.

Joseph and Mary present the infant Jesus in the Temple, there to be met by a holy man named Simeon, who recognized the Messiah, whom had been told he would see before he died.

town and the place where David had been born, for the tax census that had been called by the Romans. There Mary gave birth. It was now rumored abroad that a child who would be 'King of the Jews' had been born: three strangers from the east were making enquiries. Naturally, Herod, King of Judea, was alert to the threat this might have to his throne, and he attempted to find the child. When the visitors from the east departed without advising him, and his searchers failed, Herod issued a command to execute all children under two years of age in the Bethlehem area. But Joseph, warned in a dream that this was about to happen, fled by night, taking Mary and the child to Egypt, where they awaited God's word to return. Upon the death of Herod, they came back but went to Nazareth, fulfilling the prophecy that Jesus would be called a Nazarene.

Joseph and Mary had taken Jesus to the Temple in Jerusalem for his purification ceremony; and thereafter they made the journey there to celebrate the Passover. On one occasion, when Jesus was still a child, they began their return journey without realizing that their twelve-year-old son was not with the group of pilgrims with whom they were traveling. Turning back, they found Jesus in the Temple talking and questioning the teachers. Thereafter, Jesus grew to manhood working in his father's carpentry shop before setting out on his ministry; and Joseph is mentioned no further in the Bible. He had four other sons, James, Joses, Simon and Judas, and an unknown number of daughters. (*Matthew 1, 2, Luke 2:4–7*)

JOSEPH BARSABBAS See Barsabbas.

JOSEPH OF ARIMATHEA A wealthy and respected member of the Jewish council in Jerusalem, who was a secret follower of Jesus and did not consent to the Sanhedrin's verdict on Christ's fate. He approached Pontius Pilate to ask for Jesus' body after the Crucifixion, that he might give it proper burial. For this he appears to have provided his own family sepulcher. Jesus' body was taken down from the cross, wrapped in a linen shroud and taken to the empty tomb, which was closed with a large round piece of stone. A romantic tradition tells of Joseph's subsequent voyage to England, bearing the Holy Grail, the chalice used at the Last Supper, which engendered a number of medieval legends. (*Matthew 27:57, 59, Mark 15:43,45, Luke 23:50, John 19:38*)

JOSES Brother of James the Less, son of Mary, who is named as one of the women before the cross at the Crucifixion. (*Matthew 28:56, Mark 15:40,47*)

JOSES Half-brother of Jesus, son of Joseph and Mary, brother also of James, Judas and Simon. (*Matthew 13:55, Mark 6:3*)

JUDA The father of Simeon in the genealogy of Christ (*Luke 3:30*) and the father of Joseph in the same genealogy.

JUDAS Apostle. See Thaddaeus.

JUDAS Half-brother of Jesus, son of Joseph and Mary, brother also of James, Joses and Simon. (*Matthew 13:55, Mark 6:3*)

JUDAS BARSABBAS Prominent Christian of Antioch who went with Paul and Barnabas to Jerusalem to discuss the issue of preaching to the Gentiles, and with Silas returned to Antioch to inform the church elders there of the decision. (*Acts 15*)

JUDAS ISCARIOT Son of Simon and the only disciple who was not of Galilee. His name has become a byword for betrayal. There is no mention of Judas until late in the Gospels. It was Judas who objected to Martha anointing Jesus' feet with spikenard, saying that the ointment, which was expensive, should have been sold and the money given to the poor – not that he cared for the poor, says the Gospel according to John, but because he was a thief. (*12:4–6*)

As the Passover approached, 'Then entered Satan into Judas surnamed Iscariot, being of the number of the twelve', and he went to the priests in Jerusalem offering to betray Jesus to them while he was alone and away from the crowds. (*Luke 22:3–6, Mark 14:10*) At the Last Supper, Jesus announced to the disciples that one of their number would that night betray him, and John was prompted by Peter to ask who it would be. 'Jesus answered, He it is, to whom I shall give a sop, when I have dipped it. And when he had dipped the sop, he gave it to Judas Iscariot, the son of Simon. And after the sop Satan entered into him. Then said Jesus unto him, That thou doest, do quickly. Now no man at the table knew for what intent he spake this unto him. For some of them thought, because Judas had the bag, that Jesus had said unto him, Buy those things that we have need of against the feast; or, that he should give something to the poor. He then having

Right: Joseph of Arimathea, and the women who were before the cross, wrap the body of Jesus in linen at the sepulcher.

Jesus kisses Jesus, the sign awaited by those who came to arrest him.

received the sop went immediately out: and it was night.' (*John 13:24–30*)

Later, as Jesus prayed in the Garden of Gethsemane, Judas came with 'a great multitude with swords and staves, from the chief priests and elders of the people' and kissed Him as a sign to the priests' men, and they seized Him. (*Matthew 26:47–9, Mark 14:43–5, Luke 22:47–8, John 18:2–5*) The following morning, Judas repented and returned the thirty pieces of silver he had been paid, casting them down before the priests, who did not put the money back into the treasury, for 'it was the price of blood'; instead they took the money to buy a potter's field to be used for the burial of strangers; it became known as 'the field of blood'. According to *Matthew 27: 3–5*, Judas then went and hanged himself; according to *Acts 1:16–19*, when the apostles were deciding upon a replacement for Judas, Peter told them that Judas purchased the field himself and 'fell headlong', whereupon 'all his bowels gushed out'.

JULIA A Christian at Rome to whom Paul sent greetings in *Romans 16:15*.

JULIUS Roman centurion who took Paul from Caesarea to Rome. He treated Paul with respect, allowing him off the ship at Sidon to visit friends. At Myra, in Lycia, they transferred to a ship from Alexandria bound for Italy but made very slow progress across the eastern Mediterranean. When they touched at an anchorage called The Fair Havens, near Lasea on the southern coast of Crete, Paul questioned the wisdom of attempting the longest part of the journey, almost due west, as the weather was becoming bad, but Julius preferred the advice of the master and owner (to whom 'time was money') that they should proceed. Paul was right: bad weather pursued them, culminating in a great storm on the fourteenth night. Paul reassured the passengers and crew that all would be well, but the prospects cannot have appeared good. Making for land, the ship ran aground and began to break up. The soldiers aboard wanted to kill the prisoners, including Paul, in case they escaped, but Julius refused. All escaped to dry land, which was the island of Melita (Malta). Here they were well treated for three months while waiting for another Alexandrian ship to sail for Syracuse and then up the west coast of Italy to Rome, where Julius delivered Paul to the captain of the guard. (*Acts 27, 28:16*)

JUNIA A Christian in Rome mentioned in Paul's Epistle to the *Romans, 16:7*: 'Salute Andronicus and Junia, my kinsmen, and my fellow prisoners, who are of note among the apostles, who also were in Christ before me.'

JUPITER Sovereign god of the Romans. At Iconium, Barnabas and Paul were mistaken for gods, which vexed the two apostles greatly: 'And they called Barnabas, Jupiter; and Paul, Mercurius, because he was the chief speaker. Then the priest of Jupiter, which was before their city, brought oxen and garlands unto the gates, and would have done sacrifice with the people.' (*Acts 14: 12–13*)

JUSTUS BARSABBAS See Barsabbas.

LAZARUS Brother of Mary and Martha, Jesus' close friends who lived in Bethany. He fell sick and the two sisters sent a message to Jesus, who was not in Judaea at that time. After two days, by which time Lazarus had died, Jesus set out for Bethany – against the advice of his disciples, who pointed out that last time they were in Judaea they were nearly stoned. At Bethany they were greeted by Martha, to whom Jesus said that her brother would rise again. Martha thought he meant at the resurrection, but Jesus corrected her: 'I am the resurrection, and the life: he that believeth in me, though he were dead, yet shall he live: And whosoever liveth and believeth in me shall never die.' Mary arrived, saying that if only Jesus had been there, Lazarus would not have died. Luke reports that Jesus groaned inwardly, for even these friends and followers found it hard to believe fully that he could raise their brother. Lazarus's tomb was a cave. Jesus called Lazarus forth. 'And he that was dead came forth, bound hand and foot with graveclothes: and his face was bound about with a napkin.' (*John 11*) The news of this caused a sensation, and the Jewish leaders became determined to kill Jesus. When Jesus went to Jerusalem at the beginning of Passion

Left: Jesus raises Lazarus from the dead – 'he cried with a loud voice, Lazarus, come forth. And he that was dead came forth, bound hand and foot with graveclothes: and his face was bound about with a napkin. Jesus saith unto them, Loose him, and let him go.' (John 11:43–4)

week, crowds gathered not only to see Jesus but Lazarus also, who had been raised from the dead, and the chief priests decided they should make an end of him too. (*John 12:9–10, 17–18*)

The parable of Lazarus; dogs lick his sores.

LAZARUS A beggar who featured in one of Christ's parables demonstrating that the wealthy shall go to hell while the poor go to heaven. The rich man has come to be known as Dives, meaning 'wealthy'. (*Luke 16:19–31*)

LEBBAEUS One of the apostles (*Matthew 10:3*), surnamed Thaddaeus, and probably the same as 'Judah the brother of James'. (*Luke 6:16, Jude 1*)

LEVI Two of the ancestors of Christ. (*Luke 3:24, 29*)

LEVI Son of Alphaeus (*Mark 2:14, Luke 5:27, 29*); called also Matthew in *Matthew 9:9*.

LINUS One of Paul's friends at Rome. (*II Timothy 4:21*).

LOIS Grandmother of Timothy. (*2 Timothy 1:5*).

LUCAS A fellow-laborer of Paul. (*Philemon 24, Colossians 4:14*)

LUCIUS of Cyrene. A kinsman of Paul, and one of the prophets and teachers at Antioch. (*Acts 13:1, Romans 16:21*)

LUKE Evangelist who wrote the third Gospel and the *Acts of the Apostles*. He was a physician (*Colossians 4:14*) and accompanied Paul on some of his journeys. The first distinct reference to him is in *Acts 16*, when he joined Paul at Troas (*8, 10–13*). Paul left Luke in Philippi and was joined by him at the same place seven years later (*20:3–5*). He accompanied Paul to Jerusalem (*Acts 21:17*) and to Rome (*27, 28*). He is mentioned in the *Epistles to the Colossians* (*4:54*), to *Philemon* (*1:24*), and *II Timothy 4:11*, which were all written in Rome. Possibly an early convert to Christianity, and not a direct eyewitness to the events he described, Luke addressed both his books to one Theophilius, who is believed to have been a Gentile Christian.

LYDIA A Christian woman of Thyatira: 'And a certain woman named Lydia, a seller of purple,

Luke the Evangelist.

Paul's bucolic first conversation with Lydia: 'And on the sabbath we went out of the city by a river side, where prayer was wont to be made; and we sat down, and spake unto the women which resorted thither.' (Acts 16:13)

of the city of Thyatira, which worshipped God, heard us: whose heart the Lord opened, that she attended unto the things which were spoken of Paul. And when she was baptized, and her household, she besought us, saying, If ye have judged me to be faithful to the Lord, come into my house, and abide there.' (*Acts 16:14–15*)

LYSANIAS tetrarch of Abilene. (Luke 3:1)

LYSIAS, CLAUDIUS The chief captain of the Roman garrison in Jerusalem, who rescued Paul from the mob, and, after hearing the charges against him, sent him to Caesarea to be tried by Felix. (*Acts 21:35; 23:33*) He purchased his Roman citizenship. (*Acts 22:28*)

M

MALCHUS A servant of the High Priest Caiaphas present at the arrest of Jesus in Gethsemane. Peter cut off his right ear, and Christ touched the ear, healing him. (*Luke 22:49–51; John 18–10*)

MARK (Marcus; his Jewish name was John) Evangelist, author of the second Gospel. Nephew of Barnabas, he accompanied Paul and Barnabas on a number of missionary journeys. His mother Mary lived in Jerusalem and was a Christian. (*Acts 12:12, 17*)

Barnabas and Paul took him with them to Antioch (*Acts 12:25*), and he accompanied them on their first missionary journey as far as Perga in Pamphylia (*13:2–13*) before he returned to Jerusalem. Some years later, when Paul proposed to Barnabas that they should revisit the cities where they had preached the Gospel, they disagreed about taking Mark with them. Paul refused to take him because he had left them before, and chose Silas; so Mark went with his uncle Barnabas to Cyprus, his native country. He was with Peter when he wrote his first Epistle, but he was again with Paul during his first imprisonment at Rome. (*Colossians 4:10, Philemon 24*) After this he was with Timothy in Ephesus. (*II Timothy 4:11*)

The Gospel of Mark is generally thought to have been the first of the Gospels to be written, providing much material that is almost identical in the others, shortly after Peter's death in Rome. Mark is seen as the disciple and 'interpreter' of Peter, who looked upon him as his spiritual son. (*I Peter 5:13*) It is the shortest of the Gospels and appears to be aimed at a Gentile readership outside Palestine. (*Acts 12:12,25, 13:13, 15:36–9, Colossians 4:10, Philemon 24, Peter 5:13, II Timothy 4:11*)

MARTHA Sister of Mary and Lazarus, Jesus' close friends who lived in Bethany, whom he visited often. On one visit, while Martha was busy serving food, Mary sat at Jesus' feet and listened to him. When Martha complained about having to do all the work, Jesus gently

Peter cuts off Malchus's ear.

replied: 'Martha, Martha, thou art careful and troubled about many things: But one thing is needful: and Mary hath chosen that good part, which shall not be taken away from her.' (*Luke 10:38–42*) When Lazarus fell sick, the sisters sent for Jesus, but their brother was dead by the

Jesus reproves Martha for calling her sister away from Him.

time he arrived. Martha met Jesus outside the town, and he told her Lazarus would rise from the dead. At first she thought he meant at the resurrection, and he had to explain that 'he that believeth in me, though he were dead, yet shall he live'. (*John 11*) Jesus stayed with the family at Bethany during Passion week. (*John 12:1ff*)

MARY The Virgin Mary, mother of Jesus. *The Gospel of Luke* tells us that 'the angel Gabriel was sent from God unto a city of Galilee, named Nazareth, To a virgin espoused to a man whose name was Joseph, of the house of David; and the virgin's name was Mary.' Gabriel explained to Mary that she was to bear the Son of God, and his name was to be Jesus. Mary protested, 'How shall this be, seeing I know not a man? And the angel answered and said unto her, The Holy Ghost shall come upon thee …' He also told her that her cousin, Elisabeth, was six months with child, and Mary hastened to share her news. She stayed with Elisabeth for about three months, after which Elisabeth gave birth to the child that would be John the Baptist. (*Luke 1*)

When it was nearly time for Mary to give birth, a tax census decreed by the Romans

Mary, mother of Jesus and Elisabeth (sitting), mother of John the Baptist.

caused Mary and Joseph to make the journey to Joseph's home town, Bethlehem, 'the city of David'. Here Jesus was born, and when Mary's days of purification were over (according to the law) she and Joseph took the child to present him to the Lord and offer sacrifice, where

Mary is told by the archangel Gabriel that she will bear the Son of God.

Mary waits as Joseph tries to find a room at an inn in Bethlehem.

they met a devout man named Simeon, to whom it had been revealed 'by the Holy Ghost, that he should not see death, before he had seen the Lord's Christ.' Both he and an aged prophetess called Anna recognized the child and gave thanks to the Lord.

When three 'wise men from the east' came looking for the child that was said to be King of

Mary cradles the child Jesus as the three 'wise men from the east' pay homage and present gold, frankincense, and myrrh.

Above left: The holy family flee to Egypt to avoid Herod's wrath.

Above: 'And the child grew, and waxed strong in spirit, filled with wisdom: and the grace of God was upon him.' (Luke 2:40)

Left: The marriage at Cana, where Jesus turns water into wine.

Joseph, forewarned of this by an angel, took Mary and Jesus to Egypt, where they stayed until the death of Herod. They then settled in Nazareth, making annual pilgrimages to Jerusalem at Passover. (*Luke 2*)

When Jesus had grown to manhood and had been baptized by John, he began his ministry, gathering disciples and preaching. Mary is mentioned when Jesus attended a marriage at Cana in Galilee and the wine began to run out. When Mary pointed this out to Jesus, he called for six stone water pots and miraculously changed the water into wine. (*John 2:1–12*)

The four Gospels make no further mention of Mary until the Crucifixion, where, with the women who had supported Jesus and were his friends, she stood before the cross, and Jesus committed her to the care of the apostle John. (*John 19:25-27*) She is last mentioned after the

the Jews, King Herod was alerted to what he saw as a threat to his throne and, having had searches made fruitlessly in the Bethlehem area, decreed that all children there under the age of two years should be slaughtered. But

Mary Magdalene wipes Christ's feet with her hair.

Mary Magdalene is first to see the risen Christ.

Ascension, as praying in an upper room with the eleven apostles. (*Acts 1:13, 14*)

MARY MAGDALENE (Mary of Magdala, on the western shore of the Sea of Galilee) The first witness of the resurrection of Christ, Mary has traditionally been seen as a model of penitence. She is first identified in the narrative of Christ's ministry in *Luke 8:2* as a woman who 'had been healed of evil spirits and infirmities, Mary called Magdalene, out of whom went seven devils', so she was evidently seen as being possessed by evil spirits. Tradition – but not the Bible – links her story to that of a 'sinful woman' in *Luke 7:37–9*: 'And, behold, a woman in the city, which was a sinner, when she knew that Jesus sat at meat in the Pharisee's house, brought an alabaster box of ointment, And stood at his feet behind him weeping, and began to wash his feet with tears, and did wipe them with the hairs of her head, and kissed his feet, and anointed them with the ointment. Now when the Pharisee

which had bidden him saw it, he spake within himself, saying, This man, if he were a prophet, would have known who and what manner of woman this is that toucheth him: for she is a sinner.'

She became one of Jesus' followers and friends, giving domestic support to the disciples as they traveled about the country. She was thus one of the intimate group of women who are described in three of the Gospels as 'looking on afar off' upon the crucifixion. (*Matthew 27:56, Mark 15:40* and *John 19:25*) Later she went with Joseph of Arimathea and Mary the mother of Joses to the sepulcher to place the body in the tomb. (*Mark 15:47*)

During the Sabbath, the priests set a watch on the tomb to ensure no one removed the body, but the following day Mary Magdalene came with several of the other women, including Joanna and Mary the mother of James, to anoint the body with sweet spices. They found the tomb empty. (*Matthew 28:1*,

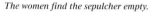

The women find the sepulcher empty.

The body of Jesus is taken down from the cross.

Luke 24:10) According to *Mark 16:9*: 'Now when Jesus was risen early the first day of the week, he appeared first to Mary Magdalene, out of whom he had cast seven devils.' *John 20:11–18* tells of Mary's visit to the tomb alone; finding it empty, she ran to tell Simon Peter and John. When they departed, 'Mary stood without at the sepulchre weeping: and as she wept, she stooped down, and looked into the sepulchre ... And when she had thus said, she turned herself back, and saw Jesus standing, and knew not that it was Jesus. Jesus saith unto her, Woman, why weepest thou? whom seekest thou? She, supposing him to be the gardener, saith unto him, Sir, if thou have borne him hence, tell me where thou hast laid him, and I will take him away. Jesus saith unto her, Mary. She turned herself, and saith unto him, Rabboni; which is to say, Master. Jesus saith unto her, Touch me not; for I am not yet ascended to my Father: but go to my brethren, and say unto them, I ascend unto my Father, and your Father; and to my God, and your God. Mary Magdalene came and told the disciples that she had seen the Lord, and that he had spoken these things unto her.'

MARY Mother of James and Joses. She was one of the group of women who ministered to the domestic needs of Jesus and the disciples but is only mentioned at the Crucifixion and sepulcher. During the Crucifixion, 'many women were there beholding afar off, which followed Jesus from Galilee, ministering unto him: Among which was Mary Magdalene, and Mary the mother of James and Joses, and the mother of Zebedee's children.' (*Matthew 27:56*; also *Mark 15:40*) She accompanied Mary Magdalene and Joseph of Artimathea when they took Jesus' body to the tomb (*Matthew 27: 61, Mark 15:47*), and on the day after the Sabbath came with the other women to anoint the body with sweet spices only to discover the tomb empty. (*Matthew 28:1, Mark 16:1ff and Luke 24:10*)

MARY Mother of (John) Mark the Evangelist, author of the second Gospel. Mark's mother is referred to just once, in *Acts 12:12*; her house in Jerusalem was evidently one of the early meeting places for the Christians, and it was here that Peter came after he had been miraculously released from prison: 'And when he had considered the thing, he came to the house of Mary the mother of John, whose surname was Mark; where many were gathered together praying.'

MARY Sister of Martha and Lazarus, Jesus' close friends in Bethany. When Lazarus fell ill, she and Martha sent for Jesus, but Lazarus was dead by the time Jesus arrived. Martha met him outside the town, while Mary waited at the house then met Jesus at the grave, where Jesus called Lazarus back from the dead. (*John 11*) During Passion week, Jesus stayed with the family at Bethany, and on the first night, when Martha served them food, Mary 'anointed the feet of Jesus, and wiped his feet with her hair: and the house was filled with the odour of the ointment.' (*John 12:1ff*)

Left: Jesus calls Matthew, the tax collector in his booth, to follow Him.

MARY Wife of Cleopas. One of the group of women who looked after the everyday needs of Jesus and the disciples, she is named in *John 19:25* as standing by the cross with her sister, the mother of Jesus, and Mary Magdalene. They were together at His burial and came to bring spices on the morning of the resurrection.

MATTHEW Apostle and Evangelist, son of Alphaeus. The Gospels of Mark and Luke refer to him as Levi. A tax-collector, or publican (from the Latin, meaning a civil servant) Matthew worked for the Romans; he thus followed an occupation despised by most Jews, who considered him a 'sinner'. So it came as a shock when Jesus recruited Matthew from his tax booth to follow him and become a disciple. (*Matthew 9:9, Mark 2:14, Luke 6:27–8*) Being a tax collector made him a relatively wealthy man, and he gave a grand feast with Jesus as guest of honor. There were many of his associates there, which provoked some criticism from the pharisees and scribes: 'And it came to pass, that, as Jesus sat at meat in his house, many publicans and sinners sat also together with Jesus and his disciples: for there were many, and they followed him. And when the scribes and Pharisees saw him eat with publicans and sinners, they said unto his disciples, How is it that he eateth and drinketh with publicans and sinners? When Jesus heard it, he saith unto them, They that are whole have no need of the physician, but they that are sick: I came not to call the righteous, but sinners to repentance.' (*Mark 2:14–17*) Matthew's is the first of the Gospels, but since much of the material is practically identical to that in Mark, it is thought that Mark was one of his sources. *The Gospel According to Matthew* was written with Jews in mind, rather than Gentiles as in the case of Mark, and concentrates upon Jesus as the Messiah, with Old Testament references, and as a teacher. Matthew is listed among the disciples in the Gospels in *Matthew 10:7, Mark 3:18, Luke 6:15* and *John 1:13.*

MATTHIAS Apostle, chosen by the assembled disciples after the Resurrection to replace Judas Iscariot and make the number up to the original twelve, in preference to Joseph or Justus Barsabbas. This was done by casting lots. (*Acts 1:23–6*)

MERCURIUS (Mercury) Roman or Italic god of circulation and movement (of goods, people and words), and thus patron of shopkeepers and transporters of goods. At Iconium, Barnabas and Paul were mistaken for gods, which caused the two apostles to tear their clothes in near-apoplectic frustration – 'And they called Barnabas, Jupiter; and Paul, Mercurius, because he was the chief speaker. Then the priest of Jupiter, which was before their city, brought oxen and garlands unto the gates, and would have done sacrifice with the people.' (*Acts 14: 12–13*)

MESSIAH See Jesus Christ.

NATHANAEL A native of Cana in Galilee, described by Christ as 'an Israelite indeed, in whom is no guile' and identified with Bartholomew. (*John 1:45*)

NICODEMUS A pharisee of Jerusalem who was a secret follower of Jesus. Nicomedus came to talk to Jesus by night, fearing that his interest in Jesus' message would lessen his influence in the Sanhedrin, of which he was a member. (*John 3:1–21*) Nicodemus had difficulty in grasping the importance of what Jesus was saying, but when the priests later condemned Jesus, Nicodemus interjected: 'Doth our law judge any man, before it hear him, and know what he doeth?' (*John 7: 50–1*) After the Crucifixion, Nicodemus brought a mixture of myrrh and aloes and helped Joseph of Arimathaea take Jesus' body to the tomb and bind it in linen cloth. (*John 19:39–42*)

ONESIMUS A slave of Philemon, a Christian of Colosse, who escaped from his master, and was converted at Rome by Paul, who lent him back to Philemon, bearing the Epistle of that name. Paul affectionately calls him 'my son' and offers to repay any wrong Onesimus may have done to his master. Tychicus accompanied him with the *Epistle to the Colossians*. (*Colossians 4:7–9, Epistle to Philemon*)

ONESIPHORUS A Christian who befriended Paul at Rome and at Ephesus. (*II Timothy 1:16–18; 4:35*)

Onesimus returns to his master, Philemon, bearing a letter from Paul.

Left: Nicomedus's night visit to Jesus.

P·Q·R

PARMENAS One of the seven disciples (with Stephen, Philip, Prochorus, Nicanor, Timon, and Nicolas) elected to become deacons – to take over the administrative burdens of the early church, which were interfering with the apostles' principal work in spreading the Gospel. This generally involved looking after the financial affairs of the early church as well as caring for widows and the poor. (*Acts 6:5*)

PATROBAS A Christian in Rome to whom Paul sent a greeting in *Romans 16:14*.

PAUL/SAUL Second only to Jesus himself, Paul is the most significant figure in the New Testament; indeed, it is largely due to his evangelism that Christianity became a religion distinct from Judaism that spread beyond the Holy Land. His writings constitute the earliest

Left: Paul (then named Saul) watches the stoning of Stephen.

Right: Paul's conversion on the road to Damascus to persecute the Christians there. 'And as he journeyed, he came near Damascus: and suddenly there shined round about him a light from heaven: And he fell to the earth, and heard a voice saying unto him, Saul, Saul, why persecutest thou me? And he said, Who art thou, Lord? And the Lord said, I am Jesus whom thou persecutest: it is hard for thee to kick against the pricks.' (Acts 9:3–5)

Christian literature, some actually predating the Gospels.

Born a pharisee Jew in Tarsus, his original name was Saul, and his father was a Roman. He is first mentioned in *Acts 7:58, 8:1* as a witness to the stoning of Stephen, and his conversion from persecutor to believer on the road to Damascus is one of the most dramatic episodes in the New Testament. (*Acts 9:1–31, 22:5–16,*

26:12–18) Paul's induction into the evangelical community at Damascus was effected by Barnabas, and the two men began to preach farther afield, into Asia Minor and Cyprus. Their experiences, including many illuminating anecdotes, are vividly related in *Acts*.

His role in determining the apostles' decision to convert non-Jews was crucial (*Acts 15:1–35*); thereafter his travels with Barnabas, Silas and

other companions including Timothy made many converts even as far as Greece and Macedonia. Their activities, however, were not always well received, engendering riots, as in Iconium, where Paul was stoned (*Acts 14:19*), Philippi (*Acts 16:22*) and Ephesus (*Acts 19:24–41*); while they were detained by the authorities at Philippi (*Acts 16:23*) and Corinth (*Acts 18:12–17*); then finally in Jerusalem (*Acts 21:27ff*). There he was prosecuted by the priests, which led to his incarceration for more than two years until he appealed to Rome for justice (*Acts 25*). His voyage there was interrupted by shipwreck at Malta. (*Acts 27*) In the imperial capital, he spent two years under house arrest but was allowed to preach. (*Acts 28*) According to tradition he was executed as part of the persecutions under the Emperor Nero.

Scenes from the life of Paul. Above left: In Troas, Paul has a vision of a Macedonian asking the apostles to preach in Macedonia. Above right: imprisoned in Philippi, an earthquakes opens the doors to the prison, terrifying the guard, who is later baptized.

His importance as an evangelist is immense, but so too are his writings (Epistles), which are not treatises or histories but genuine letters – to the Galatians, two to the Corinthians, the Romans, two to the Thessalonians, the Ephesians, the Philippians, the Colossians, and personal letters to Philemon, Timothy and Titus. Their importance to the theology of the church has been profound, and they also reveal the great network of Christian workers he had created in Syria, Asia Minor and Greece.

PAULUS, SERGIUS Roman proconsul in Cyprus during the visit of Paul and Barnabas. He enquired about Paul and his message and was converted after Paul, invoking the name of the Lord, struck blind the interfering sorcerer Elmyas. (*Acts 13:7, 12*)

PERSIS A Roman Christian woman and friend of Paul, to whom he sent greetings in *Romans 16:12*.

Right: 'I have fought the good fight.' The last days of Paul, in prison in Rome.

Above left: Paul travels from Jerusalem to Caesarea under heavy escort because of the threats to his life. Above right: Shipwrecked on Malta, the survivors make a fire. A poisonous snake bites Paul's hand to no effect.

PETER (Simon Peter) (*Mark 1:16*) Peter was one of the three or four most important characters in early Christianity and is generally regarded as the leader of the apostles. A Galilean fisherman, married and living with his wife and family in Capernaum, he was the brother of Andrew, who brought him to meet Jesus. Peter was the first to declare belief in Christ's divinity: 'He saith unto them, But whom say ye that I am? And Simon Peter answered and said, Thou art the Christ, the Son of the living God. And Jesus answered and said unto him, Blessed art thou, Simon Barjona: for flesh and blood hath not revealed it unto thee, but my Father which is in heaven. And I say also unto thee, That thou art Peter [Cephas, 'rock' in Greek], and upon this rock I will build my church; and the gates of hell shall not prevail against it. And I will give unto thee the keys of the kingdom of heaven.' (*Mark 16:15–19*)

One of the 'inner circle' of disciples, with James and John, he was present at the raising of Jairus's daughter (*Mark 5:37–43*) and at the

Peter attempts to emulate Christ and walk upon the water, but his faith fails him, and Jesus holds him up.

221

Above left: The Transfiguration, which only Peter and the 'inner circle' of disciples witnessed.

Above: Peter recognized as a follower of Jesus after Jesus' arrest. He fulfills Jesus' prediction that he would betray Him thrice before cock crow.

Left and above right: In the aftermath of the Crucifixion and Resurrection, Peter and John heal and teach in the Temple area.

Above far right: Such activities incurred the wrath of the religious authorities, who cast them into prison. But an angel appeared and threw open all the doors.

Transfiguration (*Mark 9:2*): 'Jesus taketh with him Peter, and James, and John, and leadeth them up into an high mountain apart by themselves: and he was transfigured before them. And his raiment became shining, exceeding white as snow; so as no fuller on earth can white them. And there appeared unto them Elias with Moses: and they were talking with Jesus. And Peter answered and said to Jesus, Master, it is good for us to be here: and let us make three tabernacles; one for thee, and one for Moses, and one for Elias. For he wist not what to say; for they were sore afraid.' (*Mark 9:2–6*)

He was with the other two in Gethsemane on the night of Christ's arrest, unable to keep awake as Jesus prayed. (*Mark 14:32–42*) After Jesus was led away to be interrogated, the disciples followed at a distance. Jesus had predicted that Peter would deny him thrice before the cock crowed. 'And as Peter was beneath in the palace, there cometh one of the maids of the high priest: And when she saw Peter warming himself, she looked upon him, and said, And thou also wast with Jesus of Nazareth. But he denied, saying, I know not, neither understand I what thou sayest. And he

went out into the porch; and the cock crew. And a maid saw him again, and began to say to them that stood by, This is one of them. And he denied it again. And a little after, they that stood by said again to Peter, Surely thou art one of them: for thou art a Galilaean, and thy speech agreeth thereto. But he began to curse and to swear, saying, I know not this man of whom ye speak. And the second time the cock crew. And Peter called to mind the word that Jesus said unto him, Before the cock crow twice, thou shalt deny me thrice. And when he thought thereon, he wept.' (*Mark 14: 66–72*)

On the third day, alerted by the women that the tomb was empty, he and John 'ran unto the sepulcher; and stooping down, he beheld the linen clothes laid by themselves, and departed, wondering in himself at that which was come to pass.' (*Luke 24:12*) With the other disciples he later saw the risen Jesus himself.

After the Ascension he assumed a leading role among the apostles in carrying forth the message, preaching and healing, then boldly defending his faith when challenged by the priests in Jerusalem (*Acts 4:1–21*). When their activities provoked the priests to action, they 'laid their hands on the apostles, and put them

Peter's vision at Joppa. This and the baptism of Cornelius convinced Peter about the correctness of admitting Gentiles to the church.

in the common prison. But the angel of the Lord by night opened the prison doors, and brought them forth, and said, Go, stand and speak in the temple to the people all the words of this life.' (*Acts 5:18–20*)

In admitting the centurion Cornelius to the faith (Acts 10), he opened the way to the Gentiles, hotly debating with Paul about evangelising non-Jews. (*Galatians 1:18, 2:11, 14*) He was guided in this by a vision that clarified the lack of need for the Jewish dietary constraints: 'as they went on their journey, and drew nigh unto the city, Peter went up upon the housetop to pray about the sixth hour: And he became very hungry, and would have eaten: but while they made ready, he fell into a trance, And saw heaven opened, and a certain vessel descending unto him, as it had been a great sheet knit at the four corners, and let down to the earth: Wherein were all manner of fourfooted beasts of the earth, and wild beasts, and creeping things, and fowls of the air. And there came a voice to him, Rise, Peter; kill, and eat. But Peter said, Not so, Lord; for I have never eaten any thing that is common or unclean. And the voice spake unto

him again the second time, What God hath cleansed, that call not thou common. This was done thrice: and the vessel was received up again into heaven.' (*Acts 10:9–16*)

According to tradition he ended his days a martyr in Rome, where he is said to have been crucified (at his own request upside down, since he deemed himself unworthy to die in the same way as Jesus) during the persecutions of the Emperor Nero. As such he was seen by the church as the first bishop of Rome, and his tomb lies beneath the magnificent basilica that bears his name.

PHANUEL A man of the tribe of Aser and the father of the prophetess Anna, who gave thanks in the temple at seeing the child Jesus. (*Luke 2:36, 38*)

PHILEMON A man of means in Colosse who was converted by Paul at Ephesus and afterwards entertained fellow Christians for worship at his house. The personal letter that bears his name is the shortest of Paul's writings. It asks Philemon, Paul's 'beloved and fellow worker' to receive Onesimus no longer as a slave but as a Christian brother. (*Epistle to Philemon*)

PHILETUS A heretical preacher who, with Hymenaeus, taught erroneously about the resurrection. (*II Timothy 2:17–18*)

PHILIP One of the earliest of the twelve disciples, whom Jesus approached rather than Philip coming forward – Jesus simply said 'Follow me' (*John 1:43–49*) – after which he brought Nathanael to Jesus. He came from Bethsaida in Galilee, but his name is Greek rather than Hebrew; later when a party of Greeks came to see Jesus, it was Philip whom they approached as intermediary. (*John 12:20–2*) At the feeding of the five thousand, he was the disciple who expressed doubts whether so few loaves and fishes would feed five thousand people. (*John 6:5–7*) In tradition, he died a martyr at Hieropolis, being flogged, imprisoned and crucified.

PHILIP One of the seven deacons chosen by the apostles (*Acts 6:1–1*), he later became a successful evangelist and among those expelled from Jerusalem in the persecution after the death of Stephen but who was then involved in missionary activity (*Acts 8:5–12, 26–40*) that included an encounter with an Ethiopian official. It was at his home in Caesarea that Paul encountered Agabus, who predicted Paul's deliverance to the Gentiles by the Jews. (*Acts 21:8*)

PHILIP A son of Herod the Great and first husband to Herodias. (*Matthew 14:3, 16:13, Mark 6:17, 8:27–30* and *Luke 3:19*)

PHILIP Another son of Herod the Great, mentioned in *Luke 3:1* as Tetrarch of Ituraea and Trachonitis.

PHILOLOGUS A believer in Rome to whom Paul sent greetings in *Romans 16:15*.

PHLEGON A believer in Rome to whom Paul sent greetings in *Romans 16:14*.

PHOEBE A deaconess of Cenchraea, near Corinth, who took Paul's Epistle to the Romans. In *Romans 16:1–2*, Paul commends her Christian merits to the recipients, saying that she had been 'a succourer of many, and myself also'.

PHYGELLUS Cited by Paul in his last letter, *II Timothy 1:15*, as one of those in the province of Asia who had turned away from him and his teaching.

PILATE, PONTIUS The Roman procurator of Judaea at the time of Christ's ministry and

Philip and the Ethiopian. 'And he arose and went: and, behold, a man of Ethiopia, an eunuch of great authority under Candace queen of the Ethiopians, who had the charge of all her treasure, and had come to Jerusalem for to worship, Was returning, and sitting in his chariot read Esaias [Elijah]the prophet ... And Philip ran thither to him, and heard him read the prophet Esaias, and said, Understandest thou what thou readest? And he said, How can I, except some man should guide me? And he desired Philip that he would come up and sit with him ... Then Philip opened his mouth, and began at the same scripture, and preached unto him Jesus.' After his instruction, Philip baptized the Man 'and he went on his way rejoicing'. (Acts 8:27–39)

Crucifixion, whose reputation in the eyes of Jewish historians is poor – they attest to his insensitivity to Jewish beliefs, and *Luke 13:1* refers to a massacre carried out in his name. It fell to Pilate to decide the fate of Jesus when the Sanhedrin condemned him. Mark reports Pilate as simply the judge carrying out sentence. Both Luke and John emphasize how Pilate found Jesus to be innocent and only agreed to his death because of the insistence of the Jews *(Luke 23; 13–25; John 19:12–l6)* and his fear of insurrection. *Matthew 27:24* portrays his symbolic washing of hands as he relinquished responsibility for Jesus' death. He was recalled to Rome in AD 36.

PORCIUS FESTUS Governor of Judea who sent the apostle Paul to Rome. The essential problems of the region with which his predecessor, Felix, had wrestled – banditry and terrorism and increasing friction between Herod Agrippa and the high priests – continued during his term of office. Upon his arrival in Jerusalem, the priests began lobbying Festus to bring Paul from Caesarea, where he had been in prison for two years, their secret plan being to have him killed on the way.

Pilate washes his hands, symbolically surrendering the decision about Jesus' fate to the crowd.

Festus, however, made them accompany him to Caesarea and put their case, which he found unproven. When asked whether he would be tried in Jerusalem, Paul replied: 'I stand in Caesar's judgement seat,' and said he had done no wrong to the Jews – as a Roman citizen, he appealed to Caesar. A further private interview with Festus, Herod Agrippa II and his sister Berenice could find no fault in Paul, so Festus put Paul on a ship bound for Rome. Festus died in office a few years later. *(Acts 25–6)*

PRISCILLA (Prisca) Roman-born wife to Aquila, a tent-maker of Pontus who had migrated to Rome. They were expelled by the Edict of Claudius (which was provoked by continual rioting between Jews and Christians in Rome). The couple met Paul in Corinth and were converted. Paul lodged with them in Ephesus for some time, and they developed business interests together. Church meetings were also held at their home. Priscilla was the more fervent evangelist of the two and taught the Gospel to the preacher Apollos. *(Acts 18:2, 18; Romans 16:3, 1 Corinthians 16:19,* and *2 Timothy 4:19)*

PROCHORUS One of the seven disciples chosen as deacons (with Stephen, Philip, Parmenas, Nicanor, Timon, and Nicolas). Their role was to take over the administrative burdens of the early church, such as financial affairs and caring for widows and the poor. *(Acts 6:5)*

PUBLIUS (Poplius) Chief official on the island of Melita (Malta) when Paul was shipwrecked there en route to Rome. He welcomed the stranded travelers and entertained them at his nearby estate. Paul performed a miracle there, curing Publius' father of a fever and dysentery. *(Acts 28:7–8)*

PYRRHUS The father of Sopater of Berea, in Macedonia. *(Acts 20:4)*

QUIRINIUS (Cyrenius) A Roman who became governor of Syria after the deposition of Archelaus. *(Luke 2:2)*

RHODA A servant girl of Mary the mother of Mark. She answered the door when Peter was delivered from prison, but through sheer excitement refused to admit him for a time. 'And as Peter knocked at the door of the gate, a damsel came to hearken, named Rhoda. And when she knew Peter's voice, she opened not the gate for gladness, but ran in, and told how Peter stood before the gate. And they said unto her, Thou art mad. But she constantly affirmed that it was even so. Then said they, It is his angel. But Peter continued knocking: and when they had opened the door, and saw him, they were astonished.' (*Acts 12:13–16*)

Priscilla, tent-maker, friend of Paul and an evangelist in Ephesus.

S

SALOME Daughter of Herodias and Herod Boethus. At the birthday banquet for King Herod Antipas, Herodias' third husband, the young Salome danced and so pleased the King that he offered her anything she wished. Salome consulted her mother, who saw her opportunity to avenge herself upon the preacher who had openly criticized her marriage, John the Baptist. 'And she went forth, and said unto her mother, What shall I ask? And she said, The head of John the Baptist. And the king was exceeding sorry; yet for his oath's sake, and for their sakes which sat with him, he would not reject her. And immediately the king sent an executioner, and commanded his head to be brought: and he went and beheaded him in the prison, And brought his head in a charger, and gave it to the damsel: and the damsel gave it to her mother.' (*Matthew 14:6–11, Mark 6:21–8*)

Left: Salome dances for her step-father: her reward will be the head of John the Baptist.

Right: Salome, mother of James and John, with the other women before the cross.

Below right: Paul and Silas, released from prison by an angel, confront an awe-struck jailer.

SALOME Mother of James and John, wife to Zebedee, a fisherman of Galilee. With her sons, she was an early follower of Jesus and was one of the women who took care of Jesus while he was working in Galilee. The request that James and John should sit either side of Jesus in Heaven came from her. (*Matthew*

20:20, Mark 10:35–41) She was one of the group of women at the crucifixion that also included Mary Magdalene and Mary mother of James and Joses – 'women looking on from afar off'. (*Mark 15:40–1*) At first light on the day after the sabbath they made their way to Christ's sepulcher to anoint the body with sweet spices and found the tomb empty save for an angel who told them that the disciples would see the risen Lord in Galilee. (*Mark 16:1*)

SECUNDUS A Christian of Thessalonica mentioned in *Acts 20:4*.

SERGIUS PAULUS Pro-consul of Cyprus who was converted by Paul. (*Acts 13:5–12*)

SILAS A prominent Christian of Antioch who journeyed with Paul and Barnabas to Jerusalem to attend the meeting where they discussed the issue of preaching to the Gentiles. He returned to Antioch with Judas Barsabbas to inform the church elders there of the decision. (*Acts 15*).

SIMEON A Christian prophet in the Church at Antioch, surnamed Niger (black) and therefore possibly of African birth (*Acts 13:1*)

SIMEON A righteous man who was told by the Holy Spirit that he should not see death until he had seen Jesus Christ; he saw the child at his presentation in the Temple. (*Luke 3:30*)

SIMON A Jew of Cyrene who carried the heavy cross which Christ could no longer bear. He was 'father of Alexander and Rufus'. (*Matthew 27:32, Mark 15:21, Luke 23:26*)

SIMON A Joppa tannerwith whom Peter stayed at the time he cured Tabitha. (*Acts 9:43*)

SIMON A leper of Bethany in whose house Jesus' feet were anointed from an alabaster box. (*Matthew 26:6–13, Mark 14:3, 9*)

SIMON A sorcerer of Samaria whose conduct was sternly rebuked; he was converted by Philip. (*Acts 8:9–24*)

SIMON Apostle, sometimes called Simon the Zealot (indicating that he belonged to the nationalistic Zealot sect, which had strongly held political beliefs of Jewish patriotism) or Simon the Lesser, also called the Canaanite, reflecting his connection with Cana in Galilee. (*Matthew 10:4, Mark 3:18, Luke 6:15, Acts 1:13*) He traveled widely and is traditionally linked with Jude, both being martyred in Persia.

SIMON Father of Judas Iscariot. (*John 6:71, 13:2, 26*)

Left: Simeon recognizes the Messiah when Joseph and Mary present the child at the Temple.

Right: Simon of Cyrene shoulders the burden of the cross after Christ's fall.

SIMON Half-brother of Jesus, son of Joseph and Mary, brother also of James, Joses and Judas. (*Matthew 13:55, Mark 6:3*)

SIMON PETER Apostle: see Peter.

SOPATER A Christian of Berea and kinsman of Paul, who accompanied him into Asia. (*Acts 20:4–6; Romans 16:21*)

SOSTHENES Head priest at the synagogue in

Corinth who was injured during the disturbance following Gallio's dismissal of Jewish accusations against him. (*Acts 18:17*)

STEPHEN The first Christian martyr, stoned to death. He was one of the deacons (with Parmenas, Philip, Prochorus, Nicanor, Timon and Nicolas) elected to carry out administrative duties for the apostles, but he was also a formidable preacher – a man 'full of faith'. (*Acts 6:5, 8*) After speaking in a synagogue

'called the synagogue of the Libertines' where there were 'Cyrenians, and Alexandrians, and of them of Cilicia and of Asia, disputing with Stephen', he was arrested and made a stout defence to the charge of blasphemy. 'Then they cried out with a loud voice, and stopped their ears, and ran upon him with one accord, And cast him out of the city, and stoned him: and the witnesses laid down their clothes at a young man's feet, whose name was Saul. And they stoned Stephen, calling upon God, and saying, Lord Jesus, receive my spirit. And he kneeled down, and cried with a loud voice, Lord, lay not this sin to their charge. And when he had said this, he fell asleep.' (*Acts 6:8–15, 7*) The Saul of this story was later to become the apostle Paul.

STEPHANAS A Christian of Corinth. His was the first household in Achaia to be converted to Christianity, by Paul; he is mentioned later as visiting Paul in Ephesus with Fortunatas and Achaicus. (*II Corinthians 1:16, 16:15, 17*)

SUSANNA A woman who, together with Mary Magdalene, Joanna, and others, ministered to Jesus. (*Luke 8:3*)

The first Christian martyr, Stephen, who was stoned.

T·U·V·W

TERTIUS The amanuensis whom Paul employed to write his Epistle to the Romans. (*16:22*)

THADDAEUS Apostle, identified in various Gospels and manuscripts variously as Judas, Jude, Labbeus and Lebbus, and possibly the writer of the Epistle bearing his name. *John 14:22* refers to him thus: 'Judas saith unto him, not Iscariot, Lord, how is it that thou wilt manifest thyself unto us, and not unto the world ...' while *Matthew 10:3* has 'Lebbaeus, whose surname was Thaddaeus', and *Luke 6:16*, 'Judas the brother of James'. Nothing more is known of him, but tradition tells of his death by crucifixion in Ephesus.

THOMAS Apostle, also called Didymus and 'Doubting Thomas' for his questioning of Jesus' appearance after the Resurrection. At the Last Supper, he was one of the disciples closely questioning Jesus concerning what was about to happen: 'Thomas saith unto him, Lord, we know not whither thou goest; and

Thaddeus.

Doubting Thomas is convinced at last that this is the risen Jesus.

how can we know the way? Jesus saith unto him, I am the way, the truth, and the life: no man cometh unto the Father, but by me. If ye had known me, ye should have known my Father also: and from henceforth ye know him, and have seen him.' (*John 14:5–7*) He was not with the other disciples when Jesus showed himself to them after the Resurrection: 'The other disciples therefore said unto him, We have seen the Lord. But he said unto them, Except I shall see in his hands the print of the nails, and put my finger into the print of the nails, and thrust my hand into his side, I will not believe. And after eight days again his disciples were within, and Thomas with them: then came Jesus, the doors being shut, and stood in the midst, and said, Peace be unto you. Then saith he to Thomas, reach hither thy finger, and behold my hands; and reach hither thy hand, and thrust it into my side: and be not

The young Timothy with his mother Eunice and grandmother Lois.

faithless, but believing. And Thomas answered and said unto him, My Lord and my God. Jesus saith unto him, Thomas, because thou hast seen me, thou hast believed: blessed are they that have not seen, and yet have believed. (*John 20:25–9*) He was also with other disciples when Christ appeared to them at the Sea of Galilee. (*Matthew 10:3, Mark 3:18, Luke 6:15, John 11:16, 21:1–2*) There is a tradition that he later took the Gospel to Persia and India.

TIBERIUS CAESAR Emperor of Rome, successor to Augustus, and his step-son. It was during his reign that the events in the New Testament describing the activities and deaths of John the Baptist and Jesus Christ took place. (*Luke 3:1*)

TIMON One of the seven deacons of the early church (with Stephen, Philip, Prochorus, Nicanor, Parmenas and Nicolas), whose role was essentially administrative. (*Acts 6:5*)

TIMOTHY A disciple of Paul, and his companion on some of his journeys. His mother, Eunice, and his grandmother, Lois, were also Christians (*II Timothy 1:5*); his father was a Greek. (*Acts 16:1*) He probably lived at Lystra, where Paul took and circumcised him, that he might not give offence to the Jews. (*Acts 16:3*) He attended Paul on his journey through Phrygia, Galatia, and Mysia also to Troas, Philippi, and Berea (*Acts 17:14*). He followed Paul to Athens, whence he sent him to Thessalonica. (*17:55; 18:5, I Thessalonians 3:2*) After this he was with Paul at Corinth. (*1 Thessalonians 1:1, 2 Thessalonians 1:1*) He was with Paul at Ephesus (*Acts 19:22*), from where he was sent to Macedonia. Later he went with Paul into Asia (*20:4*) and was with him for some time. He shared Paul's incarceration in Rome (*Philippians 1:1, Hebrews 13:23*) and was subsequently in Ephesus (*II Timothy 4–5*); he is possibly the 'angel' of the church at Ephesus mentioned in *Revelations 2:1–7*.

TITIUS JUSTUS A Christian Gentile of Corinth in whose home, next to the synagogue, Paul stayed. (*Acts 18:7*)

TITUS A Greek convert and associate of Paul (*II Corinthians 8:6, 23, 12:18*). He was not circumcised (*Galatians 2:3*). Titus traveled widely, including to Corinth and the Adriatic, and was put in charge of Christian affairs on Crete. (*Titus 1:5*) He was the recipient of the epistle from Paul that bears his name.

TYRANNUS A teacher or philosopher at Ephesus, in whose school Paul disputed daily for some two years. (*Acts 19:9*)

URBANE A Christian at Rome and a helper of Paul. (*Romans 16:9*)

Z

ZACCHAEUS A chief tax-gatherer at Jericho who, being short of stature, climbed into a tree in order to see Jesus above the press of the crowd around him. Jesus saw him in the branches above and asked him to come down, saying that he would stay at his house. The crowd criticized Jesus for being a guest at the house of a much-despised tax man, but 'Zacchaeus stood, and said unto the Lord; Behold, Lord, the half of my goods I give to the poor; and if I have taken any thing from any man by false accusation, I restore him fourfold. And Jesus said unto him, This day is salvation come to this house, for so much as he also is a son of Abraham.' (*Luke 19:1–10*)

ZEBEDEE Father of the apostles James and John; a Galilean fisherman and husband of Salome. (*Matthew 4:21; 27:56 Mark 15:40*)

ZECHARIAH Father of John the Baptist. When the archangel Gabriel appeared to him in a vision at the Temple, he protested that both he and his wife, Elisabeth, were too old to have children, in consequence of which Gabriel struck him dumb until the birth. (*Luke 1:5–23*)

ZENAS A lawyer whose services Paul requested in his letter to Titus. (*Titus 3:13*)

Right: The archangel Gabriel appears to Zechariah.

Left: Jesus tells Zacchaeus to come down from the tree in which he sat in order to see Him.

Characters in the Holy Bible
with No Recorded Names

These are some of the many people in the Bible who are not accorded names
in the narrative but whom tradition or contemporary and apocryphal sources have named.

THE OLD TESTAMENT

LOT'S WIFE is not named in the Bible, but according to the apocryphal *Book of Jasher* (*19:52*) was called Ado (Edith). She is the subject of a well-known story in *Genesis*: as God prepared to destroy Sodom and Gomorrah, He told Lot and his family: 'Escape for thy life; look not behind thee ... But his wife looked back from behind him, and she became a pillar of salt.' (*Genesis 19:17,26*) (See page 111)

LOT'S DAUGHTERS. One is named in the apocryphal *Book of Jasher* (*19:24*) as Paltith in a story concerning the wickedness of the inhabitants of Sodom. When a stranger who came to the city for refuge was refused succor, Paltith smuggled victuals to him but was discovered and burned to death. Her two sisters fled Sodom with Lot when the Lord destroyed Sodom and Gomorrah: 'And Lot went up out ... and dwelt in the mountain, and his two daughters with him ... And the firstborn said unto the younger, Our father is old, and there is not a man in the earth to come in unto us after the manner of all the earth: Come, let us make our father drink wine, and we will lie with him, that we may preserve seed of our father ... Thus were both the daughters of Lot with child by their father. And the firstborn bare a son, and called his name Moab: the same is the father of the Moabites unto this day. And the younger, she also bare a son, and called his name Benammi: the same is the father of the children of Ammon unto this day.' (*Genesis 19:30–8*) (See page 111)

PHARAOH'S DAUGHTER has been identified by various names, including Thermutis (Josephus), Merrhoe (Eustatius of Antioch), Merris (Eusabius) and Bithiah (Jewish tradition). She was the savior of Moses, who had been set afloat in a basket on the Nile in a plan to circumvent the death sentence on new-born male Hebrews. 'And the daughter of Pharaoh came down to wash herself at the river ... and when she saw the ark among the flags, she sent her maid to fetch it.' She decided to adopt the boy, but have a Hebrew nurse him (that Hebrew, although she did not know it, was Moses's mother) 'And the child grew, and she brought him unto Pharaoh's daughter, and he became her son. And she called his name Moses ...' (*Exodus 2:5–10*)

PHARAOH'S MAGICIANS, defeated by Aaron, are identified in the New Testament in *II Timothy 3:8* – 'Now as Jannes and Jambres withstood Moses, so do these also resist the truth ...' When Moses and Aaron appeared before Pharaoh the first time, God told Aaron to throw down his staff. 'And Moses and Aaron ... did so as the Lord had commanded:

Thermutis's maid brings forth the babe from the basket.

Above: Jannes and Jambres watch as Aaron's staff-turned-into-a-serpent eats theirs

and Aaron cast down his rod before Pharaoh ... and it became a serpent. Then Pharaoh also called the wise men and the sorcerers: now the magicians of Egypt, they also did in like manner with their enchantments. For they cast down every man his rod, and they became serpents: but Aaron's rod swallowed up their rods.' (*Exodus 7:8–12*) Jannes and Jambres were well-known at the time.

MOSES'S CUSHITE WIFE. Subsequent to his marriage to Zipporah in Midian, Moses took another wife, who became the subject of criticism from his brother and sister as the Hebrews wandered in the wilderness: 'And Miriam and Aaron spake against Moses because of the Ethiopian woman whom he had married ...' (*Numbers 12:1*) Her name may have been Tharbis, or Adoniah (according to the apocryphal *Book of Jasher*).

THE WITCH OF ENDOR. According to an ancient Jewish commentary on the Bible, she was called Zepheniah. After the death of Samuel, Saul feared that he could not count on the support of God in his struggle against the Philistines. So he sought out 'a woman that hath a familiar spirit', a necromancer who would be able to conjure up the spirit of Samuel, and went to her in disguise. When the spirit of Samuel appeared, Saul asked what he should do, since God had abandoned him; the spirit of Samuel replied: 'Because thou obeyedst not the voice of the Lord, nor executedst his fierce wrath upon Amalek, therefore ... to morrow shalt thou and thy sons be with me: the Lord also shall deliver

the host of Israel into the hand of the Philistines. Then Saul fell straightway all along on the earth, and was sore afraid, because of the words of Samuel ...' Zepheniah had compassion for the King and baked unleavened bread, which she persuaded Saul to eat. When Saul met the Philistines in battle, he was indeed defeated and slain. (*I Samuel 28*)

THE NEW TESTAMENT

THE THREE WISE MEN. (The Magi) These illustrious travelers have provided one of the great traditional tales of Christmas. According to *Matthew 2*, they came 'from the east' guided by a star in search of 'he that is born King of the Jews'. They began their search in Jerusalem, and their coming aroused much interest in King Herod, to whom this appeared threatening. Having ascertained from the When the three wise men found the stable, 'they saw the young child with Mary his mother, and fell down, and worshipped him: and when they had opened their treasures, they presented unto him gifts; gold, and frankincense, and myrrh.' In tradition the visitors are named Balthasar, Melchior and

Balthasar, Melchior and Caspar inquire about the baby born to be King of the Jews.

Caspar, and often referred to as 'three kings'; but *Matthew* does not actually state that they were kings or that there were three of them; this number has been inferred from the number of their gifts.

THE SHEPHERDS AT THE CRIB. Only the *Gospel of Luke* contains this story, which has become another important element of the Christmas narrative. An angel appeared to shepherds watching their flocks and told them: 'I bring you good tidings of great joy ... For unto you is born this day in the city of David a Saviour, which is Christ the Lord. And this shall be a sign unto you; Ye shall find the babe wrapped in swaddling clothes, lying in a manger ... And they came with haste, and found Mary, and Joseph, and the babe lying in a manger.' (*Luke 2:8–18*) The shepherds are not named in *Luke*, but according to the apocryphal Syrian *Book of the Bee* they were Asher, Zebulun, Justus, Nicodemus, Joseph, Barshabba and Jose.

THE WOMAN CURED OF AN ISSUE OF BLOOD. One of the many healing stories during Jesus's ministry concerns a hemorrhaging woman. 'When she had heard of Jesus ... touched his garment .. And straightway the fountain of her blood was dried up ...' Jesus turned: 'Who touched my clothes? ... But the woman fearing and trembling ... came and fell down before him, and told him all the truth. And he said unto her, Daughter, thy faith hath made thee whole; go in peace, and be whole of thy plague.' (*Mark 5:25–34*) In some Christian traditions, including the apocryphal *Acts of Pilate*, she is identified with a woman named Veronica (Latin) or Berenice (Greek), who is said to have given Christ her veil, as he carried the cross to Golgotha, for him to wipe his forehead.

THE SAMARITAN WOMAN AT THE WELL OF SYCHAR. At Sychar, Jesus encountered a woman whom Eastern Orthodox tradition names Photina. When he asked her for a drink of water from the well, she responded: 'How is it that thou, being a Jew, askest drink of me, which am a woman of Samaria? for the Jews have no dealings with the Samaritans. Jesus answered ...

Above: The shepherds. 'And when they were come into the house, they saw the young child with Mary his mother, and fell down, and worshipped him.' (Matthew 2:11)

If thou knewest the gift of God, and who it is that saith to thee, Give me to drink; thou wouldest have asked of him, and he would have given thee living water ... Whosoever drinketh of this water shall thirst again: But whosoever drinketh of the water that I shall give him shall never thirst ...' The woman told him: 'I know that Messias cometh, which is called Christ: when he is come,

Above: Veronica offers Christ her veil on the road to Calvary.

he will tell us all things. Jesus saith unto her, I that speak unto thee am he.' She spread the word and many Samaritans came to listen to Him. 'And many more believed because of his own word; And said unto the woman, Now we believe ... for we have heard him ourselves, and know that this is indeed the Christ, the Saviour of the world.' (*John 4*)

THE WIFE OF PONTIUS PILATE. Various names have been attributed to the wife of the Roman procurator of Judaea who sat in judgement on Jesus, including Claudia and Procula. Her part in the New Testament is short: 'When he was set down on the judgment seat, his wife sent unto him, saying, Have thou nothing to do with that just man: for I have suffered many things this day in a dream because of him.' (*Matthew 27:19*) But the priests, manipulating the mob, prevailed.

THE TWO THIEVES CRUCIFIED WITH CHRIST are named in the apocryphal *Acts of Pilate* as Dismas and Gestas, or Gesmas; other names have included Zoathan and Chammata, Joathas and Maggatras, and Titus and Dumachus. One of whom has been called 'the penitent thief': 'And one of the malefactors which were hanged railed on him, saying, If thou be Christ, save thyself and us. But the other answering rebuked him, saying ... we receive the due reward of our deeds: but this man hath done

Above: Stephaton relieves Christ's thirst.

nothing amiss. And he said unto Jesus, Lord, remember me when thou comest into thy kingdom. And Jesus said unto him, Verily I say unto thee, To day shalt thou be with me in paradise.' (Luke 23:39–43)

THE ROMAN SOLDIERS AT THE CROSS. Two of the soldiers who administered the crucifixion have received names: Stephaton is the name traditionally associated with the guard who offered Christ vinegar: 'Jesus knowing that all things were now accomplished, that the scripture might be fulfilled, saith, I thirst. Now there was set a vessel full of vinegar: and they filled a spunge with vinegar, and put it upon hyssop, and put it to his mouth. When Jesus therefore had received the vinegar, he said, It is finished: and he bowed his head, and gave up the ghost.' (*John 19:28–30*) It was customary to break the legs of crucified men to hasten death, 'But when they came to Jesus, and saw that he was dead already, they brake not his legs: But one of the soldiers with a spear pierced his side, and forthwith came there out blood and water. (*John 19:33–4*) Longinus is the name given in the apocryphal *Gospel of Nicodemus* to the soldier who wielded the spear, subsequently called the Holy Lance.

Dismas and Gestas are crucified beside Jesus, while Longinus looks on.